How Effective Sermons Advance

How Effective Sermons Advance

BEN AWBREY

RESOURCE *Publications* • Eugene, Oregon

HOW EFFECTIVE SERMONS ADVANCE

Copyright © 2011 Ben Awbrey. All rights reserved. Except for brief quotations in critical publications or reviews, no part of this book may be reproduced in any manner without prior written permission from the publisher. Write: Permissions, Wipf and Stock Publishers, 199 W. 8th Ave., Suite 3, Eugene, OR 97401.

Scripture taken from the NEW AMERICAN STANDARD BIBLE, Copyright © 1960, 1962, 1963, 1968, 1971, 1972, 1973, 1975, 1977, 1995 by The Lockman Foundation. Used by permission. www.Lockman.org

Chapter 1—Sermon Structure's Cornerstone: The Sermon Proposition, was extracted from the book *How Effective Sermons Begin*, Mentor, 2008. Used by permission.

Resource Publications
An Imprint of Wipf and Stock Publishers
199 W. 8th Ave., Suite 3
Eugene, OR 97401

www.wipfandstock.com

ISBN 13: 978-1-60899-970-5

Manufactured in the U.S.A.

Contents

Foreword by Paige Patterson / vii
Preface by R. Albert Mohler Jr. / xi
Introduction / xiii

1 Sermon Structure's Cornerstone: The Sermon Proposition / 3

2 Sermon Structure as a Text Driven Derivative / 31

3 Sermon Structure as a Necessity, Not a Luxury / 65

4 Sermon Structure as a Necessity, Not a Liability / 99

5 Sermon Structure as Statements of Theological Principle / 121

6 Sermon Structure and Textual Congruity / 149

7 Sermon Structure's Stylistic Components / 191

8 Sermon Structure's Functional Results / 255

9 Sermon Structure's Functional Means / 273

Bibliography / 299

Foreword

In *Arabian Sands*, Wilfred Thesiger spreads a verbal canvass in which he paints a vivid picture of what has become known as the "Empty Quarter" in the Arabian Peninsula. This is the desert of all deserts where one may suddenly find himself sinking into quicksand; but if he is searching for the liquid of life, he either knows exactly where he is going and has provisions to get there, or else he—like many others who have ventured into this desert—will never venture out. The scarcity of water in the Empty Quarter reminds me of the infrequency with which one finds genuine biblical preaching in the churches of our era. The sparseness of anything that could be called meaningful life in the Empty Quarter has its double in the churches of the land as a result of the infrequent appearance of those spiritual oases where the Bible is actually taught.

In this volume, Ben Awbrey, Associate Professor of Preaching at Midwestern Baptist Theological Seminary in Kansas City, Missouri, has provided the finest conceivable instruction on *How Effective Sermons Advance*. This second volume follows a highly successful and helpful volume one, *How Effective Sermons Begin*, published in 2008. For a good many preachers, *How Effective Sermons Advance* will be a book, to change the metaphor above, that will resemble throwing ice water into the face of a nearly frozen man. Many contemporary preachers will allege that the message of the book, and the stratagem enjoined upon the preacher is dated and totally ineffective in the postmodern milieu. But for many tortured church members who are forced to wander some Saharan wilderness of contemporary, shallow preaching, this volume will be ice water to the parched throat of the thirsty believer who wishes spiritual refreshment; and it will be life-saving water for those who are lost and need to know the Savior. Awbrey's position, which he unpacks for his readers in the following pages, is based upon the contention that the information provided on the pages of Holy Scripture is not optional. Awbrey believes that the text of Holy Scripture was given from God as special revelation and that the Word of God is "sealed forever in heaven" (Psalm 119:89). Consequently, he believes that the best preaching in any day is still what has most often been referred to as "exposition." While I certainly have no quibble with that term, I prefer to note simply that Awbrey promotes "biblical preaching," which is defined as the careful teaching of all aspects of the special revelation with application of didactic narrative, as well as hortatory passages for the lives and eternities of those who hear the preacher. In order to accomplish this task, Awbrey's determined conviction is that a sermon needs to have structure.

The argument presented in this compelling volume does not attempt to superimpose on the biblical text some pedantic external mode but seeks to discover the structures that are provided in the sacred text itself. Awbrey does this while carefully avoiding the error of removing the personality of the preacher since he believes in the incarnational delivery of the message of God in every generation. There is no attempt on Awbrey's part to clone preachers but rather the determination to insist that sermon structure is in fact a necessity and not a luxury, inspiring the title of the third chapter. Reasons for this position are provided in both the fields of communication in general and specifically in theology.

Subsequent chapters demonstrate that commitment to structure, far from being a liability, is a desirable asset and that the structure of the sermon actually serves as the statement of theological principle. Furthermore, Awbrey demonstrates visibly that the congruity of the text itself is at stake. Toward the end of the volume he also discusses stylistic components that should be present in an appropriately structured sermon and proceeds in a most perceptive way by anticipating the results that arise from well-structured discourse for preacher, congregation, and the contemporary church as a whole.

Throughout the entire volume, Awbrey has first provided the principles that ought to be part of a structured approach to preaching; and then, not content to leave his readers with theory alone, he has provided superb examples of the craft he advocates. These examples, which act as illustrations to cast light on the theories advanced in this volume are among the most helpful additions to the book and are reasonably rare in books on homiletics. In the process of the preparation of the volume, Awbrey demonstrates a rather remarkable grasp of numerous fields of investigation from theology to hermeneutics to the latest in homiletical theories and the advocates of those theories. But in the end, Awbrey is his own man, advocating a method of proclaiming the unsearchable riches of Christ, which is uniquely biblical.

One of the most amazing accomplishments of this volume is a feature that will combine both insight and inspiration. Most preachers with whom I have visited during my fifty years in ministry, when asked about preaching from the book of Proverbs, muster a rye smile and mutter something under their breaths about the fact that most of it is "not really preachable." Proverbs seems to be a fine book of religious aphorisms, but what in the earth could it possibly have to do with preaching? At the first of every chapter Awbrey uncovers in Proverbs a veritable gold mine for the preacher. He has marshaled from its wisdom ten to fifteen verses, that have a direct impact upon the preaching of the Word. By the time I finished reading the manuscript, I wondered why homiletitians have not insisted that their students virtually memorize the book of Proverbs as a precursor to the faithful preaching of the Word of God. One cannot help but conclude that a thorough grasp of the message contained in the proverbs of Solomon and the other contributors to that book would have made possible the avoidance of a thousand common mistakes in the pulpit.

In the midst of a generation that seems determined to abandon genuine biblical preaching, Ben Awbrey's *How Effective Sermons Advance* becomes a critically important volume. The concepts that he is advocating are those to which I have been committed for most of my ministry. Nevertheless, I found the book both stimulating and challenging, and I express my gratitude to this professor of homiletics at Midwestern Seminary for his labor of love in producing this volume. In short, if you want to learn how to do genuine biblical preaching and you are unselfish enough to desire that the congregations who hear you preach grow in the nurture and the admonition of the Lord, this is one book that cannot be optional. With gratitude to God and to its author, I warmly commend it to you.

Paige Patterson
President
Southwestern Baptist Theological Seminary
Fort Worth, Texas

Preface

Evangelicals now face a fascinating and troubling dilemma. We repeatedly declare our commitment to preaching, but there seems to be little consensus about what constitutes authentic and faithful Christian proclamation. As a populist movement, Evangelicalism is often exemplified by an unfortunately superficial and tragically insubstantial diet of preaching. One of the key symptoms of this expositional distress is the lack of adequate structure in biblical exposition.

Just as any building requires architecture and engineering, an expository message requires structure and form. An adequate building is made both safe and functional by engineering and architecture that simultaneously create the structural integrity of the building and remain largely out of view. In other words, just as the blueprint and engineering schematics lead to a beautiful building, careful attentiveness to expositional structure is required in order to achieve a powerful and faithful sermon.

This metaphor demands our attention to the issue of structure, but it also reminds us that no one admires a building primarily for its engineering. Those who look upon a magnificent building or bridge admire its style, force, functionality, and beauty. In the crowd there may well be a number of engineers and architects who take an inordinate interest in the structural design of what others admire in terms of its total force. Similarly, the structure of the sermon does not exist in order to draw attention to itself, but rather, to provide an adequate means of conveying biblical truth that will serve to enable the preacher to proclaim the Word of God while "rightly dividing the Word of truth."

In this important book, Ben Awbrey provides a primer on sermonic structure. *How Effective Sermons Advance* presents an enlightening and inspiring guide to sermon structure. Ben Awbrey understands the importance of structure—that is why he wrote this book. At the same time, his commitment is to the expositional preaching of the Word of God, and not to structure as an end in itself. This book is an important contribution that is especially noteworthy and helpful in this age of so much evangelical superficiality.

I am often perplexed by the number of preachers who declare themselves to be committed to expository preaching, but who seldom seem to achieve their goal. Thankfully, they hold to the absolute inerrancy and infallibility of the Bible, and even to a faithful understanding of verbal inspiration. Nevertheless, they seem to lack the equipment and knowledge necessary to move from an understanding of the text to an adequate proclamation of that text in an expositional message. As Ben Awbrey reminds us, a faithful interpreter of Scripture needs an adequate sermonic structure in order to preach a faithful expository sermon.

If there is the danger of inadequate attention to sermonic structure—and there is—there is also the danger of substituting a fixed sermonic structure for the responsibility to fit sermonic structure to each biblical text. The skilled and faithful preacher will be attentive to the different forms of literature found in the Bible. A parable is not a psalm, and an historical narrative is not structured as a proverb. As found in the Bible, all of these are given to us for preaching, but each text demands a structure that is both faithful and adequate to its own form and genre. This means that slavish devotion to one sermonic structure—no matter how comfortable—can be disastrous to faithful exposition.

I am particularly encouraged by the publication of this book and by the influence of Ben Awbrey. He represents a generation of young expositional preachers who are committed to the perpetuation of faithful Christian preaching in this generation. In *How Effective Sermons Advance*, as in his earlier book, *How Effective Sermons Begin*, Ben Awbrey demonstrates a deep understanding of the homiletical challenge and a passionate commitment to the exposition of Scripture. This book will be not only helpful, but inspiring to those who are committed to the preaching task. All those who love the church of the Lord Jesus Christ and prize the calling of preaching will welcome this book as a sign of good things to come.

R. Albert Mohler Jr.
President, Southern Baptist Theological Seminary

Introduction

Surely you have heard a preacher reference and use in his sermon the following type of sermon structure: "As we examine our text this morning I want you to see the man, the motive, the ministry, the mission, and the means." I certainly have witnessed such a demonstration on numerous occasions. In fact, I had experienced this kind of thing so often I thought it was perfectly acceptable and would have never imagined that there could be a more productive product to be desired. However, even before I made a thorough research project upon sermon structure I realized, upon hearing a rather uncommon but far more descriptive demonstration of sermon structure in preaching, that there was indeed a better product that could be achieved. Subsequent research in the field of homiletics regarding sermon structure has verified that such a product not only could but should be provided. This is my position as well. The type of sermon structure depicted above, though unquestionably common, is unquestionably deficient. Since a better effort and effect can be achieved then it must be provided in our preaching. My purpose for this book is to provide the case, the procedure, and the product for better sermon structure to be incorporated in the proclamation of God's Word.

Perhaps an example would be helpful at this point to indicate the kind of difference that can and should be made in our preaching in reference to sermon structure. Instead of the non-descriptive version of "As we examine our text this morning I want you to see the man, the motive, the ministry, the mission, and the means" a more suitable rendition would be: "As we examine our text this morning I want you to see 5 characteristics of the servant whom God uses greatly in His Kingdom work." The fivefold structure, cast in a more suitable fashion, would be: "God greatly uses servants who have been tested severely and approved thoroughly." "God greatly uses servants who seek only to glorify Him in their lives." "God greatly uses servants who fervently love fellow believers." "God greatly uses servants who are burdened for the lost and committed to win them to Christ." "God greatly uses servants who sacrifice much in their opportunity to serve Him."

The latter outline is preferable because it is far more descriptive than the former. Instead of the naked injunction of "we will see the man" there is a more detailed statement, one that actually says something significant about this "man," namely, the important characteristic about this servant as one who has been tested severely and approved thoroughly. Something about the man is actually indicated, something that is meaningful even though the text has not been expounded yet the hearers can grasp truth about the kind of man that God greatly uses in His Kingdom work. The attempt to "see the man" is homiletical gamesmanship; it conveys very little, it states nothing the hearers need to know. And so it is for each of the remaining four points of the sermon. "The motive" is a poor substitute for "God greatly uses servants who seek only to glorify Him in their lives." This statement reveals what is the motive of the servant God greatly uses in His Kingdom work rather than using the term "motive" yet indicating nothing about the motive. The empty phrase of "the ministry" says nothing about the ministry even though the word is articulated, but the statement of "God greatly uses servants who fervently love fellow believers" defines the ministry of one used greatly by God. "God greatly uses servants who are burdened for the lost and committed to win them to Christ" communicates so much more than "the mission" could ever entail. "The means" bears no potential to reveal the truth that "God greatly uses servants who sacrifice much in their opportunity to serve Him."

A redeeming word is needed for the common but poor rendition of sermon structure indicated above by "the man, the motive, the ministry, the mission, and the means." Such alliterated categories can be used with the more descriptive statements and are profitable when employed in conjunction with them. But the attempt to use the alliterated categories independent of the more descriptive statements is inadequate because they are "starter quality" as opposed to "final quality" expression of thought. The combination of starter quality alliterated categories and final quality descriptive statements can be achieved and is a worthwhile product to pursue. Notice how this could be done by the following: "The text initially gives us insight regarding the man. The man himself is described for us in how God has worked and continues to work in his life. What is it that we need to know about the man whom God uses greatly in His Kingdom work? Here it is: God greatly uses servants who have been tested severely and approved thoroughly." Both the alliterated category and the descriptive statement receive priority and each one makes a contribution to what must be understood clearly from the passage. The remaining four alliterated categories and their descriptive statement counterparts could be combined productively so that the alliterated categories serve the purpose of a folder and the descriptive statement acts as a document that is filed in the folder.

The liability of the deficient sermon structure typified by the man, the motive, the ministry, the mission, and the means is that when the sermon is over and the hearer is reflecting upon the sermon, the hearer may be able to remember the alliterated categories and some of the insights offered in the exposition of the passage and that is it! But what will they be able to remember definitively about the man? They will remember nothing definitively because they were told nothing in particular, no timeless truth, no theological principle, about the man. Certainly we would expect that the text would be treated with care and many details of the text would be discussed, but no particular insight regarding the man would be achieved because none was offered. The best case scenario then would be this—the hearer would have to derive some meaning about the man on his own because the preacher never did make a particular declaration about the man. The tragedy is that the preacher never synthesized a timeless truth, a statement of theological principle, from all the details discovered from the text. In his study, he fell short of doing what he needed to do—make sense of the passage for himself, to come to grips with valuable insights from the passage for his own life. Therefore, in the pulpit he will be just as irresponsible to his hearers by not articulating clear, timeless truths or statements of theological principle that they need to know from this passage. In short, he cannot be of help to clarify the text to his hearers because he could not even clarify the text for himself.

I have heard sermons that were truly excellent in every regard except for the sermon structure. I had to figure out what the preacher was trying to say in all the stuff he was saying. Sometimes, I just could not do this. Comprehension eluded me just as certainly as it had eluded the preacher who was preaching to me. At other times, I was able to pull the details together and discover what the preacher had been trying to say but was unable to discover for himself and thus unable to state for his hearers—final quality descriptive statements about the passage. But my "after the sermon achievement" in making sense of what was said was a hollow victory because my thought process was to this effect, "I wish you could figure out what you are trying to say before you try to say it!" *I strongly suggest that a preacher figure out what he is trying to say before he says it!* Sermon structure composed of anything other than final quality statements, statements of theological principle, is sufficient evidence that the preacher really doesn't understand what he is trying to say! There is no room for this in preaching if one is striving for excellence in preaching!

If there is any cause, any endeavor, any field in which excellence should be sought, shouldn't it be in the cause of proclaiming the God of the Word through the Word of God? Many lesser causes are infused with a greater pursuit for excellence than the pursuit for excellence demonstrated in the preaching of those who serve as ambassadors of God. Take, for example, the Hallmark Corporation in Kansas City, Missouri, who has articulated the following:

> For us, excellence is an aspiration, an attitude, a pursuit, a way of life.
> Excellence is all of us working together, aspiring to the fullness of our potential,
> Always in pursuit of higher standards, determined to do every thing we do,
> Somehow better than it ever has been done before.
> Excellence is found in the caring, in the trying, in the doing.
> It is our objective. We seek it with dedication.
> Excellence is the Hallmark of this Corporation.[1]

The Hallmark Corporation states, "This pledge was composed by the employees of Hallmark. It expresses our commitment to bring you the very best."[2] Very impressive, and this for the cause of producing greeting cards! Excellence is at home at the Hallmark Corporation while mediocrity is at home in the pulpit! My challenge to you is for the pursuit of excellence in your preaching, and specifically, excellence in your sermon structure.

Sermon structure is the essential substance of what the preacher will be saying in the sermon. It must never be the case that what the preacher will say, in essence, in his sermon is still beyond his ability to grasp! The opportunity to preach is an opportunity for a preacher to expound the meaning of a biblical text which has been understood thoroughly and will be explained clearly by him. Poor sermon structure provides evidence that the preacher did not understood the text as thoroughly as he should have when he was in his study and did not express it as clearly as he should have when he was in his pulpit. This book is intended to help preachers develop and deliver sermon structure that will help them to clearly and thoroughly express the essential meaning of the texts they preach and to preach them with a higher degree of excellence because of the sermon structure used in their preaching.

ENDNOTES

1. This excerpt was extracted from a television commercial for Hallmark Greeting Cards, based in Kansas City, Missouri. The commercial ran during a Hallmark Hall of Fame Special Presentation of *The Tenth Man*, aired on Sunday evening December 11, 1988 by the CBS television network.
2. Ibid.

Words to Live and Preach By

The Diligent Man's Satisfaction

*Poor is he who works with a negligent hand,
but the hand of the diligent makes rich.*
PROVERBS 10:4

*He who tills his land will have plenty of bread,
but he who pursues worthless things lacks sense.*
PROVERBS 12:11

*A man will be satisfied with good by the fruit of his words,
and the deeds of a man's hands will return to him.*
PROVERBS 12:14

*A lazy man does not roast his prey,
but the precious possession of a man is diligence.*
PROVERBS 12:27

*The soul of the sluggard craves and gets nothing,
but the soul of the diligent is made fat.*
PROVERBS 13:4

*Hope deferred makes the heart sick,
but desire fulfilled is a tree of life.*
PROVERBS 13:12

*Have I not written to you excellent things of counsels and knowledge, to
make you know the certainty of the words of truth
that you may return words of truth to him who sent you?*
PROVERBS 22:20-21

Do you see a man skilled in his work?
He will stand before kings;
he will not stand before obscure men.
Proverbs 22:29

He who tills his land will have plenty of food,
but he who follows empty pursuits will have poverty in plenty.
Proverbs 28:19

1

Sermon Structure's Cornerstone

The Sermon Proposition

THE SERMON PROPOSITION AND the sermon structure are linked inseparably since both serve to provide a synopsis of the sermon. The sermon proposition has been called "the essence of the sermon in a sentence"[1] and rightly so since the proposition bears the essential thrust of the sermon confined to one brief statement. The sermon structure, on the other hand, may be referred to as the blueprint of the sermon's essence since it will detail the major principles and clarifying assertions of the biblical text to be preached. Of course, the sermon proposition is stated and repeated in the sermon introduction and, therefore, as of the introduction of the sermon the hearers can understand the subject-matter to be treated in the sermon and how the subject will be treated by the preacher.[2] However, they can understand these in only the most general way through the means of a stated sermon proposition in the sermon introduction. The sermon structure provides for the hearers a more definitive treatment of the sermon proposition in the body of the sermon. The sermon structure depicts the major and minor thrusts of the sermon and the biblical text that will be explained via the sermon. Obviously then the sermon structure must represent an accurate depiction of the development of the biblical passage. Therefore, the biblical text must drive the preparation of the sermon's structure in an expository sermon.

Since the sermon structure is the unfolding of the sermon proposition, it is essential to focus attention on the sermon proposition in order to understand it well before we consider sermon structure. For an understanding of the other elements of a sermon introduction examine the book *How Effective Sermons Begin*.[3]

ORGANIZATION AND PREACHING

In all preaching, expository preaching and all such preaching that would never be confused as an attempt to explain a passage of Scripture, this much is certain: the preacher must know what he will be talking about in the sermon and what he will be saying about whatever he will be talking about in the sermon—this is his most basic responsibility of cognition. Additionally, he must be able to help those who will hear him preach discern what he will be talking about and what he will be saying about that subject-matter—this is his most basic responsibility of communication. "The hearer does not cling to a speaker who, undertaking to guide him, seems to be ignorant whither he is going."[4] It is through the means of a sermon proposition and the structure of the sermon that these matters are achieved effectively. The most basic conception for a well-designed sermon is the "embodiment and extension of an important idea, of which the first element is a clearly defined subject and the second element is structural assertions concerning the subject."[5]

Clarity regarding the subject-matter of the sermon as well as the treatment of the subject-matter must be communicated in the sermon introduction. The sermon introduction is the necessary place for the hearers to understand the subject-matter of the sermon and the treatment the subject will receive by the preacher on this preaching occasion.

In the introduction of the sermon the preacher states and repeats, at least one time, the sermon proposition. Through a clearly articulated statement of the sermon proposition the congregation will know what the preacher will be preaching on and, in a general way, what he will say about the subject. Only in the body of the sermon will the hearers understand fully and specifically what the preacher is saying about the subject-matter of the text as he expounds the text with the help of the sermon structure derived from the passage to be preached. The old adage of "tell them what you are going to tell them, tell them, and then tell them what you told them" cannot be set aside in preaching without sacrificing a degree of clarity.

One of many things to be done in a sermon introduction is to clearly communicate to the hearers what you will be saying in the sermon they are about to hear. In other words, the sermon introduction is the place in the sermon where the preacher tells the hearers what he will be talking about in the sermon. In the body of the sermon he will tell them the meaning of the passage. And among other responsibilities the preacher has in the sermon conclusion is to tell them what he has told them in the sermon. The expositor of Scripture owes it to his hearers to inform them, as of the sermon introduction, what he will be addressing in his sermon. If the hearers of a sermon cannot discern what the preacher will be talking about before he begins to preach the body of the sermon he has failed them because he simply has not afforded them the basic information they need in order to follow a sermon with understanding.

Notice, for example, G. Campbell Morgan's clear indication of how his text of Matthew 16:21 will be treated as he preached his sermon *The Pathway of the Passion*. In Morgan's final two paragraphs of his sermon introduction he said:

> As I have said, Matthew summarizes all the teaching from Caesarea Philippi to Calvary in these words: "He must go unto Jerusalem, and suffer many things of the elders and chief priests and scribes, and be killed, and the third day be raised up." In that summary there are three matters which demand our attention. The first is that of the *compulsion*: "He *must* go unto Jerusalem." The second is that of the *course* marked out: "suffer . . . and be killed." The third is that of the *consummation*: "and the third day be raised up."[6]

It would have been easy for Morgan's hearers to discern how the reputable expositor was going to treat the pathway of Christ's passion by the three matters of the compulsion, the course, and the consummation of his journey to Jerusalem. Although this portion of the introduction could have attained greater clarity through a more thoroughly synthesized sermon proposition and structure, Morgan's three matters of Christ's compulsion, course, and consummation provide some indication as to the subject-matter of the sermon.

Unfortunately, however, such clarity commonly is neither advocated nor practiced in preaching today. For example, consider the sermon introduction of Fred Craddock's *expository*[7] sermon from Acts 2:2-21 entitled *On Being Pentecostal*. The intended treatment of the passage and clarity for what the sermon would be about was indicated by one vapid, vacuous sentence—"And that's what I'd like for us to do; think again about Acts 2 and Pentecost."[8] In reality, Acts 2 was not dealt with at all except to say that a very large crowd was present, being made up of Jews from every nation under heaven, along with converts to Judaism and other visitors. So this proposition, at best, indicates that Acts 2 will receive treatment that is so uncertain that it can only be indicated by the phrase "think again about Acts 2 and Pentecost." There is no clarity conveyed about the meaning of the text of Acts 2:2–21, that is, how it would be divided and how each division would be developed. Even though it may be understood that the sermon is to be about Pentecost, there is no indication as to what will be said about Pentecost.

The sermon proposition is an entity of the sermon introduction. The development of the proposition, the sermon structure, is the conceptual framework of the body of the sermon, and therefore, guides the exposition of the text. Though the sermon structure works with the sermon proposition, only the sermon proposition will be considered in this chapter. However, it is of little or no value to have a clearly stated proposition in the introduction if there is not a tight, logical, and obvious connection between the sermon structure in the body of the sermon that corresponds to the sermon proposition. After all, the sermon structure is simply the sermon proposition unfolded in a point by point manner. Therefore, much attention will be given to the goal of producing sermon outlines for the sermon body that will be helpful to the preacher and the congregation in subsequent chapters. Our specific goal in this chapter is to understand how to develop a clear proposition that will be helpful to the preacher and the congregation in the introduction of the sermon.

CLARITY OF THE SERMON PROPOSITION

Clarity is a chief component for both the sermon structure and the sermon proposition. Since 1912, through J. H. Jowett's oft-quoted statement insisting upon clarity in the sermon's proposition, propositional clarity has been a cornerstone element of homiletical instruction. Specifically, Jowett wrote:

> I have a conviction that no sermon is ready for preaching, not ready for writing out, until we can express its theme in a short, pregnant sentence as clear as a crystal. I find the getting of that sentence is the hardest, the most exacting, and the most fruitful labour in my study. To compel oneself to fashion that sentence, to dismiss every word that is vague, ragged, ambiguous, to think oneself through to a form of words which defines the theme with scrupulous exactness,—this is surely one of the most vital and essential factors in the making of a sermon: and I do not think any sermon ought to be preached or even written, until that sentence has emerged, clear and lucid as a cloudless moon. Do not confuse

obscurity with profundity, and do not imagine that lucidity is necessarily shallow. Let the preacher bond himself to the pursuit of clear conceptions, and let him aid his pursuit by demanding that every sermon he preaches shall express its theme and purpose in a sentence as lucid as his powers can command.[9]

A more appropriate and definitive call for clarity for a sermon proposition has never been written to date.

Clarity regarding the sermon proposition is not just a good idea and something to be attained, if possible. It is truly essential. Donald L. Hamilton has stated the case well as he wrote, "A sermon without a clear proposition is like a ship without a rudder or an automobile without a steering wheel. Keeping it on course will be very difficult, if not impossible!" The result of a sermon without a clear proposition will be an unclear purpose, an unclear direction, and an unclear argument. The audience may feel a sense of frustration since effective communication has been hindered by a lack of preciseness. The preacher himself may also be frustrated as he is unable to present clearly that which he desires to present.[10]

THE ARDUOUS TASK OF CONSTRUCTING CLEAR SERMON PROPOSITIONS

The starting point for a clear, effective sermon proposition and its related outline is very diligent work. Halford Luccock expressed the reality of this very well as he insisted that the preacher must "toil like a miner under a landslide." This expression enlarges on two axiomatic realities of preaching—that the preaching ministry must rest on a life of study, and secondly, that "real study and the creative work coming from it and running along with it are painfully hard."[11] Don McDougall comments upon the hard work necessary to craft the sermon proposition and structure, specifically, as well as being a good expositor of the Bible, in general.

> Good expositors of the Bible have disciplined themselves to work hard and long. Nowhere is that discipline and hard work more demanding and rewarding than in determining the central idea (the sermon proposition) and structure of the passage.[12] Undoubtedly, there are some great natural athletes. When it comes to the field of expositors, however, probably no such thing as a great natural expositor exists. To be a true and acknowledged expositor of the Word requires discipline. It takes hard work and

thorough preparation for which there are no substitutes. A lot of time and effort must be spent establishing the central idea and determining the outline of a passage.[13]

A clear, effective sermon proposition like everything else that is a part of good preaching will not be easy to achieve but it must be achieved. If a preacher cannot achieve clarity at this juncture he can never be clear in his preaching and a lack of clarity exacts a costly price to be paid in the process of preaching. As Augustine wrote, "Who does not realize that a person who is not understood cannot be listened to either with pleasure or with obedience?"[14]

However, even if one fully subscribes to this most beneficial counsel, it seems to me that a very important question needs to be raised and answered regarding propositional clarity. The question is simply this—how is clarity achieved in writing a sermon proposition? Is it simply working diligently to craft a carefully articulated statement that is to be uttered from the pulpit in such a way that the congregation will not miss it nor misunderstand it?

Surely the careful construction and forceful declaration of the sermon proposition must be a starting point for propositional clarity. William G. T. Shedd comments on both of these factors. He contends that the proposition should be stated in the most concise manner possible. It is, or should be, the condensation and epitome of the whole discourse, and should, therefore, be characterized by the utmost density of meaning. Additionally, the proposition should be stated in the boldest manner possible. Every teaching, or tenet, of revelation, ought to be laid down with a strong confidence of its absolute truthfulness. When the proposition of a sermon is a legitimate derivative from a passage of Scripture, it ought to be expressed in such a manner as to preclude all hesitation, doubt, or timidity, in the phraseology. A weighty conciseness, and a righteous boldness, ought to characterize the terms, and form of the proposition.[15]

Even as these general assertions are understood and applied to the development and delivery of a sermon proposition, I suggest that the very character of the propositional statement is significant if it is to engender clarity and integrity between the propositional statement announced in the introduction and the sermon structure or outline of the message to be articulated in the body of the sermon. Constructing the propositional statement that is clear and appropriate for the passage is seldom an easy assignment.

All propositional statements, even when finely crafted, are not created equal. Not all clear propositions wield the same ability to supply the needed coherence to the outline of the sermon body. The plural noun proposition distinguishes itself in its inherent ability to be easily identified in the introduction as well as relating to the outline in the sermon body in a tight, logical way.

PLURAL NOUN PROPOSITIONS

In his book *Design for Preaching*, Grady Davis argues for a necessary understanding on behalf of a congregation as they hear one preach—an understanding that is sufficient only as two "structural questions" are effectively answered by the data supplied to them by the preacher. These questions are: What is the man talking about? and, What is he saying about it?[16] These two questions are the framework for congregational understanding in the context of preaching. The preacher can be clear about these matters in the pulpit only if he has gained personal clarity about these matters in his study. A sound sermon must be the embodiment of an organic relatedness of thought that establishes one subject and elaborates upon that subject in an identifiable way. The simple necessity of such sermonic cohesiveness however does not guarantee its presence in a message. Davis's lament for the absence of such organic soundness in preaching, as well as his insistence upon it, is justified.

> It may seem childishly simple to say that every sermon consists of only two things: what is talked about, and what is said about it, a subject with one or several predicates. To say it is indeed simple; to act on it must be very difficult, judging by the evidence. A man who has been to college and seminary, a man who has preached for years, can speak as if he never heard of this primary fact... No overlay of brilliant or witty talk, apt quotations, choice anecdotes, can hide a misshapen body of thought. There is no way to correct these elemental faults of design except to keep pressing the question, "What am I to talk about? What must be said about it?"
>
> To learn to preach, a man must develop his sense of form, his feeling for the shape and organic structure of a thought. This is the first step in learning. To feel the shape and structure of his idea is also the first and chief task in preparing any given sermon, down to the last one a man will preach before he dies. No man ever graduates from this, or gets above it.[17]

In the proclamation of a sermon that is truly sound, any listener should be able to report accurately the pastor's sermon—this is what he was talking about and this is what he said about it.

In general terms, this minimally constitutes clarity in preaching—the ability of a hearer to articulate what the preacher was talking about and what he said about it. But the question must be raised, is minimal clarity sufficient for preaching? I strongly affirm that minimal clarity is inadequate! Instead of listeners being able to state in general terms what the preacher was talking about and what he said about it, they should be able to recite with some degree of specificity what he actually said regarding the subject-matter. Is it possible for a listener to recover both the general thrust of the sermon as well as the more important specific statements the preacher made pertaining to the subject-matter of the sermon? I believe it is not only possible but it is essential for listeners to be able to do this, having heard a sermon. However, this will be possible only if the listener is allowed to discern a statement of the general thrust of the sermon, to discern how many specific statements will be incorporated to clarify the general thrust of the sermon, and to discern the specific clarifying statements of the general thrust of the sermon. These conditions are fulfilled best through the usage of a plural noun proposition.

BENEFITS OF A PLURAL NOUN PROPOSITION

Many authors and professors of preaching agree that a sermon proposition bearing a plural noun or keyword has a distinct advantage to produce a strong sermonic structure by unlocking the divisions most notable for an exposition of a particular text and sermon.[18] In his book *Power in Expository Preaching*, Faris D. Whitesell enumerates seven benefits of using the plural noun propositional approach in expository preaching. He lists these benefits as follows:

> 1) to classify, label, or catalogue the main points, keeping them all in one category; 2) to point the direction you intend to follow with your thesis; 3) to give unity to the sermon; 4) to aid in parallel construction of main points; 5) to test the main points proving whether or not they fit the outline; 6) to link the main points together, tying them into a neat bundle; 7) to make the sermon easier to memorize and easier for the hearers to remember.[19]

A former professor of mine, Craig Skinner, presents a strong advocacy for plural noun propositions as he writes: "I have examined many hundreds of volumes, including many in the general preaching and secular fields, for this study and found nothing of any quality in terms of valid sermon structure other than this thesis-interrogative-keyword approach." He contends that the thesis-interrogative-keyword approach, or the plural noun proposition approach, is the finest developed for expository preaching and is in full accord with the best ideas in contemporary speech theory and educational psychology. He deemed it appropriate to insist that any sermon without a thesis, expressed or implied, cannot be a sermon, as it advocates no basic truth. Additionally, Skinner insists that most good sermons, on analysis, will be found to have affinity with the (thesis-interrogative-keyword) structure.[20]

Without the use of a keyword, or plural noun, a sermon proposition degenerates into a factual yet simple statement rather than a worthwhile sermon proposition which causes people to want to know more about the subject-matter contained in the propositional statement.[21]

THE BASIS OF A PLURAL NOUN PROPOSITION

The basic presupposition of the plural noun propositional approach in preaching is that the proposition will be expanded by dealing with more specific truths derived from the text. In other words, there will be structure in the message, that is, the proposition will be unfolded by two or more points in the sermon.

Since there will be more than one line of advancement of the subject-matter of the proposition, there must then be a plural noun in the proposition. The plural noun will correspond to the divisions of thought in the sermon structure. For now we can think of them as "main points" or "sermon points" or "points of sermon structure" but in the following chapters we will understand the main points to be "statements of theological principle."

In order to understand sermon propositions, we must understand that a sermon will always have a plurality of points. In preaching, a preacher will always be saying various things (the points of the sermon structure) about the one thing he is preaching about (the sermon proposition). To truly say one thing about something will either be no sermon at all, or a sermon that is incredibly brief. On the other hand, however, if one does more than say one thing about something, he will be advancing thought. Shedd made the case for the necessity of plural sermon points by arguing that there are two things in rhetoric—the statement of a thing and the development of the thing stated. The statement of a sermon proposition cannot be the development or amplification of the proposition. The development or amplification of the proposition is the main points of the sermon. Likewise, the statement of a main point of a sermon is not the development or amplification of the main point. The development or amplification of the main point is the substructure. Every sermon must contain main points which flow out of each other and yet are distinct from each other. If this is not the case, then there is no development, no progress or none of the elements of oratory.[22]

Advancement of thought can take place in two very distinct ways. A preacher can advance thought in a rambling, disorderly way that is hard to establish the precise advancement being made of the proposition. Or, he can advance the subject-matter in a clear, orderly fashion so that the development of the proposition can be clarified by the more specific thoughts upon the subject-matter.

To argue for a one point sermon is to misunderstand the difference between a sermon proposition and a sermon point. One author, in the attempt to advocate "one-point communication," effectively establishes the necessity for multi-point communication. He writes:

> The older three-point sermon style should be abandoned in this hard-hitting day of single-emphasis communication. This is not to say, however, that the sermon outline might not have several piers that support the argument. It's just that these points of supporting logic should not be allowed to develop separate themes. They should all contribute to building a single emphasis, which the sermon develops from the lone theme it champions.[23]

The author is quite right in his assertion that "the lone theme," or the proposition, should be championed by the "several piers that support the argument," or sermon points. Again, his assertion that "these points of supporting logic should not be allowed to develop separate themes" only underscores the very purpose of a sermon outline regarding a sermon proposition—to develop it, not to distract from it. Sermon points that do not develop the proposition constitute an ineffective, flawed structure. The solution to poor structure is not an attempt to have no structure at all.

EXAMPLES OF PLURAL NOUN PROPOSITIONS

Perhaps some examples of non-plural noun propositional statements versus plural noun propositional statements will help to distinguish and compare the two approaches. In each couplet of propositional statements, a non-plural noun proposition will be given in italics followed by a plural noun proposition in bold faced print with the plural noun underlined. For reference purposes, the following four examples will be referred to as couplet 1, couplet 2, couplet 3, and couplet 4.

Couplet 1

"Parents should be pleasing to God in the raising of their children."

"In this chapter we discover 3 qualities of parents who are pleasing to God in the raising of their children."

Couplet 2

"Those who suffer persecution are blessed by God."

"In his Sermon on the Mount, Jesus affirms that those who suffer persecution are doubly blessed as persecution brings to them 2 benefits."

Couplet 3

"It is important to correct a faulty understanding of sin."

"In our passage this morning we will find 3 correctives for the most common misunderstandings regarding sin."

Couplet 4

"The Christian life is often not as fulfilling as it could be."

"Joyful, responsible living as a child of God is conditioned upon compliance to the 3 requirements we shall see in this text."

ASSESSMENT OF PLURAL NOUN PROPOSITIONS

Several observations are immediate. The non-plural noun propositions are briefer. The non-plural noun propositions do not suggest the intended treatment the subject-matter will be given in the sermon. There is no number used in the non-plural noun propositional statement which informs the hearers how many points will be discussed in the sermon regarding the subject-matter. Obviously, the plural noun propositions tend to be longer than a non-plural noun attempt to say the same thing. However, the longer statement of the plural noun proposition is certainly worthwhile as it conveys much in the few additional words.

It is important to understand that the non-plural noun statements are a significant start in the formulation of a sermon proposition, specifically, a plural noun proposition. These significant starter-statements possess an inherent weakness in that they do not and cannot shoulder the load necessary to make a more definitive declaration regarding the subject-matter, treatment, and structure of the sermon to be delivered.

I couldn't agree more with the thoughts of a popular and powerful preacher of the early to mid-nineteenth century who noted that, "the turning of certain leading thoughts, as they arise, into propositions, marks the rate of progress, indicates direction, and blazes one's way through the forest." He continued, "We never have the full use of language, as an instrument of thought, unless we cause our thoughts to fall into assertory shape."[24] Even though the previous thoughts were not made with plural noun propositions as a frame of reference, they are uniquely relevant to them.

How then does one construct a plural-noun proposition? In order to facilitate the understanding and implementation of plural noun propositions, I will provide a step-by-step process for making plural noun propositions out of non-plural noun statements for all four of the couplets mentioned above.

CRAFTING A PLURAL NOUN PROPOSITION

In the previous examples of non-plural noun propositions, the basic statements found in them are what may be called the thesis, theme, or central idea of the biblical passage and, therefore, the sermon. I will use to term "thesis" to refer to these non-plural noun statements.

The process of crafting a plural noun proposition includes eight steps. These steps do not formulate a rigid sequence of events that must be followed. For example, the amount of major assertions can be identified (step three) and the development of each of the main points can be charted (step seven) before the plural noun is clearly discerned (step five) or the statements of the main points are fashioned (step four). In this case, step seven occurs before steps five and four are completed. Additionally, step five has been accomplished before step four is finalized. Synthesis must be done but there is no invariable step by step occurrence in its achievement. One should only be satisfied with the fact of its occurrence not the sequence of occurrence. The eight steps are enumerated as such only as an attempt to typify a common sequence of events.

The first step for establishing a plural noun proposition for a sermon is to synthesize a basic understanding of a passage, the thesis. This is critical, remembering that this statement supplies the answer to the question, "What is this passage about?"

With the thesis of the passage in mind, the second step is to understand how the thesis is developed and treated in the passage. In other words, the development of the thesis will be the answer to one of the following interrogatives: who, what, when, where, why, or how. Deciding which interrogative, when supplied to the thesis, best reflects the truths of the text as answers to the interrogative supplied to the thesis. The determination of this interrogative, which is to be supplied to the proposition and is indicative of the passage, is the completion of the second step.

The third step is to identify how many components are unified by the plural noun thus establishing how many main points the sermon will contain. Having diagrammed the passage the major assertions of the text can be identified with relative ease.

The crafting of the sermon points of the passage is the fourth step. Having decided which interrogative best describes the treatment of the thesis, one can craft the actual statements of the main components of the text, which become the main points of the sermon, so that these main point statements both answer the interrogative and reflect the understanding of the passage.

The fifth step is to discern the plural noun that most accurately unifies the points of the sermon, each of which, answer the interrogative supplied to the basic thesis statement of the passage. The answering of the interrogative supplied to the basic thesis and the reflection of the passage, that is, the unifying concept of each of the statements of theological principle or sermon points must be accomplished by the plural noun.

The sixth step is to be certain that there is an actual and accurate correlation between the basic proposition of the sermon, the supplied interrogative, the statements of the sermon points, the amount of main points contained in the passage, and the plural noun of the sermon proposition.

The seventh step is to discover the development of the main points of the sermon according to the content of the passage and reflect the development of the main points by establishing sub points for the main points of the passage.

The eighth step is to modify, revise, or correct the statements of the plural noun proposition, the main points, and the substructure through the best exegesis and most thorough study of the passage one can accomplish.

Now let's apply these steps to the thesis statements of the four couplets given above. For example, in couplet three, the non-plural noun propositional statement "It is important to correct a faulty understanding of sin" is an excellent thesis statement for the biblical passage of Matthew 5:21–26. Having established this as a thesis statement for the passage, the thesis is interrogated by determining which of the interrogatives best describe the treatment the Lord provides for the subject-matter.

According to what the Lord says in this passage it seems appropriate to understand his instruction as a response to the implied interrogative "how." With the interrogative "how" supplied to the thesis "It is important to correct a faulty understanding of sin" one gets the resulting thesis question—"How does one correct a faulty view of sin?" This question is critical since Jesus depicts 3 common misperceptions regarding sin and supplies the needed understanding to correct these misperceptions. Thus, the Lord is supplying "correctives" to the prevalent problem of a faulty view of sin. Specifically, he supplies 3 of these correctives as he indicates 3 common misperceptions regarding sin. Therefore, the resulting plural noun proposition would be something like, "In our passage this morning we will find 3 <u>correctives</u> for the most common misunderstandings regarding sin."

This plural noun proposition suggests the following: the sermon to be preached will have 3 points, each sermon point will infer a misconception of sin commonly held by Jesus' disciples and the multitude who heard him preach, and each sermon point will be a corrective to a common misperception of sin. The sermon structure correlating to this plural noun proposition would be:

I. To have a correct understanding of sin you must identify sin as an internal disposition.
II. To have a correct understanding of sin you must equate sin against man as sin against God.
III. To have a correct understanding of sin you must act to minimize the consequences of your sins.

In regards to the first couplet, "Parents should be pleasing to God in the raising of their children" is a good thesis statement for the passage of 1 Samuel 1. This chapter deals with the birth and lineage of Samuel through his godly parents Elkanah and Hannah. However, an important clarifying comment must be offered regarding using the aforementioned thesis for preaching from I Samuel 1. The primary intent of the chapter is to reveal the particular circumstances of the birth of this one who would be used by God greatly in the life of the nation Israel. It is only through the details of Samuel's birth and lineage that insight regarding the godliness of his parents is apparent. The fact of his birth and lineage, how God miraculously controlled them is primary. The condition of his parents' godliness, though factual, is secondary. I am not arguing that the secondary significance of Samuel's parents would be inappropriate treatment of the passage as long as the orientation material of the sermon introduction brings out the primary focus of a sovereign, omnipotent, covenant keeping God miraculously affecting the birth of this prophet of God.

In reading this chapter, 3 things are apparent about Samuel's parents, especially his mother: although imperfect, they are devoted to God; to accomplish their purpose in life they are dependent upon God; and in the raising of their child they are dedicated to God. Elkanah and Hannah serve as a good model for parents who wish to be pleasing to God in the raising of their children. What was true for them should be true for all parents who know the Lord, that is, they should be pleasing to him in their task of raising their children. But the question is "what" does it take to be parents who are pleasing to the Lord? What qualities constitute parents who please God? What are the hallmarks or qualities that epitomize the lives of parents with whom God is well-pleased?

The interrogative "what" will be crucial for establishing a plural noun proposition that will accurately depict the thesis of this passage as well as the observable qualities of Samuel's parents. With the interrogative "what" supplied to the thesis "Parents should be pleasing to God in the raising of their children," one may derive the thesis question "What is necessary to be parents who are pleasing to God in the raising of their children?" The three qualities that can be observed regarding Elkanah and Hannah help to construct the plural noun proposition—"In this chapter we discover 3 <u>qualities</u> of parents who are pleasing to God in the raising of their children." This plural noun proposition obviously portends of 3 sermon points, each one being a quality of Samuel's parents and all parents who would be pleasing to God in the raising of their children.

   I. God is pleased with parents who are devoted to him in spite of their imperfections.
   II. God is pleased with parents who are dependent upon him to accomplish their purpose in life.
   III. God is pleased with parents who are dedicated to him in the training of their children.

In the second couplet we find a statement that will be a thesis for a plural noun proposition. The statement, "Those who suffer persecution are blessed by God" is a thesis for a message preached from Matthew 5:10–12. Jesus makes two statements regarding the blessedness of those who suffer persecution. Even though persecution and blessedness have a definite spiritual connection they do not pose an initial logical connection. The significant interrogative in this passage is "why."

When the interrogative "why" is supplied to the thesis—"Those who suffer persecution are blessed obey God" the interrogative question is—"Why is it that those who suffer persecution are blessed by God?" In general, the answer is because persecution is indeed a beneficial reality. More specifically, the answer is given by the plural noun proposition "In his Sermon on the Mount, Jesus affirms that those who suffer persecution are doubly blessed as persecution brings to them 2 <u>benefits</u>." The following 2 sermon points would attend this propositional statement:

   I. Believers are benefited when persecuted because persecution bears a proof of citizenship in the kingdom of heaven.
   II. Believers are benefited when persecuted because persecution brings a promise of reward in the kingdom of heaven.

As to the fourth couplet, "The Christian life is often not as fulfilling as it could be" is a thesis statement that will serve as the crux of a plural noun proposition—"Joyful, responsible living as a child of God is conditioned upon compliance to the 3 <u>requirements</u> we shall see in this text." Either the interrogative "when" or "who" could be applied to the thesis statement, each of them providing a slight distinction in the phraseology of the sermon points. If the interrogative "when" is used, then the sermon structure would be as follows:

I. Joyful, responsible living results when you pray persistently for the unique necessities of your life.

II. Joyful, responsible living results when you trust unquestionably in the perfect faithfulness of your God.

III. Joyful, responsible living results when you strive exclusively for the equitable treatment of your neighbor.

If the interrogative "who" is applied then a slight emphasis may be discerned in the following structure:

I. Joyful, responsible living is experienced by those who pray persistently for the unique necessities of their lives.

II. Joyful, responsible living is experienced by those who trust unquestionably in the perfect faithfulness of their God.

III. Joyful, responsible living is experienced by those who strive exclusively for the equitable treatment of their neighbor.

Though different interrogatives may be supplied to the thesis, the main points will be altered in a marginal way. Actually, the different interrogatives make emphatic what would be understood clearly by the structure that would unfold from the thesis if controlled by the other interrogative.

In the main points that unfold from the thesis controlled by the interrogative "when," what is emphatic is the resulting reality that occurs as certain conditions are met by an individual. In the main points that unfold from the thesis controlled by the interrogative "who," what is emphatic is a description of the kind of individual who experiences the reality.

Unacceptable Words to be used as Plural Nouns

In the formulation of a plural noun proposition it is never acceptable to use the word "things" as a plural noun. Warren Wiersbe warns that the word "things," when used as a key word in a sermon proposition, is "too broad" and it "isn't likely to attract much interest."[25] This is certainly true but, beyond that, it must be recognized that the word simply is not declarative. It says nothing.

Moreover, when the word "things" is used as a plural noun it strongly suggests that the preacher really has not been able to synthesize the passage well enough so that he can articulate productively what he would like to talk about. No preacher would want to advertise that. In fact, if he is going to talk about "things," to what degree can the listener be certain as to what the preacher will be saying about his subject-matter? The answer is zero degree of certainty about the treatment of the subject-matter outside of the obvious fact that four "things" indicates that the sermon will have four points.

The number accompanying the plural noun indicates to the listeners how many points will be contained in the sermon. If "things" is used to convey to the listeners how many points will be contained in the message then the word is worthless since it essentially means "points" and that is understood already by the number used in the propositional statement. The word "points" is just as useless as a plural noun since it is equivalent to "things" and either word can, at best, only relate to the sermon outline and not the sermon proposition.

A plural noun proposition is not beneficial if it is used simply to indicate that a preacher has a number of "things" to say or a number of "points" to make about the subject-matter of a biblical text. Therefore, the words "things" and "points" must never be used as the plural noun in a plural noun proposition.

Unadvisable Words to be used as Plural Nouns

Additionally, two other words, "aspects" and "truths," must be severely curtailed in usage. Anything can be an aspect of something. An aspect of something asserts as fact that there is a relationship but a relationship that cannot be described in more definitive terms. When using the word "truths" as the plural noun for a sermon proposition, the extent of disclosure being made to the congregation is that what is being communicated is not falsehood. In other words, the preacher is saying first and foremost about the subject-matter he will be preaching upon is, "I will not be lying to you about this issue." It goes without saying that a preacher will not be fabricating falsehood about the subject-matter of the sermon. Therefore, "truths" declared about any subject-matter is no great disclosure. Truths should be declared about every subject of every sermon. We, then, could preach "truths" for every subject of every sermon we will ever preach.

"Truths" and "aspects" must see extremely limited duty in plural noun propositions. Granted, they may be used, but they must be used sparingly. Using these two terms is like playing for a tie in a football game. If that is the best you can do then you do it, but you can't feel very good about it—although you did not lose, you clearly did not win. So it is when we preach about truths and aspects of something.

THE HEARER'S PERCEPTION OF SERMONIC INTEGRITY

A more objective, as well as practical, way to help assure that there is a comprehensible integrity between the sermon proposition and the sermon structure is to make certain the congregation has identified the preacher's proposition when it is stated in the introduction of the sermon. The preacher must state the proposition clearly. Yet again, what is stated clearly and what is stated unclearly incorporates some subjectivity.

Clarity as perceived by the preacher is a different matter than clarity as perceived by the congregation. Because of the hard work done by the preacher, having discovered and written out a propositional statement in his study, then clearly announcing this statement in the pulpit as he introduces the sermon, the preacher may assume, quite incorrectly, that he has made himself clear on the matter. Such an assumption will inevitably lead the preacher astray.

The truth is, no matter how intentional the preacher is, no matter how clear he desires to be, no matter how well he articulates the propositional statement, not everyone will get it! The stated proposition will not be grasped by all the first time it is communicated, regardless of how clearly it was communicated! Therefore, the preacher must repeat the propositional statement at least once.[26] He is well advised to repeat his proposition several times in the introduction of the sermon.

REPETITION OF PLURAL NOUN PROPOSITION

When I preach, I strive to provide in every sermon introduction at least 3 statements the sermon proposition. Having stated the proposition the first time, I will state it again immediately without any other material intervening and I will state it exactly as I did the first time. Later on in the introduction I will state the proposition for the third time, perhaps with a little diversity of statement to avoid redundancy while attempting to secure comprehension. Repetition is the first crucial factor for a clear propositional statement.

Placement of the statement is the second crucial factor for clarity in a sermon proposition statement. The last statement of the sermon introduction is significant. It must accomplish two tasks: it must conclude the sermon introduction and it must signal the transition to the sermon body. Only the sermon proposition contains the means by which both tasks can be accomplished with conceptual and functional clarity. Therefore, the very last sentence of the sermon introduction will be final statement of the sermon proposition, whether it is the second time or the fifth time the proposition is declared.

It is virtually impossible for one to be too clear, but it is incredibly easy to not be as clear as one must be in informing the congregation as to what the sermon will be about. Repeated statements of the sermon proposition and placement of the final repetition of the sermon proposition are two crucial factors for clarity in a sermon proposition.

However, repetition and placement cannot determine clarity, unconditionally. No matter how many times a verbose, hazy, uncertain concept is stated, it will not be perceived as being clear to those who hear it. In order to make compact, definitive statements about a subject, one must master the subject. That is, he must understand his subject thoroughly. Therefore, the third crucial factor for sermon proposition clarity is a thorough understanding of what the sermon will be about as reflected in a descriptive, definitive, distinguishable statement. A descriptive, definitive, distinguishable statement which is repeated in the sermon introduction and ends the introduction are the three factors by which a preacher helps his hearers apprehend with clarity his sermon proposition.

SERMON PROPOSITION QUALITY

What is it that constitutes a proposition and structure that may fairly be described as "good?" A good proposition and structure, which works the same for the preacher as well as his listeners, is qualified as "good" if it is "specific enough to get their hands on it, interesting enough for them to want to stay with it, and so full of life and anticipation that they can't let go of it."[27]

A Three-fold Threat to Sermon Proposition Quality

Warren Wiersbe is insightful as he surfaces three possible problems regarding sermon propositions which militate against the prospect that a proposition will be a good one. Wiersbe cautions against the problems of predictability, departure from the biblical text or an inaccurate guide to the biblical text, and irrelevance toward the hearers.

The first area of caution lies in the fact that, although a sermon proposition helps to forge out a clear outline, yet there may be an attending predictability and sameness of treatment for texts because of a sermon preparation that has grown mechanical. He points out that through the proposition, timeless truths will be supplied for the sermon but these may vary in character from one sermon to the next taking on the form of affirmation, or question, or exclamation, or exhortation.[28]

Second, care must be taken in the construction of the sermon proposition so that the statement is directed toward the understanding and treatment the text will receive by means of the sermon structure. He rightly insists that the proposition "unifies the *content* of the sermon, so it discourages the preacher from covering too much territory or wandering off into foreign lands."[29] Additionally, he suggests that "The development of the message grows out of the union of the text and the proposition" and "If the proposition is what it ought to be, it will contain the 'homiletical DNA' that will determine how the message develops."[30]

Third, the propositional statement will be directed toward life because "an outline isn't a message any more than a recipe is a meal or a blueprint is a house."[31] If the proposition and the structure flowing from it is as it should be, then they will be statements "about God and human life" touching "people where they live" making "people see, think, feel, and want to obey" the text expounded to them.[32]

A Three-fold Task for Sermon Proposition Quality

A good proposition must communicate the biblical writer's message. Therefore, it must be discovered by the preacher in diligent study of the passage but it must not be created by the preacher. According to Don McDougall, a preacher must comply with a three-fold task in order to have a good sermon proposition. He must:

1. find the author's central theme
2. build a message around that theme, and
3. make that theme the central part of all we have to say.[33]

A Three-fold Test for Sermon Proposition Quality

The quality of the sermon proposition can be tested by asking the following three questions.

Does the sermon proposition depict the central idea of the text? Since it is the responsibility of the preacher to discover the central idea of the passage, which will become his sermon proposition, how does one go about discovering the central idea of the text? McDougall suggests three ways the central idea of the passage can be discovered. The central idea of the passage can be found from a single statement in the passage, from the larger context of the passage, and from recurring ideas in the passage.[34]

Does the sermon proposition reflect the attributes of accuracy, specificity, conciseness, interest, and relevance?

Does the sermon proposition provide actual insight as to what the sermon will be about?

The sermon proposition fills a significant part in a sermon. It must be a reliable guide to the hearers informing them of the direction, scope, and content of the sermon. Therefore, the desire and ability to do good work in constructing the sermon proposition statement is important. The inability to do good work in constructing a good sermon proposition will be costly for the one who preaches as well as the ones who hear him preach. When a sermon is preached and no one knows, with a great deal of certainty, what the sermon was about it will inevitably be the situation that the preacher's sermon proposition and structure were poorly crafted and communicated. On the contrary, good work in crafting the sermon proposition not only accurately portrays what the message will be about but such work becomes the cornerstone for qualitative sermon structure, the foundation for clear communication. As of the sermon introduction, where the sermon proposition is stated and repeated, the sermon proposition statement will be an invaluable aid for clarity if it has been constructed well. A well constructed sermon proposition is an accurate one sentence statement of the text's essence that will be unfolded by sermon structure that reveals point by point the meaning of the text. This can only happen if the structure of the sermon has actually been derived from the passage, that is, if the structure of the sermon is text driven.

CONSIDER THE FOLLOWING QUESTIONS

1. What is the preacher's most basic responsibility of cognition? What is his most basic responsibility of communication?
2. What is the most basic conception of a well-designed sermon?
3. What is the old adage for preaching that cannot be set aside without sacrificing clarity?
4. What are the two axiomatic realities of preaching suggested by Halford Luccock and the expression he used to represent these realities?
5. What areas of preaching, according to Don McDougall, require an expositor's most demanding discipline as well as a lot of time and effort in order to establish?
6. How do hearers respond to a preacher who lacks clarity in his preaching, in the view of Augustine?
7. What did William G. T. Shedd say in reference to the expression and characteristics of a sermon proposition that is a legitimate derivative from Scripture?
8. What are Grady Davis's two structural questions which form the framework for understanding in the context of preaching?
9. How does the use of a plural noun proposition and the structure unfolding from it make a contribution to constitute more than the minimal clarity sufficient for preaching?

10. What are the seven benefits for using a plural noun proposition, according to Faris D. Whitesell?

11. What is the basic presupposition that a plural noun proposition makes regarding the sermon structure?

12. How do Shedd's "two things in rhetoric" necessitate a plurality of sermon points?

13. How is the sermon proposition discussed most profitably?

14. In what way does sermon structure contribute to the discussion of the text?

15. What is important to understand about non-plural noun propositional statements, how are they referred to, and what is their inherent weakness?

16. What are the eight steps involved in crafting a plural noun proposition?

17. What words are unacceptable, what words are unadvisable for usage as a plural noun and why are they so?

18. What constitutes the difference between the preacher and his hearers regarding perceived clarity of the sermon proposition?

19. What are the three factors by which a preacher helps his hearers apprehend the sermon proposition with clarity?

20. What constitutes a "good" sermon proposition and structure?

21. What is the three-fold threat to sermon proposition quality?

23. What is the three-fold task for sermon proposition quality?

24. What is the three-fold test for sermon proposition quality?

ENDNOTES

1. Bryson and Taylor, *Building*, 63–68.
2. My conviction is that the role of a pastor is reserved for men only. The preacher of the Word, as a pastor-teacher, is a role exclusively reserved for men. God does and will use gifted women to speak to other women. However, for the sake of simplicity, I will use the male gender in referring to the "preacher."
3. Awbrey, *Begin*, 317–42.
4. Davies, *Papers*, 233.
5. Davis, *Design*, 29.
6. Morgan, *Westminster Pulpit, Volume VII*, 76–77.
7. Cox and Cox, *Best Sermons I*, In the preface of this book the editor and associate editor write: "This book is the fruit of an attempt to bring together some of the best efforts of contemporary preachers to articulate their messages for congregations." The book includes sermons categorized under the headings of evangelistic, expository, doctrinal/theological, ethical, pastoral, and devotional. This sermon was one of ten which were deemed "expository" by the editor and associate editor.
8. Ibid., 67.
9. Jowett, *Preacher*, 133–34.
10. Hamilton, *Handbook*, 42.
11. Luccock, *Workshop*, 211.
12. McDougall, "Central Ideas," 225–56.
13. Ibid., 241.
14. Augustine, *On Christian Teaching*, 141.
15. Shedd, *Homiletics*, 183–84.
16. Davis, *Design,* 24.
17. Ibid., 26.
18. See Skinner, *Teaching Ministry,* 161–71; Perry, *Guide*, 27–36; Koller, *Without Notes*, 72–75.
19. Whitesell, *Power*, 61.
20. Skinner, *Teaching Ministry,* 169.
21. Davis, *Secrets*, 42.
22. Shedd, *Homiletics*, 193–94.
23. Miller, *Marketplace*, 146.
24. Alexander, *Thoughts*, 95.
25. Wiersbe, *Dynamics*, 64.
26. Hamilton, *Handbook,* 64.

27. Wiersbe, *Dynamics*, 61.
28. Ibid., 65.
29. Ibid., 60.
30. Ibid., 62.
31. Ibid., 62.
32. Ibid., 61.
33. McDougall, "Central Ideas," 229.
34. Ibid., 229–33.

Words to Live and Preach By

The Wise Man's Quest

When I was a son to my father, tender and the only son in the sight of my mother, then he taught me and said to me, "Let your heart hold fast my words; keep my commandments and live; acquire wisdom! Acquire understanding! Do not forget, nor turn away from the words of my mouth. Do not forsake her, and she will guard you; love her, and she will watch over you."
PROVERBS 4:3–6

Take my instruction and not silver, and knowledge rather than choicest gold. For wisdom is better than jewels; and all desirable things cannot compare with her.
PROVERBS 8:10–11

The fear of the Lord is the instruction for wisdom, and before honor comes humility.
PROVERBS 15:33

How much better it is to get wisdom than gold! And to get understanding is to be chosen above silver.
PROVERBS 16:16

He who gives attention to the word shall find good, and blessed is he who trusts in the Lord.
PROVERBS 16:20

The mind of the prudent acquires knowledge, and the ear of the wise seeks knowledge.
PROVERBS 18:15

My son, eat honey, for it is good, yes, the honey from the comb is sweet to your taste; know that wisdom is thus for your soul; if you find it, then there will be a future, and your hope will not be cut off.

Proverbs 24:13–14

2

Sermon Structure as a Text Driven Derivative

IN THE PROCESS TO communicate, several things can occur that are highly unfortunate. The one receiving the communication may fail to understand what is being disseminated, that is, they do not understand what they should have understood. Secondly, the one receiving the communication may misunderstand what is being communicated, that is, they do not understand accurately what they should have understood.

It is frustrating to convey something that is not understood or misunderstood. The result of such failure to communicate can run the range from trivial to tragic. Failure to understand or to misunderstand the Word of God represents the greatest possible tragedy of communication. The Word of God is more than worthy of an accurate understanding of its contents every time it is preached.

One way to affect a more accurate understanding of God's Word in preaching lies in better sermon preparation, in general, and better preparation of sermon structure in our preaching, specifically. In general, this chapter is intended to deal with sermon structure, a specific aspect of sermon preparation that will allow for enhanced accuracy of understanding in the sermons we preach. Specifically, this chapter will present how a sermon's structure may be prepared that will provide an accurate understanding of a biblical text as the text itself drives the structuring of the sermon.

An expository sermon is a text driven sermon and a text driven sermon must include a text driven structure for the sermon. It is not enough to necessitate the presence of sermon structure for expository preaching but rather the necessity is to achieve sermon structure that aides the clear understanding of the exposition advanced in the act of preaching a biblical text. For this to be the case, the sermon structure must be a text driven derivative. Two requirements for sermon structure must be strenuously adhered to so that sermon structure will be a true help rather than a hindrance in preaching: it must come from the passage being preached and it must not be overdone. Either one or both of these requirements can be violated easily. Even the best of men, the Puritans, not only violated both requirements but did so in extreme fashion.

SHIFT TOWARD THE SCHOLASTIC PREACHING OF THE PURITANS

The sermons of the Puritans were composed of extensive outlines which, typically, included many main points, and many more sub points and sub-sub points. The sermon outlines of Richard Baxter's, *A Sermon Of Repentance*, and William Williams's, *The Spiritual World*, and John Bunyan's, *The Heavenly Footman*, included at the end of this section, are illustrative of Puritan preaching.

To put it bluntly, the Puritans took a good thing too far. However, in our day of pointless preaching, which has given way to rambling commentary or even multiple story-telling, clearly there is a need for a shift back toward the structured preaching of the Puritans. The shift does not need to travel the entire distance of Puritan preaching but a healthy shift in that direction would be a major, and much needed, correction for present-day preaching. An appropriate and helpful structure is needed for expository preaching, especially, since the expositor endeavors to draw out of the biblical text truths that must be clear and must be accurate expressions of the meaning of the passage from which he preaches.

An appropriate structure for preaching consists of a sermon proposition and a sermon outline, subjects which will be considered for the remaining chapters. However, before considering these issues I want to address briefly the preaching of the Puritans since they were prodigious practitioners of sermon structure.

In the effort to assess modern preaching in the timeframe of 1906, Lewis O. Brastow, a professor of practical theology at Yale University, suggested some insightful contrasts between modern preaching and the preaching of the Puritans. Although he was not advocating Puritan preaching he was fair in the characterization of their preaching, both in terms of strengths and weaknesses. However, I believe his conclusions for present-day preaching, based upon weaknesses of Puritan preaching, are without warrant. From the basis of his positive depiction of Puritan preaching, I will suggest that what is needed as a corrective measure to much present-day preaching is a major shift toward the scholastic, doctrinal, practical exposition of the Puritans. The effort here is not to advocate a duplication of their practice of preaching but to modify their basic approach and practice. The modifications are not based upon alleged contemporary or cultural necessities but upon necessities for hearers of any time and culture so that the modifications suggested would have been beneficial to the Puritan's preaching in their day just as these modifications are indispensable for present-day preaching.

Because the Reformation was a return to the Gospel of Grace as its most basic principle and to the authority of Scripture as its formal principle, there was a return to biblical preaching. In the rediscovery of biblical truth, Reformation and post-reformation preachers perpetuated the scholastic method as the form of preaching most appropriate to communicate the doctrinal insights from the passages preached.

According to Brastow, scholasticism conceived a sermon in terms of structure. A sermon was something that was built. The notion of building a sermon, the notion of a sermon as a homiletic architecture, is a scholastic conception.[1]

Secondly, Brastow maintained that the building of a structured sermon suggests that material is brought to the structure from outside of the text, and that material may not be related to the text, so that the structured sermon may be a growth by accretion. Therefore, it lacks in vital quality. When preaching rests upon external authority and gives itself to the task of defending formulated doctrines, it is very likely to import its texts from without, and to adjust them artificially to the support of these doctrines. In such external adjustments there can be no unfolding of thought from within.[2]

Finally, Brastow said that preaching that is anchored to propositional theology almost as of necessity involves itself in monotony. Therefore, scholasticism had given us a rigidly structured homiletic. Its stereotyped method was one of its most characteristic marks and most serious defects. Each sermon must defend its thesis and theological propositions by appeal to law. This leads to preaching that is "supremely doctrinal and supremely monotonous."[3]

In response to Brastow's assessed weaknesses of Puritan preaching, I suggest the following considerations. First, the scholastic conception of building a sermon is not a sound one. A better concept is *discovering* the structure of the sermon rather than building it. The difference is a vital one. Houses are built but treasure is discovered. A home-builder is not going to discover a house any more than a treasure-hunter is not going to build a treasure. In dealing with a biblical text the structure of the passage must be discovered, not built.

Second, sermon structure comes from the passage that is preached. Other passages are used in the exposition of the passage to corroborate and clarify the meaning of the passage but structure is not derived from outside passages. Therefore, the structure comes from the text and is an unfolding of the text.

Third, propositional preaching may be supremely doctrinal but doctrine in and of itself is not automatically monotonous. Certainly, there are individuals who are bored with theology either because they do not value spiritual truth, or the preachers they have heard who were doctrinal in their preaching never got to the core significance of the doctrines they handled so that their preaching was just a lot of data without any personal significance or implications. The former is inexcusable on behalf of the hearer and the latter is inexcusable on behalf of the preacher.

However, the preaching of the Puritans is marked by dominant qualities which are commonly absent from much present-day preaching, absences that prevent preaching from being a vital force in the lives of hearers. The following qualities of Puritan preaching will always be beneficial to the preaching enterprise and preaching will be less than it should be when they are absent or marginal.[4] The qualities of intellectual, pastoral, persuasive, prophetic, and Bible focused preaching were hallmarks of the Puritans.

Puritan preaching had a notable intellectual quality. As a class of preachers, the Puritans were preeminent advocates of an intelligent practice of faith. They believed biblical truth must be intellectually appropriated and edifyingly taught. The revelation of divine truth must appeal to human thought, and growth in Christian character demands an intelligent presentation of it. As a class of preachers, the Puritans were men of profound and vigorous understanding of Scripture.

Puritan preaching displayed a prominent pastoral quality. The Puritans were eminently edifying preachers. They believed the congregation committed to their charge was to be built up into strong Christian maturity. Though they had an unfailing evangelistic impulse and sought to win men to Christ in their preaching, it was their ultimate aim to develop sound Christian piety and character in the lives of believers.

Their preaching, though marked with a depth of theological understanding, was prevailingly practical. The sermons of the Puritans never failed to be abounding in practicality.[5]

Puritan preaching demonstrated a noble persuasiveness. Because their preaching was so elaborately instructive, to the degree that they were viewed as theological teachers, they were persuasive in the truths they taught. Their zeal, evidenced by the directness and forcefulness of their theological yet practical instruction, caused them to be effective in promoting change and correction in the lives of their hearers. Their strong emotional earnestness effected ethical reform in the hearers' lives. "Their preaching reached not only the consciences of men, but it undertook to reach their hearts and to subdue them to God as it subdued them to righteousness."[6]

Puritan preaching was saturated in a prophetic tone. Not only were they avid adherents to their theological beliefs, they were always ready to submit to and to require submission to the divine authority of Scripture. Modification of what God had spoken was not acceptable. They were not liberal or tolerant in theory or spirit, and were therefore, the enemies of all who were broadminded and enemies of theological latitudinarianism.[7]

Puritan preaching was anchored directly to the Scriptures. In promoting a rational faith based upon Scripture, they accounted no merit to guidelines of faith and practice that could not be defended from Scripture. Their instruction was never given without an appeal to Scripture. Their preaching, then, was an effort to interpret and apply the Bible for the edification of the Christian's thinking so as to enhance the character of their hearers and to provide guidance in their conduct.[8]

Certainly, the Puritans were not perfect preachers in that they possessed weaknesses and shortcomings. Every preacher demonstrates weaknesses and shortcomings. However, any man's preaching that can be characterized as having an intellectual and pastoral quality, possessing persuasiveness and a prophetic tone, while being anchored directly to the Scriptures is certainly preaching that has much to commend it. Even though such preaching today might be criticized by some and labeled as "scholastic" or "puritanical," I suggest such criticism and labeling is exceedingly better than the criticism and the labels that might be afforded preaching that lacks these qualities! I want to express that the scholastic preaching of the Puritans of old is far better than the unintelligible ramblings and storytelling of the anti-puritans of today!

The remaining chapters of this book dealing with the sermon proposition and sermon structure. These are the devices which ensure a scholastic cast to one's preaching. And, to be sure, these devices are offered because the same beliefs and motives which guided the Puritans—that the preaching of Scripture must be perceptible, persuasive, and practical. Perceptible, persuasive, practical explanation of Scripture is desired by those seeking to live pleasingly to the Lord and such teaching is certainly consistent with true expository preaching. For now, it will be helpful to see the highly structured outlines of Puritan preaching by means of an example of the work of three Puritan preachers—Richard Baxter, William Williams, and John Bunyan.

A Sermon of Repentance from Ezekiel 36:31 by Richard Baxter.[9]

Introduction

1. The remembering of their own iniquities, and loathing themselves for them, is the sign of a repenting people and the prognostic of their restoration, so far as deliverance may be here expected.

2. It is not all kind of remembering that will prove you penitent.

    (1) It is a remembering from a deep conviction of the evil and odiousness of sin.

    (2) It is a remembering with abhorrence and self-loathing.

    (3) It is a remembering that leadeth to a resolved and vigilant forsaking.

3. It is not all self-loathing that will signify true repenting.

    But the self-loathing of the truly penitent hath these following properties:

    (1) It proceedeth from the predominant love of God, whom we have abused and offended.

    (2) It is much excited by the observation and sense of his exceeding mercies, and is conjunct with gratitude.

    (3) It continueth and increaseth under the greatest assurance of forgiveness, and sense of love, and dieth not when we think we are out of danger.

(4) It containeth a loathing of sin as sin, and a love of holiness as such, and not only a love of ease and peace, and a loathing of sin, as the cause of suffering.

(5) It resolveth the soul against returning to its former course, and resolveth it for an entire devotedness to God for the time to come.

(6) It deeply engageth the penitent in a conflict against the flesh, and maketh him victorious, and setteth him to work in a life of holiness, as his trade and principal business in the world.

(7) It bringeth him to a delight in God and holiness, and a delight in himself, so far as he findeth God and heaven, and holiness within him.

Part One: This must be the self-loathing that must afford you comfort, as a penitent people in the way to restoration.

1. Self-loathing containeth these common acts
   (1) Accusing and condemning thoughts against ourselves.
   (2) It containeth a deep distaste and displeasure with ourselves, and a heart rising against ourselves.
   (3) As also a holy indignation against ourselves, as apprehending that we have played the enemies to ourselves and God.
   (4) It possesseth us with grief and trouble at our miscarriages, so that, a soul in this condition is sick of itself and vexed with its self-procured woe.

2. Note, also, that when self-loathing proceedeth from mere conviction, and is without the love of God and holiness, it is but the tormentor of the soul, and runs it deeper into sin, provoking men here to destroy their lives; and in hell it is the never dying worm.

3. Note, also, that it is themselves that they are said to loathe, because it is ourselves that conscience hath to do with, as witness, and as judge.

4. Note, also, that it is not for our troubles, or our disgrace, or our bodily deformities, or infirmities, or for our poverty and want, that penitents are said to loathe themselves, but for their iniquities and abominations.

- (1) This loathing is a kind of justice done upon ourselves, and therefore is exercised, not for mere infelicities, but for crimes.
- (2) It is sin that is loathed by God, and makes the creature loathsome in his eyes; and repentance conformeth the soul to God, and therefore causeth us to loathe as he doth, and on his grounds.
- (3) There is no evil but sin, and that which sin procureth; and therefore it is for sin that the penitent loathes himself.

5. Note, also, that till repentance, there was none of this remembering of sin, and the loathing of themselves.

- (1) Inquire, then, whether there be none among you that live a sensual, careless life, clothed with the best, and faring deliciously every day in rioting and drunkenness, chambering and wantonness, strife and envying, not putting on Christ, nor walking in the Spirit, but making provision for the flesh, to satisfy the lusts thereof.
- (2) Inquire whether there be none among you, that, being strangers to the new birth, and to the inward workings of the Spirit of Christ upon the soul, do also distaste a holy life, and make it the matter of your reproach, and pacify your accusing consciences with a religion made up of mere words, and heartless outside, and so much obedience and your fleshly pleasures will admit, accounting those that go beyond you, especially if they differ from you in your modes and circumstances, to be but a company of proud, Pharisaical, self-conceited hypocrites, and those whom you desire to suppress.
- (3) Inquire also whether there be none among you that let loose your passions on your inferiors, and oppress your poor tenants, and make them groan under the task, or at least do little to relieve the needy, nor study not to serve the Lord with your estates, but sacrifice all to the pleasing of your flesh, unless it be some inconsiderable pittance, or fruitless drops, that are unproportionable to your receivings.
- (4) Inquire whether there be none that live the life of Sodom, in pride, fullness of bread, and idleness; and that are puffed up with their estates and dignities, and are strangers to the

humility, meekness, patience, and self-denial of the saints; that ruffle in bravery, and contend more zealously for their honor an preeminence than for the honor and interest of the Lord.

Part Two: The loathing of yourselves in your own eyes, for all your iniquities and abominations.

1. A converted soul hath a new and heavenly light to help him to see those matters of humbling use which others see not.

2. He hath the knowledge of sin and of himself.

3. He hath seen by faith the Lord himself; the majesty, the holiness, the jealousy, the goodness of the eternal God whom he hath offended, and therefore must needs abhor himself.

4. He hath tasted of God's displeasure against him for his sin, already.

5. He hath seen Christ crucified, and mourned over him.

6. He hath foreseen, by faith, the end of sin, and the doleful recompense of the ungodly; his faith beholdeth the misery of damned souls, and the glory which sinners cast away.

7. The true convert hath had the liveliest taste of mercy, of the blood of Christ, of the offers and covenant of grace, of reprieving mercy, of pardoning mercy, of healing and preserving mercy, and of the unspeakable mercy contained in the promise of everlasting life; and to find that he hath sinned against all this mercy, doth constrain him to abhor himself.

8. It is only the true convert that hath a new and holy nature, contrary to sin; and, therefore, loathes himself because his nature is contrary to his sin.

9. The true convert is one that is much at home; his heart is the vineyard which he is daily dressing; his work is ordinarily about it; and, therefore, he is acquainted with those secret sins, and daily failings, which ungodly men, that are strangers to themselves, do not observe, though they have them in dominion.

10. Lastly, a serious Christian is a workman of the Lord's, and daily busy at the exercise of his graces, and, therefore, hath occasion to observe his weaknesses, and failings, and from sad experience is for to abhor himself.

If you be not brought to loathe yourselves, it is not because there is no loathsome matter in you. And to instigate you hereunto, let me further reason with you.

1. You can easily loathe an enemy; and who hath been a greater enemy to any of you than yourselves? Another may injure you; but no man can everlastingly undo you, but yourselves.

2. You abhor him that kills your dearest friends; and it is you by your sins that have put to death the Lord of life.

3. Who is it but yourselves that have robbed you of so much precious time, and so much precious fruit of ordinances, and of all the mercies of the Lord?

4. Who is it but yourselves that hath brought you under God's displeasure: Poverty could not have made him loathe you, nor anything besides your sins.

5. Who wounded conscience, and hath raised all your doubts and fears? Was it not your sinful selves?

6. Who is it but yourselves that hath brought you so near the gulf of misery, and endangered your eternal peace?

7. Consider the loathsome nature of your sins; and how, then, can you choose but to loathe yourselves?

    (1) It is the creature's rebellion or disobedience against the Absolute Universal Sovereign.

    (2) It is the deformity of God's noblest creature here on earth, and the abusing of the most noble faculties.

    (3) It is a stain so deep that nothing can wash out but the blood of Christ.

    (4) The church must loathe it, and must cast out the sinner as loathsome, if he remain impenitent; and none of the servants of the Lord must have any friendship with the unfruitful works of darkness.

    (5) God himself doth loathe the creature for sin, and for nothing else but sin.

But we are much afraid of God's departure, when we see how common self-love is in the world, and how rare this penitent self-loathing is.

1. Do they loathe themselves that on every occasion are contending for their honor, and exalting themselves, and venturing their very souls, to be highest in the world, for a little while?
2. Do they loathe themselves that are readier to justify all their sins, or at least to extenuate them, than humbly confess them?
3. Do they loathe themselves for all their sins that cannot endure to be reproved, but loathe their friends and the ministers of Christ that tell them of their loathsomeness?
4. Do they loathe themselves that take their pride itself for manhood, and Christian humility for baseness, and brokenness of heart for whining hypocrisy of folly, and call them a company of priest-ridden fools that lament their sin, and ease their souls by free confession?
5. Do they loathe themselves for all their sins, who loathe those that will not do as they, and speak reproachfully of such as run not with them to the same excess of riot?
6. Do they loathe themselves for all their sins, that love their sins even better than their God, and will not, by all the obtestations, and commands, and entreaties of the Lord, be persuaded to forsake them?

Part Three: Having called you first to remember your misdoings, and secondly to loathe yourselves in your own eyes for them, I must add a third, that you stop not here, but proceed to reformation, or else all the rest is but hypocrisy.

Conclusion

"The sum of our requests"

1. That holiness may be encouraged, and the overspreading profaneness of this nation effectually kept down.
2. That an able, diligent ministry may be encouraged, and not corrupted by temporal power.

3. That discipline may be seriously promoted, and ministers no more hindered by magistrates in the exercise of their office than physicians and schoolmasters are in theirs.

4. We earnestly request that Scripture sufficiency, as the test of our religion and only universal law of Christ, may be maintained.

"This I would beg of you as on my knees"

1. As for the sake of Christ, whose cause and people it is that I am pleading for.

2. For the sake of thousands of poor souls in this land, whose salvation or damnation will be much promoted by you.

3. For the sake of thousands of the dear servants of the Lord, whose eyes are waiting to see what God will do by your hands.

4. For your own sakes, who are undone if you dash yourselves on the rock you should build on, and set against the holy God, and turn the cries of his servants to heaven for deliverance from you.

5. For the sake of your prosperity, that they may not be bred up in ignorance or ungodliness.

6. For the honor of the nation and yourselves, that you turn by all the suspicions and fears that are raised in the land.

7. For the honor of sound doctrine and church-government, that you may not bring schism into greater credit than now you have brought it to deserve shame.

8. Lastly, I beg this of you, for the honor of sovereignty, and the nation's peace.

This sermon by Richard Baxter was chosen as illustrative of Puritan preaching due to the fact that he is cited by Wiersbe and Perry as the "Best known of the Puritan preachers" and was referred to as "the 'English Demosthenes.'"[10] This sermon, as representative of a Puritan sermon outline certainly is excessive, but it is not excessive in the amount of divisions included in a *typical sermon by Baxter or other Puritans* in their preaching.

However, examples of less-extensive sermon outlines include William Williams's outline for his sermon from Daniel 12:2, entitled

The Spiritual World,[11] and John Bunyan's, *The Heavenly Footman*, from 1 Corinthians 9:24. Even these less-extensive sermon outlines will seem excessive to us and rightly so. Sermon structure that is suitable for today cannot begin to compare with the sermon outlines of the Puritans, even the relatively briefer sermon outlines of the Puritans as those exemplified below.

William Williams's outline for his sermon from Daniel 12:2, entitled *The Spiritual World*, was as follows.

I. We shall give some proofs of the existence of the world to come.
   1. We can look upon the nature of the human soul as a proof of it.
   2. The functions of the soul.
   3. God's moral government of the world.
   4. The general dealings of God with men in this world prove the existence of a future one; while, if we deny it, the dispensations of God become quite inexplicable.
   5. We have the more sure word of prophecy on the subject—the express testimony of God as to the existence of that world.

II. The nature of the world to come.
   1. It is a spiritual world.
   2. It is a world in which a wonderful expansion of man's faculties and powers will take place.
   3. Whatever be the strongest bent of a man's nature here will be the strongest bent of his nature there.
   4. It will be a world where every man will fully develop the characteristic bias of his nature.
   5. It is a world without any intermixtures.
   6. It is a world of rewards and punishments.

III. The principles and sources of happiness and misery in that invisible world.
   1. The moral principles of the heart.
   2. The witness of the conscience.

3. The memory of the past.

4. Another element of blessedness in the invisible world will be the recognition of friends there.

5. Approbation and disapprobation is also another of these elements.

6. Again, fellowship with one another is one of the elements of happiness and misery in the other world.

7. Another of these elements is the view that will be obtained of the character and dispensations of God.

8. The approbation and disapprobation of God; His will and favor on the one hand, His wrath and resentment on the other.

IV. This world is of everlasting duration.

1. It is a continuous duration.

2. It is an undiminishing duration.

3. All its things have the same stamp and image.

Deductions

1. We are all related to this world we have been speaking of.

2. It is clear that it is the mind that makes heaven and hell; the mind is the home of happiness or misery—and the moral disposition of the heart of the source of the one and of the other.

3. It is impossible for anyone to exert too much care and self-denial in order to win heaven and avoid hell.

4. Let us think much of that world.

The sermon outline of John Bunyan's *The Heavenly Footman* from 1 Corinthians 9:24 was as follows.[12]

1. Running as Fleeing
2. Running as Pressing
3. Running as Continuing

   The reasons for the running

   (1) Because all or everyone that runneth doth not obtain the prize;

Sermon Structure as a Text Driven Derivative 45

(2) Because, you know, that tho a man do run, yet if he do not overcome, or win, as well as run, what will they be the better for their running?

(3) Because the way is long, and there is many a dirty step, many a high hill, much work to do, a wicked heart, world, and devil to overcome;

(4) They that will go to heaven they must run for it; because, as the way is long, so the time in which they are to get to the end of it is very uncertain;

(5) They that will have heaven, they must run for it; because the devil, the law, sin, death, and hell follow them.

(6) They that go to heaven must run for it; because perchance the gates of heaven may be shut shortly.

(7) Lastly, because if thou lose, thou losest all, thou losest soul, God, Christ, heaven, ease, peace, etc.

Pray tell me, therefore, how I should run. That thou mayest indeed be satisfied in this particular, consider these following things.

The first direction: If thou wouldst so run as to obtain the kingdom of heaven, then be sure that thou get into the way that leadeth thither.

The second direction: As thou shouldst get into the way, so thou shouldst also be much in studying and musing on the way.

The third direction: Thou must strip thyself of those things that may hang upon thee, to the hindering of thee in the way to the kingdom of heaven.

The fourth direction: Beware of by-paths; take heed thou dost not turn into those lanes which lead out of the way.

The fifth direction: Do not thou be too much in looking too high in thy journey heavenward.

The sixth direction: Take heed that you have not an ear open to everyone that calleth after you as you are in your journey.

The seventh direction: Be not daunted tho thou meetest with never so many discouragements in thy journey thither.

The eighth direction: Take heed of being offended at the cross that thou must go by before thou come to heaven.

The ninth direction: Beg of God that He would do these two things for thee: First, enlighten thine understanding; And, secondly, inflame thy will.

The tenth direction: Cry to God that He would inflame thy will also with the things of the other world.

1. The saints of old, they being willing and resolved for heaven, what could stop them?
2. See again, on the other side, the children of the devil, because they are not willing, how many shifts and starting-holes they will have.

Lest in thy running thou should not lose thy way, remember to:

1. Get into the way.
2. Then study on it.
3. Then strip, and lay aside everything that would hinder.
4. Beware of by-paths.
5. Do not gaze and stare too much about thee, but be sure to ponder the path of thy feet.
6. Do not stop for any that call after thee, whether it be the world, the flesh, or the devil.
7. Be not daunted with any discouragements thou meetest with as thou goest.
8. Take heed of stumbling at the cross.
9. Cry hard to God for an enlightened heart, and a willing mind, and God give thee a prosperous journey.

Provocation:

If this will not provoke thee, consider thus,

1. Thy soul is thine own soul, that is either to be saved or lost.

2. If thou lose thy soul, it is thou also that must bear the blame.
3. That, if thou wilt not run, the people of God are resolved to deal with thee even as Lot dealt with his wife—that is, leave thee behind them.
4. Will it not be a dishonor to thee to see others looking more after heaven than thee?

Again, the Puritans took a good thing too far. The extensiveness of their many levels of thought and the weightiness of their sermons seem overwhelming. Structure is good, but too much of it prevents a hearer from gaining a clear reception and retention of what is being preached.

ADVANCED PLANNING

I have never been a practical advocate of advanced planning of sermons nor am I an advocate of advanced sermon preparation. In theory, I am all for a preacher preparing himself to preach before the week previous to the preaching event. My track record indicates the reality that this is something I have not accomplished in actual practice. I have discovered that, for a pastor who preaches multiple times each week, advanced sermon preparation is very general at best. If a preacher is not re-preaching sermons he has already prepared and preached before, it is very difficult to know with a substantial amount of specificity what the treatment of subject-matter will be for sermons months ahead of the preaching occasions. Consider for example, Calvin Miller's recommendation and appraisal of advanced sermon planning and preparation. He writes,

> I recommend an annual view of sermon preparation, which means that the pastor should take a block of time during the year to plan his preaching for the next fifty-two Sundays. My annual sermon planning time comes usually in the week between Christmas and New Year's. I take the calendar, type off the fifty-two Sundays of the coming year by date, and begin to fill in the blanks with my sermon title, text, and outline for those Sundays ... During this planning week I try to outline (and *only* outline) and "textify" these sermons. I then place them in a file folder so that I can look back over them as I plan my year of preaching. Through the successive weeks of the year, I repeatedly refer to this file, gather illustrations to place in each of the separate file folders, and augment the sermon's content between the time of its

first outlining and its actual preaching. Sometimes I have felt like my long-range preaching plan was not well thought through and find I must scrap a portion of it midyear and substitute something else. Overall, my long-range planning directs my year.[13]

What Miller is advocating seems to be attainable for an expository preacher in a limited way. That is, when an expositor is preaching through a biblical book, he may be able to work ahead by diagramming passages he will be preaching weeks before he will deliver them to his congregation. The limited benefit of advanced preparation I have experienced has been precisely at this point. In diagramming a biblical text, I may diagram beyond what I will be able to preach in the next sermon or two and, therefore, through this advanced work I may be able to gain a great deal of certainty as to the subject-matter of future messages, albeit messages for the very near future, and how the messages will be structured. This is not done intentionally, according to a plan to work ahead beyond the next sermon. There are times, in fact, where a diagrammed passage, intended to be one sermon becomes a short series of sermons. In such cases, one diagrammed passage becomes advanced preparation, though only initial preparation, but still advanced preparation for sermons weeks before their actual delivery. This occurs with no intentionality, no plan to work ahead. In the process of preparation it simply becomes obvious that I have bitten off more than I can chew for the next sermon. This, then, is unplanned yet limited advanced preparation.

Expository preaching, that is, the verse-by-verse preaching through a book of the Bible, presents some opportunity for advanced preparation of sermon propositions and structure. Spurgeon too understood the rather natural connection between advanced planning in sermon preparation along with the preaching of a series of sermons. However, he denounced both in theory and practice, both for himself and for others.[14]

Despite Spurgeon's arguments against advanced preparation and serial preaching, it must be acknowledged that he was neither an expositor nor was he one whose homiletical capabilities should be described by any other term than "genius." Men of lesser abilities may be served well by the advantages that advanced preparation and series preaching provides, even if the advanced preparation is limited to the next sermon or the next few sermons. I concur with Lloyd-Jones regarding the reticence for attempting to propose an advanced preaching plan. He writes,

> It is right both to preach on odd texts and a series; and, in any case a series can be broken into. Indeed a series should always be broken into if you feel a particular pressure on your spirit urging you to do so. That is why I would never print a program of what I proposed to preach even for the next three months. You cannot tell what you should do—at least I could never tell.[15]

Lloyd-Jones's reluctance was based upon not wanting to be presumptuous to know with certainty what he should preach and actually propose such a course for preaching months ahead of time. As Lloyd-Jones suggests, since a series can be broken into, the idea that the plan may have to withstand some deviation is not a problem for advanced preparation.

The problem I have with advanced preparation is a logistical one. The logistical problem has to do with the difficulty to take a large section of a biblical book, provide careful study for the book to understand accurately what the author is talking about and what he is saying about what he is talking about, and doing this for many texts in a short amount of time. My experience has proven to me that an accurate depiction of a passage, one in which I can have confidence that this, indeed, is indicative of the meaning of the passage and one I can preach with conviction, consumes much time. In fact, it consumes more time and effort than I could ever give to a plan to develop accurate depictions of many passages in a couple of weeks.

Stephen Rummage, in his book *Planning Your Preaching* distinguishes the planning process from the preparation process. Exegesis and developing the completed sermon are part of the preparation process, not the planning process.[16] Rummage is correct and his insight brings to light my contention with advanced sermon planning, that is, it really doesn't consist of advanced preparation. It is only planning and planning is not preparation. Planning without preparation does not seem to me to be much of a plan. Any plan for preaching that I can attain is limited to whatever advanced preparation I may be able to achieve. The liability then with advanced planning is that it does not incorporate preparation. With a plan in place, one must limit preparation in order to stay on track with one's plan, or be willing to have one's plan repeatedly violated by weekly preparation. On many occasions, I have come to a paragraph which I thought I would preach in one sermon, only to discover that I ended up preaching the paragraph in three or four sermons. If a preaching plan were in place, it would be in disarray.

As advantageous as advanced planning may be in theory, I believe it is far more advantageous to deal accurately with the texts that one preaches. In principle, advanced planning must defer to accurate preaching based upon thorough preparation. In other words, if one preaches from a preaching plan it is far more important to deal accurately and insightfully with each text one comes to while preaching through a biblical book rather than limiting treatment of God's Word in order to stay on track with a preaching plan. The plan must not control how Scripture is preached. God's Word must not be minimized because of a man's plan for preaching.

However, if one can actually do advanced planning that incorporates advanced preparation of sermons with accuracy and thus compiles many accurate depictions of passages from which one may preach for many weeks after, how great that is! If this is actually the situation, I would only commend and encourage any man's ability to proceed in a course of advanced sermon preparation, and therefore advanced planning of sermons.

If, however, one cannot produce an accurate depiction of a passage in terms of a sermon proposition and sermon structure by the expeditious means required by the typical approach of advanced planning, then don't worry about it! This may be just an additional matter in which you have to apply the principle of "Others may, I cannot." If this is the case, then be content with preaching that is poor in terms of advanced planning but is rich in textual accuracy because you prioritize thorough preparation over long-range planning. After all, do you think God is more concerned with an advanced preaching plan of a year, half year, quarter of a year, or do you think he is more concerned with a plan that may be limited to the next week yet enables one to say with great accuracy, "Thus saith the Lord"? People may want you to know what you will be preaching about months from next week but God requires you to know what you will be preaching about the next time you preach! Since you can only preach one sermon at a time, why not be content to prioritize your preaching one sermon at a time?

Certainly, however, a worse-case-scenario should be that through very diligent work the week previous to delivery, the pastor must be able to know with no uncertainty what his sermon proposition will be and how that proposition will be unfolded through a sermon outline. In the sermon introduction the proposition is announced clearly and repeated at least one time. The sermon introduction should conclude with the final repetition of the sermon proposition. In the body of the sermon the proposition will be unfolded with the same clarity through clear sermon structure. Advanced preparation, not advanced planning, is responsible for producing the sermon proposition and sermon structure. When these things, the sermon proposition and sermon outline, are established and to the degree that these things are established through advanced preparation, there is truly advanced planning that is more than just a worthy concept.

DIAGRAMMING THE BIBLICAL TEXT AS ADVANCED PREPARATION

Diagramming a text is an excellent way to discover the central idea of the text and the supporting components of the central idea, which will become the proposition of the sermon and the sermon points, respectively. This is immediate preparation in which one begins to prepare sermons to be preached the next week. Beyond this critical benefit, diagramming is a profitable way in which any preacher can do short-range advanced preparation, or at least unintentional advanced preparation. Diagramming a passage which is intended to be the initial work for one sermon, only to discover that the amount of text diagrammed will in fact yield two or more messages rather than one, is perhaps a haphazard method of advanced preparation. In reality, this is unintentional advanced preparation, which may happen commonly as one preaches through a book of the Bible. However, this is not a bad thing. The preaching ministry should be the outworking of a man's diligent study through books of the Bible, for the most part. If one's diligent discovery yields more than can be accommodated in the next sermon so that one has inadvertently prepared for the following sermon as well, this is, indeed, an unforeseen blessing.

Unnecessary pressure for, and unwise commitment to, advanced planning of sermons so that one knows definitively for months ahead what one's text will be on a given day, what the sermon proposition will be, and what the structure will be, can be a real threat to true expository preaching. Such a commitment to advanced preparation motivated by a desire to achieve advanced planning for one's preaching gives evidence that one's true commitment in preaching is the projection of sermonic treatment of passages rather than the thorough discovery of passages and the imminent delivery of that which was discovered. Expository preaching will not thrive if thorough discovery of texts is supplanted by projected treatment of texts. The smooth organization of advanced planning will be paid for at the expense of shallowness in preaching. Warren Wiersbe writes, "The opportunities are limitless for the shallow preacher to manufacture a ministry that's a mile long and an inch thick."[17] Though Wiersbe was commenting upon the more shameful practice of purchasing or securing ready-made outlines for preaching, preparing one's own outlines, albeit outlines quickly and conveniently stamped out long ago for the cause of advanced planning, may still result in shallow preaching none-the-less.

The main reason for advanced planning and advanced preparation seems to be for the collection of supporting material, primarily illustrations, that can be stuffed in a file created for each of the sermon outlines created months before they are to be delivered. Therefore, texts are given a predetermined structure based upon a hasty and superficial treatment for the sake of potential illustrative enrichment in preaching. Does this not indicate that the compelling commitment in one's preaching is to provide enhanced illustrative material rather than enhanced perception of a text's meaning in one's preaching? The priority of illustrative material may be good for preaching but it is not the priority for expository preaching. Besides, one does not need to commit to advanced planning simply to be garnering illustrative material to be used in future messages. An expositor can, and should be, reading ahead in the book he is expounding so that he knows what subject-matter he will be dealing with in the future and, therefore, he can be collecting such materials to be used as needed. Therefore, the collection of illustrative material for future usage does not warrant a commitment to hasty treatment of texts for the sake of advanced planning.

It is sufficient for the expository preacher to affect short-range advanced preparation by diagramming texts several weeks before he preaches from those passages, getting an initial idea of several future sermon propositions with their attending outlines. The final form of these propositions and outlines will be determined by the most thorough exegesis of the text the preacher can muster the week before the actual delivery of the sermon. Exegetical scrutiny may necessitate modifying the proposition and structure which was based solely on the preliminary study of the passage through diagramming.

Later we will look at the process of diagramming. For now, suffice it to say that the purpose for diagramming is to synthesize the passage of Scripture from which one intends to preach. Synthesis, in its strictest sense, is defined as "the putting of two or more things together so as to form a whole" or the assembling of separate or subordinate parts into a new form. For the purpose of preaching, synthesis is done to assemble the parts of a preaching portion for an enhanced understanding. In regards to a diagrammed passage of Scripture, it is through synthesis that one may see how all of the various parts of a text relate to the text as a whole. For a preacher preparing to preach a sermon, synthesizing a passage is a five step process: one *determines* the text to be preached; one *dismantles* the text into constituent parts by diagramming the passage; one *discerns* how each of the parts of the diagrammed text are related to the whole of the text; then one *depicts* how the parts and the whole are related through a carefully worded sermon outline and sermon proposition; finally, one *details* or modifies the sermon proposition and outline to reflect exegetical insights discovered through a detailed study of the passage. Synthesis is a beneficial means by which a chosen text, once diagrammed, may yield a sermon proposition and outline.

Synthesis is not only a means by which the end-product of diagrammatical analysis, the sermon proposition and sermon structure, are obtained in his study. Synthesis is also the process by which an expositor, in the pulpit, helps his hearers understand with clarity and understanding the relationship of each part of the text to the whole of the text. In other words, through expository preaching the expositor accomplishes for his hearers what was accomplished for him in his study of the passage—how the parts of the text relate to the whole of the text.

For the expositor in the study, synthesis is a means of personal understanding of a text through diagrammatical analysis and exegesis. For the expositor in the pulpit, synthesis is a means of helping his hearers understand a text by explaining the passage through the aid of a sermon proposition and sermon outline. Therefore, when one preaches an expository sermon, the preacher is involved in the synthesis process, in behalf of his hearers, as he expounds the passage with the use of his sermon proposition and his sermon structure and helps them to understand the passage of Scripture. As Howard Hendricks explains, "It (synthesis) moves from the big picture to an analysis of the parts—breaking them down, seeing their meaning in light of the whole, and then putting them back together again so everyone walks out the door thinking, *Now I understand it and can use it.*"[18]

The expositor must first successfully synthesize the text in his study before it can be synthesized successfully in the pulpit. If the preacher cannot synthesize clearly the passage for himself in his study he will be unable to help others synthesize the passage as he preaches it. A lost guide can only lead a following of lost people! The expositor bears a two-fold responsibility for synthesis in his preaching—he must synthesize the text for himself in his study and he must synthesize the text for his hearers in the pulpit as he preaches.

INCLUSION OF MATERIAL AND SERMONIC INTEGRITY

The arranged material must contribute to the unity of the message. This must be understood as the first principle in determining whether any material should be included in a sermon. This, however, must never be construed to become the grounds for skipping any textual material of the passage. In other words, you must never think to yourself, "I will skip this phrase, this sentence, or these verses because they will make no contribution to the unity of my sermon." The contents of the biblical text do not pose a threat of disrupting the unity of the message of that text. The text is the message! If your sermon can be messed up by dealing with the text, then clearly your sermon is a messed up representation of what is the message of the text! In expository preaching, the text is a given—it is God given! The text, the message of the text, the unified message of the text is what you must bring out in your exposition. The text has a unified message but the issues are these—have you discovered it and does your sermon reflect it? If not, then you do not have a problem with the text, *you are the problem* since you do not understand the text, and *your sermon will become a problem* since it cannot represent the meaning of the text. The more you deal with the biblical text the more unity will be supplied to the sermon if the sermon is an accurate depiction of the unity and message of the text!

The unity of material to be incorporated does not have anything to do with textual content but it has everything to do with all things included as possible explanation, corroboration, illustration, or application of the text. If the material to be arranged does not make a contribution to the development of the subject-matter of the sermon proposition then unity will suffer loss. Again, if the sermon proposition is the controlling

Sermon Structure as a Text Driven Derivative

principle of the sermon, then it demands that all extraneous material, however valuable and attractive it may be in itself, must be rejected. However, if the text is the controlling principle then all material that directly or indirectly clarifies the meaning of the passage has the right of presence in the sermon. "When building an arch the idea of the arch controls. Only such stones are selected as will fit this particular arch. All other stones, no matter how fine, are rejected."[19]

Judicious discretion and vigilant discernment must be employed to prevent content from being incorporated into the sermon that would diffuse the thrust of the sermon. Whatever is not helpful to develop the theme of the sermon weakens the sermon. Woodrow Kroll wisely observed the connection between the unity of a sermon assisted through the willingness to withhold material from the sermon. He writes:

> As you gaze at the Mona Lisa or Da Vinci's Last Supper you do not see a mass of different colors. These paintings are composites of many colors or characters but we are conscious of receiving only one impression. That is because there is a unity to each painting. The impression received is not of separate parts but of a unified whole. Sermons must exhibit the same element.
>
> Like the Master's seamless robe, each of the divisions and parts of a sermon must fit together, not as a patchwork, but as a whole. If one of the component parts does not fit, it should be discarded.[20]

The willingness and ability to withhold material that would detract from the unity of the sermon is both difficult to attempt and difficult to do when attempted, but it must be done.

There is no doubt as to the subjective criteria for determining what should and should not be rejected. What one preacher deems as crucial for the advancement of the theme and the unity of the sermon, another preacher would determine that the same material should be set aside. Still, every man who preaches bears the responsibility to determine what will and will not develop sermonic unity and establish the meaning of the text and, therefore, include or disallow material into the sermon as he deems wise.

MASTERY OF CONTENT

A preacher must master the text he is preaching on or he will not be clear to those trying to understand him. His mastery of the text, that is, his understanding of the content of the passage, must be born out in his statements of his sermon proposition as well as the statements of theological principle, or the main points of the sermon. If he has not understood clearly what he is talking about, how can those who hear him understand clearly? Spurgeon wrote:

> Your doctrinal teaching should be clear and unmistakable. To be so it must first of all be clear to yourself. Some men think in smoke and preach in a cloud. Your people do not want a luminous haze, but the solid terra firma of truth... No man can hope to be felt who cannot make himself understood. If we give our people refined truth, pure Scriptural doctrine, and also worded as to have no needless obscurity about it, we shall be true shepherds of the sheep, and the profiting of our people will soon be apparent.[21]

If a preacher cannot articulate the main thoughts of the passage from which he will be preaching, he has not understood the passage sufficiently. He is still ignorant of that which he must know with certainty in order to be able to preach with clarity.

The very fact that clear, accurate, concise statements of theological principle cannot be articulated guarantees that the sermon will be swamped with vague verbiage in an attempt to, somehow, communicate what is still not understood. Again, Spurgeon's comments are appropriate concerning this issue.

> Verbiage is too often the fig-leaf which does duty as a covering for theological ignorance. Sounding periods are offered instead of sound doctrine, and rhetorical flourishes in the place of robust thought. Such things ought not to be. The abounding of empty declamation, and the absence of food for the soul, will turn a pulpit into a box of bombast, and inspire contempt instead of reverence.[22]

Mastery of a subject is verified by the ability to articulate the pivotal statements of the sermon (the points of sermon structure) in the most brief and comprehensible manner. When there is imperfect mastery of a subject, the following predicament arises—"Instead of a clear, downright statement, because he knows whereof he affirms, he expresses himself obscurely and doubtfully, because he does not certainly and positively know. Statement follows statement, and yet there is little or no progress toward the final statement."[23]

With the sermon proposition understood by the greatest amount of people possible, then and then alone is integrity between the sermon proposition and sermon structure a reality. The preacher, however, has to be just as clear in the statement of the sermon points as he was clear in the statement of the proposition. When the congregation understands the sermon proposition and structure, then they can correlate the sermon points to the proposition, understand how the preacher is developing the theme as he intended to do so, and appreciate the fact that the preacher is making progress, clear progress, because the sermon points actually deliver upon the promised treatment of the theme as announced in the propositional statement.

CLARITY AIDES POWER IN PREACHING

Clarity in the statements of the sermon proposition and the sermon structure does more than provide integrity and continuity of perceived subject-matter from the listener's viewpoint. More importantly, clarity helps to enhance the power of the preacher. Skinner writes, "Homiletic power bears direct relation to the clarity of the sermonic skeleton, or frame. Where inadequate attention is given to this, power will fail."[24]

Though power in preaching is the result of much more than clarity, clarity plays an undeniable role in establishing the perceived force of a preacher's power. When the preacher's sermon proposition is clarified and its validity enforced by every element of the sermon as it is preached, both the preacher and the congregation have an absolute confidence that they are going somewhere and getting there through the means of everything included in the content of the sermon. When such clarity is the case, it enables a preacher to "communicate best and lead others most effectively"[25] thus increasing, to no small degree, the power with which one preaches.

Clarity has a unique benefit to enhance the power of an expository preacher since it will be obvious to the listeners that what the expositor is saying is not only clarifying and validating the sermon proposition, but it is clarifying and validating the expositor's interpretation of the text since his proposition and structure is deduced from his understanding of the text he is expounding. Clarity breeds power—power to communicate what one desires to say in a sermon, and power to communicate the interpretation of a passage and power to persuade the hearers of the personal significance of the interpretation of the passage in their lives.

The substance of the sermon, the truth of God's Word, must be made clear to the hearers. The structure of one's sermon, if it is a good structure, is the essence of the substance of the sermon. The structure helps the preacher to communicate the substantial substance of the sermon with clarity and power. We have structure in our preaching, not to affect some sense of artistry or refinement for preaching. We need structure in our preaching just like a munitions maker who must create casings to house the explosive substance of his bombs and bullets. Absorb Sprugeon's much needed comments upon structure and substance.

> To divide a sermon well may be a very useful art, but how if there is nothing to divide? A mere division maker is like an excellent carver with an empty dish before him
> ... but the true minister of Christ knows that the true value of a sermon must lie, not in its fashion and manner, but in the truth which it contains ... Sermons, when criticized by judicious hearers, are largely measured by the amount of gospel truth and force of the gospel spirit which they contain. Brethren, weigh your sermons. Do not retail them by the yard, but deal them out by the pound.[26]

Spurgeon's insistence first and foremost upon the weight or the sermon's substance above the sermon's arrangement is entirely appropriate.

Clarity, power, and unity of content is the potential effect of a sermon proposition that has been discovered through the careful study of a passage so that the actual meaning of the passage is conveyed to the listeners as the preacher expounds the text with the help of the sermon proposition and structure. As Warren Wiersbe aptly commented, "Just as a river without banks becomes a swamp, so a sermon without a clear proposition becomes a rambling religious speech that tries to say so much it ends up saying nothing."[27] A proposition, as it unifies the content of a sermon, will automatically limit the extra-biblical content of the sermon.

Once the proposition and structure have been established, based upon an accurate reflection of the meaning of the passage being preached, the preacher is responsible to stick with the passage, proposition, and structure and not drift into matters outside of these parameters. The proposition and structure become the river banks in which the river of the sermon must flow.

Sermon Structure as a Text Driven Derivative

A sermon that is not held within the banks of the proposition and structure becomes a mess just as surely as a river that is not held within its banks becomes a flood. Even though a sermon proposition and structure cannot guarantee that a homiletical flood will not occur, a good proposition and structure will severely curtail the likelihood of it.

A good proposition and structure is far more than just a stated plan of attack and intended treatment of a passage, it provides incentive—the desire to flesh out and stick with the plan. It is one thing to plan the work. It is quite another to work the plan. A proposition and structure brings assurance that the work of preaching the sermon has a plan. A good proposition and structure brings assurance that the plan for preaching the sermon will be worked out.

CONSIDER THE FOLLOWING QUESTIONS

1. What two highly unfortunate problems of communication are solved effectively through sermon structure?
2. Why must sermon structure for an expository sermon be a text driven derivative?
3. What are the two requirements for sermon structure so that it will be a help rather than a hindrance?
4. Of what were the Puritans prodigious practitioners?
5. What three criticisms were advanced against the preaching of the Puritans and scholastic preachers? Identify and describe these criticisms.
6. What five dominant qualities were possessed in Puritan preaching?
7. What is the "logistical problem" with advanced preparation?
8. What is the liability of advanced planning?
9. What is the difference between advanced planning and advanced preparation?
10. What is the principle that must be honored as one preaches from a preaching plan?
11. What is the potential of diagramming passages in regards to advanced preparation?
12. How may advanced planning be a threat to expository preaching?

13. What seems to be the main motive for advanced planning and how does this contrast with the main motive for expository preaching?
14. What is the five step process of synthesis in preparing an outline from which to preach?
15. How does the synthesis process for a preacher in his study contrast with the synthesis process for a preacher in his pulpit?
16. What is the real problem when one believes that the text of Scripture threatens to mess up the unity of his sermon structure?
17. Upon what grounds must a preacher decide what material may or may not be included in an expository sermon?
18. How does one not detract from the unity of the sermon and what must be employed for this to result?
19. Why is it that deciding what material to reject or to incorporate into a sermon is a subjective matter and what is the inescapable result of such decisions?
20. How is mastery of a subject verified?
21. What does it mean, in the preaching of a sermon, that clarity breeds power?
22. Beyond the intended treatment of a passage, what does a good proposition and structure provide for a sermon?

ENDNOTES

1. Brastow, *Modern Pulpit*, 121–22.
2. Ibid., 122.
3. Ibid., 125.
4. Ibid., 227.
5. Ibid., 228–29.
6. Ibid., 229–30.
7. Ibid., 230–31.
8. Ibid., 231.
9. Fant Jr. and Pinson Jr., *20 Centuries*, vol. 2, 252–76.
10. Wiersbe and Perry, *Wycliffe Handbook*, 7.
11. Jones, *Whales*, 301–10.
12. Wiersbe, *Treasury*, 82–89.
13. Miller, *Spirit*, 204–5.
14. Spurgeon, *Lectures*, 94–96.
15. Lloyd-Jones, *Preaching*, 190.
16. Rummage, *Planning*, 85.
17. Wiersbe, *Dynamics*, 86.
18. Hendricks, *Teaching*, 64.
19. Lenski, *Sermon*, 80.
20. Kroll, *Prescription*, 149.
21. Spurgeon, *Lectures*, 77–78.
22. Ibid., 72.
23. Shedd, *Homiletics*, 139.
24. Skinner, *Teaching Ministry*, 162.
25. Ibid., 162.
26. Spurgeon, *Lectures*, 70–71.
27. Wiersbe, *Dynamics*, 61.

Words to Live and Preach By

The Results of Living as a Fool

*Through presumption comes nothing but strife,
but with those who receive counsel is wisdom.*
PROVERBS 13:10

*Every prudent man acts with knowledge,
but a fool displays folly.*
PROVERBS 13:16

*A scoffer seeks wisdom, and finds none,
but knowledge is easy to him who has understanding.*
PROVERBS 14:6

*Wisdom rests in the heart of one who has understanding,
but in the bosom of fools it is made known.*
PROVERBS 14:33

*A scoffer does not love one who reproves him,
he will not go to the wise.*
PROVERBS 15: 12

*The mind of the intelligent seeks knowledge,
but the mouth of fools feeds on folly.*
PROVERBS 15:14

*Wisdom is in the presence of the one who has understanding,
but the eyes of a fool are on the ends of the earth.*
PROVERBS 17:24

A fool does not delight in understanding,
but only in revealing his own mind.
PROVERBS 18:2

Also it is not good for a person to be without knowledge,
and he who makes haste with his feet errs.
The foolishness of man subverts his way,
and his heart rages against the Lord.
PROVERBS 19:2–3

3

Sermon Structure as a Necessity, Not a Luxury

"Much that has been said and written on 'structure' in the sermon might be put into one sentence: The power of a sermon lies in its structure, not in its decoration."[1] The author of that statement, Halford Luccock, wrote decidedly for the necessity of structure in preaching. Wayne McDill writes, "No matter what else the sermon has to commend it, it will likely flounder without a good outline to follow."[2]

Many homileticians agree that a sermon needs an outline. Sometimes a sermon may be preached without an outline but the only thing for which it may be commended is the variety it provided. But this variety from the norm may well be without the usual clarity brought forth in a sermon containing a good structure. William Evans provides an account of a preacher who departed from his typical approach of preaching with a well-structured sermon outline. He writes:

> A minister who had preached one of these (unstructured) sermons said to his elder, after the close of the service: "Do you know I did not know what I was to preach about when I went to the pulpit this morning." The elder was honest, and replied, "Do you know that no one knew what you had preached about when you had finished?"[3]

I am persuaded that preaching proclaimed through the means of a sermon outline makes for a better sermon than the same material presented without sermon structure. A sermon preached without an outline is vague and, therefore, not as effective as it would have been if it would have had structure. As one man effectively put it, "With a good chart, a common-sense sailor will find his way about the seas, while without it a genius would soon bring his vessel to shipwreck. It is the same with a preacher: if he has laid down a good chart with his divisions, he can hardly err."[4] Especially in expository preaching, when the text receives so much scrutiny, attention, and so much is said about the text in order to interpret it, a clear outline provides the needed hooks to hang all the information that is coming to the hearers. The hearers of a sermon, especially an expository sermon, simply will not understand the text as well as they would without the valuable component of sermon structure.

Jerry Vines and Jim Shaddix make a good case for structure in preaching. They argue that a wide gulf exists between good exegesis and a good sermon. The lacking distinction between the two has fostered ridicule from critics of expository preaching. Even when a preacher has a central theme, the explanation of exegetical material without organization frustrates those who listen. Accordingly, the authors assert: "You cannot afford to take your Bible bullets and toss them at your congregation. You must organize them and then systematically fire them. If you structure your sermon well, you will be far ahead in your attempt to get the biblical message across to a contemporary audience."[5] Good exegesis results in a lot of information and technical insight while a good sermon requires clear communication of insight that can be understood at the time of transmission and retained, at least temporarily, subsequent to the transmission. Therefore, sermon structure has a strategic role and plays a necessary part in a clearly communicated expository sermon.

> A well-structured sermon is a necessity if the total impact of the preacher's message is to be remembered. In the by and large, people do not remember the outlines of sermons. Often they retain very little of what is said except a particularly vivid illustration here and there, and they may remember that with the wrong application. But if a sermon is carefully structured, if the points are forcefully made, and if each point obviously relates to every other point driving toward a single conclusion, they will remember the total impact. This is the main thing.[6]

A successful transmission of textual insights to the hearers of an expository sermon requires a vehicle for clear communication, a grid of some kind, to help them organize and synthesize the data that is coming their way. Without good sermon structure, good exposition becomes a wealth of material that does not enrich the hearers as much as it should because they simply cannot grasp and retain truth that bypasses them. All this good information, which without sermon structure is minimally received, cannot result in a good sermon because clear communication, that is, communication that is received clearly by the hearers has not occurred and cannot occur. Arndt L. Halvorson argues convincingly for the necessity of a vehicle for clear communication.

> Structure is the vehicle for the message. It is the sluice gate through which the message moves. It is the path the message travels. So structure is the best guarantee that the sermon will be coherent and will have objective clarity and force. Structure is the practice of orderly thinking, essential for such a vulnerable style of communication as preaching, bereft as it is of visual aids. The listener must hear, remember, visualize, and anticipate, all at the same time, under the stimulus of spoken words ... We don't need truth in general; we need truth which can break through to our awareness, and the volitional and imaginative centers which are the vehicle of conscience. Something should happen when the Word is preached. But it usually won't if the sermon is but random thoughts, collected quotes, unorganized impressions from the text.[7]

Among other things, a good exegete needs a good sermon outline to preach a good expository sermon.

Presently there is a lamentable disdain for structure in preaching. This certainly is not surprising. In fact, it is quite consistent with the prevalent views of Scripture as non-propositional truth, and the debunking of deductive, expositional preaching. Nevertheless, the responsibility of the preacher has not changed. He must preach the Word. And because it is the Word of God that is preached, it must be preached with the utmost clarity.

The preacher must move from the exegesis of the text to the shaping of the sermon. The central proposition derived from the text and its development through supporting material must be packaged for communication. The content must be given form. The classical and traditional mode has been to project a series of main ideas and secondary ideas, major assertions and minor assertion, or main points and sub points to carry the argument. Augustine insisted that both sequentia and eloquentia are needed in effective discourse. Furthermore, Demosthenes recognized that persuasion depends as much on the order of presentation as on the strength of the argument.[8]

Still, many homileticians write in favor of preaching with a decided informality to it. This informality includes doing away with structure. Thoughtful, productive, linear thinking is to give way to a meandering oral essay. Larsen wrote, "The tendency is that pools of literary protoplasm are loosed to flow in all directions simultaneously. This is the river sermon which winds about like the Meander." The results of this emphasis in modern preaching "lead us nowhere."[9] Actually, I think preaching without clear sermon structure has led us somewhere indeed—a place of great uncertainty as to what any given passage of the Bible means generally and specifically. This is entirely intolerable!

The attempt to preach without the help of sermon structure overlooks the fact that we learn material more easily when it is organized as opposed to material that is unorganized. Organized thought has a greater power than unorganized thought.[10] Many advocate the dismissal of sermon structure at the expense of setting aside sage advice for preaching—"Disdain not the old fashion of dividing your sermons into heads; a discourse which rejects these aids to perspicuity will turn out a bewildered rhapsody, without aim or effect, order or conclusion."[11]

An unstructured sermon not only adversely affects the perceptibility of the hearers but it also affects the patience of the hearers. An unorganized sermon does not commend itself to the hearers so that they can track whatever progress the preacher may be making in his sermon. Therefore, a sermon without structure, since it is hard to track its progress—if it is actually making progress, seems to take more time to preach than it should when sermon structure is not incorporated. Therefore, the hearers who cannot make sense of what the preacher is saying, and cannot track any progress he may be making become frustrated and impatient. They just want the sermon to be done with because the sermon, seemingly, goes on and on and on with no hope of an end in sight. Like a football team that is hopelessly behind in the middle of the fourth quarter, they just want to see the clock run down to zero and to get this game over with! Charles Reynolds Brown addressed both of these weakening effects of preaching without sermon structure.

> The lack of arrangement also tends to make any sermon seem long. There was once an uneducated Irishman who picked up a pocket dictionary and started to read it through. He said afterward that the book seemed to be full of valuable information, but for the life of him, he could not get "the thread of the discourse." There are sermons which have a lot of good stuff in them, but the material is not arranged in any sort of order ... The lack of order in the arrangement of sermon material works out a similar uncertainty and confusion in the minds of the people in the pews.[12]

He continued by stating, "The mollusk can never do the work of the vertebrate. The mollusk sermon may have plenty of good soft thought in it, furnishing in abundance edible material which could be used in making a homiletic chowder. But if the sermon can neither "sit nor stand," it will fail in its effectiveness."[13] Nevertheless, some view sermon structure only as an unnecessary encroachment of the rhetorical approach of the scholastic preachers from the fifteenth and sixteenth centuries.

Wiersbe and Perry affirm that, "A powerful and direct influence on homiletics in the fifteenth century was the revived study of classical rhetoric."[14] However, it was during the time period when the Reformation was taking place that preaching was being re-established, not only through the conviction of *Sola Scriptura,* but through the writing of Erasmus who enumerated five canons of preaching: invention, *arrangement*, style, memory, and delivery.[15] In August, 1535 Desiderius Erasmus wrote "the most important work on the theory of preaching since Augustine" entitled *Ecclesiastes, sive Concionator Evangelicus* (i.e., gospel preacher).[16] Erasmus's writings directed preaching back to the principles of classical rhetoric established by Aristotle, Cicero, and Quintilian, all of whom agreed that rhetoric had five parts.[17] Aristotle systematized an approach to persuasive speaking in his *Rhetoric* in the fourth century BC.[18] Cicero addressed the five canons in several treatises written in the first century BC, especially in his *De Oratore*.[19] In the first century AD, Quintilian, in his *Institutes on Oratory* pulled together and elaborated upon the five canons of rhetoric.[20]

Because of the writing of Erasmus, who redirected preaching back to its first century roots of rhetorical preaching, it is certain that propositions, divisions, and subdivisions have been a significant part of preaching since the sixteenth century. But as with the more general work of church reformation as a whole, the more specific emphasis of rhetorical preaching was part of the great reformation in expounding the Scriptures. The canon of arrangement has been a staple of communication theory—theory advanced for the purpose to establish effective communication, as testified to by ancient writings dating back to more than two millennia.

More recently, and to the present time, the significance of sermon structure is still understood, appreciated, and advocated by some. Edmund Clowney, referring to divisions and subdivisions which must be developed according to the text and, therefore, must be aspects of the central unifying theme of the passage, wrote: "Here is freedom in preaching coupled with faithfulness to the Word of God. Here, too, is a message which comes with freshness from the Word which liveth and abideth, and reaches men's hearts with relevancy and power."[21] Most significantly, sermon structure is a benefit to both preacher and hearer in the quest to expound and understand the Bible. Therefore, sermon structure must not be viewed as a liability, it should not be viewed as a luxury, but it must be viewed as a necessity. George Jennings Davies is right as he asserted, "It may be considered as a sure rule that something is wrong, when there is a difficulty, after hearing a sermon, to give an outline of its continuous arrangement in a few concise words."[22]

Good sermon structure, because of the clarity it provides the hearers, can compensate for other weaknesses apparent in the sermon. "Structure for the sermon is as the skeleton is to the body, as the timber framework is to the house, or as the steel ribs are to the skyscraper."[23] And just as a body, a house, and a skyscraper are ruined without structure so it is in preaching that a sermon is significantly diminished without the benefits of good sermon structure.

Admittedly, sermon structure can be and has been abused. Most notably, four abuses surface—excessive uniformity in sermon structure, excessive cleverness in constructing sermon structure, excessive display of sermon structure, and excessive quantity of division in sermon structure.

The excessive uniformity in sermon structure is specific to the requirement to have three, and only three, main points in a sermon. In regards to excessive uniformity to structure it is observed that:

> There are some preachers who are absolute slaves in this respect—you must have three "heads" and three only. If you have fewer than three heads you are a bad preacher; if you have more than three you are equally a bad preacher. This is quite ridiculous, of course, but it is amazing to notice how easily one falls into habits and becomes the slave of a tradition. I was certainly brought up in this tradition of "always an introduction and three heads." People looked for them; that was the invariable custom of the preachers.[24]

Of course the devoted pursuit to craft a three point sermon is without foundation, begs to be ridiculed and must not be tolerated. One thing is certain; if a preacher always has three points in a sermon then the texts of Scripture are being manipulated to accomplish this result.

In addition, Lloyd-Jones cautioned against excessive cleverness in constructing sermon structure.

> Do not be too cleaver in your divisions, do not be too smart. This has been a real snare to many preachers. It may not be quite as true today, but certainly in the earlier part of this century there was probably nothing that did greater harm to preaching than this very thing—clever headings; slick and smart divisions in which the preacher displayed his cleverness.[25]

Obviously, a preacher is culpable if he is using the pulpit to bring praise to himself in any way, not restricted to, but certainly including the sermon structure.

Also, excessive display of sermon structure was chided as an inappropriate way of providing the much-needed framework of a sermon. "You are to have a framework—and let it show—making no vulgar display of it, as if your skeleton were exhibit A, Victim of Famine in the Ukraine; yet not allowing what you are supposed to have in hand wander hazily abroad like an indeterminate fog."[26] The structure is subservient and must function as such in order to clarify the meaning and message of the text. It must be discernable but it must serve to help the hearers understand the meaning of the text by giving them hooks to associate the meaningful details of the exposition.

Finally, as we have seen already in the sermon structure of the Puritans, one can demonstrate an excessive amount of structure by excessive division of an idea. Though the potential exists for abusing sermon structure, the potential for abuse does not constitute grounds for dismissing sermon structure. It does, however, constitute grounds for careful implementation of structure in one's preaching.

THE BENEFITS OF SERMON STRUCTURE

Although sermon structure, when it is used in preaching, can be used in such a way as to achieve diminished returns or even abused in such a fashion as to affect disgust in the hearts of some hearers. But, of course, this does not have to be the case. Structure is necessary for a sermon to be a message that has a clearly divided analysis of a text's subject-matter.

A good sermon will provide comprehensible treatment of the text and its meaning by dealing with it one division at a time. Lloyd-Jones wrote:

> I maintain that a sermon should have form in the sense that a musical symphony has form. A symphony always has form, it has its parts and its portions. The divisions are clear, and are recognized, and can be described; and yet a symphony is a whole. You can divide it into parts, and yet you always realize that they are parts of a whole, and that the whole is more than the mere summation or aggregate of the parts. One should always think of a sermon as a construction, a work which is in that way comparable to a symphony. In other words a sermon is not a mere meandering through a number of verses; it is not a mere collection or series of excellent and true statements and remarks. All those should be found in the sermon, but they do not constitute a sermon. What makes a sermon a sermon is that it has a particular "form" which differentiates it from everything else.[27]

R. E. O. White contends that there is more to be said for preaching from a clear and explicit outline than there is against it. In a phrase, the benefits of using sermon structure may be expressed as "interested comprehension."[28] Interested comprehension of the hearer due to sermon structure is functional from the earliest portion of the sermon, continues throughout the sermon as it is preached, and may be maintained after the sermon has been completed. Specifically, White suggests that there are five benefits of using an outline in preaching: mental certainty regarding the treatment the passage will receive; increased capacity to comprehend what is conveyed in the sermon; perceived clarity regarding the totality of the sermon; enhanced interest in the sermon; and clear remembering of the sermon.[29]

When the sermon structure is sound so that it works well with the text, and thus, serves to facilitate understanding of the portion of the text that will be expounded, and the process of expounding the text serves to facilitate clarity of the sermon structure, four subsequent results occur *beyond heightened comprehension*; the credibility of the preacher is intensified; persuasion is more cogent; listener satisfaction is heightened; the preacher himself is fulfilled.[30]

Because of the decline in most people's capacity to hear and retain what is conveyed in words and the increased visual character of our culture, one of the ways in which we can meet the cultural and psychological needs of our hearers is to provide a memorable outline, by which the preacher's explanations of the text may be grasped and carried away. If one should contend that an outline is a crutch for lame listeners then it must be recognized that our listeners are lame in this respect in these days. Why not be Christ-like enough to provide them the help that they need? Fenelon argued for a discourse with a strong body that could make a strong impression and be remembered better. He asked, "Why should you speak if not to persuade, to instruct, and to proceed in such fashion that the listener remembers what you say?"[31] The outline will not be all the help they need but without it, other help may be in vain.

It is true that the main purpose of preaching is the immediate response to the truth of the biblical text rather than the clear remembering of all that was said. Yet the desired response is more likely to occur and to be a lasting response if the statements of truth that evoked the response can be recalled.

The sermon outline is a set of shelves upon which the main assertions of a biblical text can be arranged in the hearer's mind. The sermon structure can be a vessel in which the hearer can retain the truths of the message and subsequently retrieve them. Why not then, help the hearers in this regard? If a preacher cannot help his hearers to understand and retain the truth of the passage because he has not understood the passage well enough to be able to afford such a serviceable sermon structure then he will be ethereal and ephemeral in the preaching of that text. If he will not, because he thinks it is beneath him to provide such structure in his preaching or because he thinks intelligent people ought not to need it, then he has ceased to be a good servant to the congregation through his preaching because of his foolish presuppositions.

The carefully arranged sermon structure enormously adds to the clarity of the entire understanding of the biblical text and, therefore, the expository sermon. The usage of many sentences expressed in a sermon always creates the possibility that the main thoughts of the text and sermon will be lost in the multitude of words, obscured and buried by the material intended to amplify and adorn them.

The hearers cannot be responsible for making sense of that which the preacher only dimly understands and presents in unclear way. If the preacher cannot arrange his sermon structure in an orderly fashion, it is indicative of the fact that he has not adequately understood that which he is preaching and is inadequately prepared to preach from his passage. We should never preach to others a sermon we cannot think through clearly. Clarity and mental grasp of the text from which we preach is not so much an issue of memory as it is an issue of faithfulness to fully prepare ourselves for the responsibility to declare God's Word. Lloyd-Jones writes,

> Take time over this (the statement of your main divisions) because the whole purpose of dividing up the subject in this way is to make it easier for the people to take in the Truth and to assimilate it. That is the sole reason for having divisions. We should not be believers in "Art for Art's sake." As we do this in order to help the people it should be done well. That is why you should take time over this. But sometimes you will find that it is extremely difficult to get exactly the right form. You have got your message, and you are beginning to see the "form" in which you are going to present it, but you cannot quite work out the divisions to your own satisfaction. I advocate taking great care over this; we must not rush it or force it.[32]

The orderly arranged sermon structure adds greatly to the hearer's interest in the sermon. The complaint that a sermon is too long or boring is due, in no small way, to the lack of progress and advancement of thought in the sermon. Good sermon structure provides the rails upon which the sermon makes progress and advances thought.

Good sermon structure affords the hearers mental relief. When one point of the sermon has been completed, and has been done so plainly in the mind of the hearers, a certain satisfaction is sensed by the hearers because of the successful progress of the sermon thus far. They anticipate and are ready to engage the next sermon point. Such ease in following a sermon through its course is a considerable part of the pleasure which good preaching imparts to an appreciative congregation.

A preacher must work hard to communicate clearly. If he fails to do his work thoroughly and well, he passes on to his hearers the burden to clarify the truth of the passage for themselves—the very thing he was never able to do. He, in effect, shirks his responsibility as he adds unnecessarily to the responsibility of his hearers. In such a condition, a preacher is not prepared adequately to preach clearly. Hendricks says, "Preparation is the best insurance you can take out on your communication. In preparation you give your message form and features. Your message needs structure; it needs to be packaged—and the ability to

Sermon Structure as a Necessity, Not a Luxury 75

package your content is what separates the men from the boys . . . in communication."³³

The ability to package content is what separates a preacher who is clear in his preaching from those who are not. In order to preach with clarity, the preacher must possess clarity about the sermon he intends to preach. Personal clarity, sufficient enough to yield an ordered outline was a necessity for Lloyd-Jones as he readily confessed:

> We are all different, I know, and one can only speak for oneself, but as far as I am concerned if my sermon is not clear and ordered in my mind I cannot preach it to others. I suppose I could stand up and talk, but that would probably muddle people rather than help them. That is why I regard this ordering and shaping of the sermon as most important, and I advocate that you should struggle with this until you get it into shape.³⁴

INTEGRITY BETWEEN THE TEXT AND THE SERMON THROUGH SERMON STRUCTURE

The matter of integrity between the text and the sermon through sermon structure is based upon three related precepts. First, a sermon must have a lone theme to be discussed (the sermon proposition) but the discussion of the lone theme of the sermon must be the theme of the text. Second, the discussion of the theme of the text, and therefore the theme of the sermon, takes place, most profitably, through the aid of sermon structure. If there is no structure, there is no clear discussion of the theme. Third, appropriate structure comes from the text, the same text, which generated the theme of the sermon.

I have witnessed many times the tragic spectacle of a preacher taking a text, allegedly for the purpose to preach that passage, only to preach a sermon that had nothing to do with the text at all. I mean, the sermon I heard had no bearing on that passage of Scripture. The text contributed only slightly to the sermon, as the preacher lifts a word of the text, from which he makes wholesale associations referencing personal experiences, contemporary events, historical allusions, etc. I am left thinking to myself, "How did that sermon come from that passage?" "Does the preacher really believe that the sermon he just preached clarified the meaning of that biblical text?" If a hearer supposes that a sermon and a biblical text are supposed to relate to one another with integrity then many times the sermon will bring disappointment because of the incongruity between the meaning of the text and the sermon that was preached from that passage. Spurgeon's insistence upon congruity between the text and the sermon is well stated.

> We insist upon it, that there must be abundance of matter in sermons, and next, that this matter must be congruous to the text. The discourse should spring out of the text as a rule, and the more evidently it does so the better; ... and there must always be a connection—a real relationship between the sermon and its text ... Some brethren have done with their text as soon as they have read it. Having paid all due honour to that particular passage by announcing it, they feel no necessity further to refer to it. They touch their hats, as it were, to that part of Scripture, and pass on to fresh fields and pastures new. Why do such men take a text at all?[35]

The "macroscopic" organic unity between text and sermon is enforced further by Spurgeon as he continued:

> Those sermons which expound the exact words of the Holy Spirit are the most useful and the most agreeable to the major part of our congregations. They love to have the words explained and expounded. Let your matter, then, be copious, and let it grow out of the inspired word, as violets and primroses spring up naturally from the sod, or as the virgin honey drops from the comb.[36]

Macroscopic organic unity, or integrity between the sermon and the text, is mediated by sermon structure that is born out of the passage. Therefore, appropriate structure takes the preacher back to the biblical text for the only justifiable discussion the theme should receive. Justifiable discussion of a theme drawn from a biblical text is predicated upon the discussion of the text.

The structured discussion of the text is better than the unstructured discussion of a text. A "running commentary" is the unstructured discussion of a text. A running commentary, though valuable, can be enhanced when there are succinct statements of truth which summarize the portions of the text to be discussed. The sermon points, then, clarify the discussion of the text.

The clear discussion of the text, understood point by point, results in a discernable advancement of the proposition of the passage. Again, if a theme is discussed, then things must be declared regarding the theme.

To say only one thing about anything is simply a declaration or inquiry about something, but saying one thing about anything is not a discussion at all. Clear structure, then, is needed for the clear advancement of a theme. R. C. H. Lenski expressed this well as he wrote: "Every discourse, deserving the name, has some kind of logical arrangement, and the better the arrangement the better the discourse."[37] When there is no structure the sermon is like a lot of building material dumped on the ground. Building material dumped at a prospective home construction site does not constitute a home any more than a bunch of words delivered upon an occasion constitutes a sermon. An ill-arranged sermon is like a house built without a blueprint. A well arranged sermon is like a first-class custom-built house, in that, it is a delight to the home-builder, to the homeowner, and to all who see and pass through it. The preacher's business, like the home-builder, is to construct a first-class product that will be a benefit and a blessing to all who encounter it.

Plural noun propositions provide the best opportunity for advancement of a theme drawn from a biblical text through a plurality of sermon points that actually discuss the passage in a point by point fashion.

INTEGRITY BETWEEN THE SERMON PROPOSITION AND THE SERMON STRUCTURE

Just as there is a macroscopic integrity between the text and the sermon preached from the text, mediated by sermon structure born out of the passage, there must also be a microscopic integrity between the sermon structure and the sermon proposition. It is the microscopic organic unity, or the integrity between the sermon proposition and its structure, that assures the listeners that they truly understand what the preacher is talking about and what he is saying about what he is talking about in reference to the text from which he preaches. The sermon proposition and the sermon structure must correspond to each other. Neither can exist in the absence of the other without greatly diminishing the integrity of the sermon. "A group of assertions not attached to a clearly defined subject makes a rambling, pointless harangue—a brushpile. A subject, however important, that is not followed by predication is not a complete idea."[38] Another writer established the necessity or sermonic unity, the relationship between the theme and parts of the sermon, as he asserted: "We can speak of real unity only when a theme is divided into its component parts. Putting it in the simplest way, unity is:

1. that there is *one thing*, the one named by the theme;
2. *all the parts* of that one thing, each in its place, none missing. A sermon of this type is a unit in the truest sense of the word."[39]

Lenski rightly establishes the fact that sermonic unity is predicated upon a sermon proposition and sermon structure that truly correspond to one another.

The sermon proposition and sermon structure must then work together to establish a basic understanding of, and to develop specific meaning for, any given subject. The main points of a sermon must function to establish the sermon proposition. The main points "define, explain, impress, or prove"[40] the sermon proposition. This can and will be done only as a preacher understands that the sermon proposition is a unifying principle of the sermon. This is true since the sermon is embodied in the proposition and the proposition dominates all the parts of the sermon.[41]

Though this seems to be a given, and it is a logical given, it is not a given in actual practice. Because there is a lack of clarity, integrity and continuity between the proposition and structure in contemporary sermons as well as sermons preached in the past, preachers must realize the problem exists and be determined to arrest the problem. The following words, though written long ago are an appropriate depiction of preaching in our day.

> One of the most common faults in preaching is want of coherence, lack of plan. A sermon may contain good ideas, interesting illustrations, and elevated language, yet leave no impression on the hearer's mind, simply because it has followed no principle of construction. One may say that order, which is Heaven's first law, is also the first law of the sermon. Hence the imperative need of a plan, a definite arrangement of material.[42]

Arrangement of material is helpful, but arrangement of material is only part of the solution to the problem. The nature of the material to be arranged is not unimportant. However, the microscopic organic unity of the sermon proposition and the sermon structure must be unquestionable.

In the last two headings related the organic unity of a sermon, we've touched on two problems observable in preaching. There is the smaller problem of a lack of a clear, cohesive connection between the sermon proposition and the sermon structure which results in communicative disunity—a sermon that does not stay on track point by point with the subject-matter promised in the sermon proposition. Then there is the larger problem of a lack of a clear, cohesive connection between the text and the sermon which results in cognitive disunity—a sermon that does not stay on track point by point with the biblical text which the sermon is supposed to be clarifying. Both are problematic and must be arrested. Communicative disunity must be arrested because it is a disservice to the people of God. Cognitive disunity must be arrested because it is a disservice to the Word of God and the God of the Word! The latter, being the more egregious problem is arrested by preaching that is a careful and accurate exposition of the biblical text, in other words, expository preaching.

A HIGH VIEW OF SCRIPTURE FOR EXPOSITORY PREACHING AND DEDUCTIVE PREACHING

A high-view of the Bible is the basis for expository preaching, specifically, and for deductive preaching in general. Ronald J. Allen and Gilbert L. Bartholomew are perceptive of this fact as they make the connection between preaching verse-by-verse and the conservative, evangelical theology of the majority of its practitioners. They write:

> The sermon as running commentary is associated primarily with preachers who have an evangelical or fundamentalist theological orientation. This association is natural. Evangelicals regard the Bible as the inspired word of God that imparts utterly essential revelation to the church and the world. The church must understand the biblical text in its fullness in order to grasp the completeness of divine revelation. Indeed, in a sense for the evangelical, theology is explaining the Bible and drawing out its implications. Running commentary is only one of many homiletical modes in evangelical circles, but it is an instructive vehicle for evangelical theology.[43]

I agree with their assessment but they leave room for one additional thrust in the practice of preaching of ardent conservative evangelicals—the declaration of statements of theological principle derived from the text that compose the timeless truths of the passage expounded in a verse by verse fashion. Allen and Bartholomew view expository preaching as a running commentary. Their assessment of expository preaching as a running commentary of verse-by-verse preaching and as the practice of men of conservative theology and a high view of Scripture is correct and praiseworthy. But, men of conservative theology and of a high view of Scripture could chart a more commendable practice of preaching, namely, verse-by-verse exposition of Scripture through the means of a well structured sermon outline.

As with Allen and Bartholomew, it seems to be a tendency of non-conservatives to view expository preaching as a running commentary and therefore, a non-rhetorical approach to preaching. Non-conservatives also seem to be reluctant to accredit structure as a viable part of expository preaching. John Killinger appeals to the fact that the great pulpiteers of the nineteenth century such as Charles Spurgeon, Henry Ward Beecher, and Phillips Brooks preached sermons that were far more rhetorical than they were expositional. As Killinger phrased it, "The last half of the twentieth century has seen a strong movement toward the recovery of genuine expository preaching." This was due to the fact that, in the thinking of Killinger, "Homileticians in conservative and fundamentalist seminaries have tended to insist to their students that expository preaching is the only Christian way to preach, and that all others are contaminated by human argument and design."[44] Design and argument are viewed by Killinger as contaminants that get in the way of genuine expository preaching.

Killinger makes such a stark distinction between an expository sermon and the developmental sermon so as to make the two mutually exclusive. Accordingly, Killinger concludes that an expository sermon is an interesting approach to preaching and has the merit of forcing the preacher to pay very close attention to the biblical text so that what is said in the sermon is essentially what the text itself purports to say. Therefore, "exegesis becomes the be-all and end-all of homiletical formation . . . restricting the preacher to a mere amplification of what the ancient writers set down. The text governs everything."[45] This is a worthy conclusion advanced by Killinger even though he was trying to present expository preaching as an inferior approach to preaching.

In Killinger's assessment, the developmental sermon is one that has a central idea or controlling purpose that is worked out through a series of progressive stages—an introduction, two, three, or four points, and a deft conclusion. According to Killinger, such development could not constitute an expository sermon. I disagree strongly with this mutual exclusion between an expository sermon and a developmental sermon. However, Killinger is correct as he asserts that this classical sermon form of the developmental sermon:

> is an eminently serviceable way of preparing and communicating a message. It has undergone subtle changes from era to era, mostly in terms of simplification. But it has remained a primary method of sermon preparation through the ages because experience has shown that it works effectively as a way of persuading people of the truth of the gospel.
>
> Every student of preaching ought to master this form, just as every artist ought in the beginning to master the use of basic art forms.[46]

Killinger is correct in his assessment of the developmental sermon's productivity and his assessment that in expository preaching the text controls everything. His error is the assumption of mutual exclusivity between the two. The text does control everything, including the sermon structure that is developed according to the development of the text that will be preached!

Before focusing on the role of the sermon outline in expository preaching I want to assert the significance of preaching verse-by-verse. This is a vivid portrayal of one's high view of Scripture. Nothing is so self evident of a deep conviction of the inerrancy and infallibility of the Bible than a man's commitment to preach all of it and to do so verse-by-verse. Verse-by-verse exposition of Scripture, where a preacher preaches through a book of the Bible week after week until that book has been expounded entirely, is a public attestation of one's trust in the veracity and authority of the entire Bible, not just some of the Bible. I agree with Albert Mohler that verse-by-verse exposition of the Bible is "a measure of our stewardship" as well as a sure way to preach "those angular texts that are just so difficult to preach."[47] But we must preach them because they too are part of God's Word and are, therefore, profitable for our preaching.

As to the reason that the Scriptures are not faithfully explained by preachers, Fenelon argued that it is much easier to paint the disorders of the world than to explain soundly the basis of Christianity. For the former, one needs only to be experienced in the doings of the world and to be able to command language. For the latter, a serious and profound contemplation of the sacred Scripture is required which few men know fully enough to explain it well. Therefore, Fenelon contended that "most sermons are the reasonings of philosophers." Sometimes Scripture is cited only as an afterthought for the sake of appearance or ornament. When this is done, Fenelon concluded about such cases, "Then it is no longer the word of God; it is the word and contrivance of men."[48]

Additionally, preaching verse-by-verse through books of the Bible, or the lectio continua method of expository preaching, reflects the resoluteness of the expositor's commitment to provide understanding of the Bible. This understanding is affected as the expositor brings microscopic understanding of Scripture through the thorough treatment of verses and macroscopic understanding of Scripture through the thorough treatment of entire books of the Bible in preaching from the same book for whatever time is necessary for the completion of the book. Fenelon made a powerful argument for preaching through books of the Bible as he wrote:

> One can preach sermons upon the Scripture without explaining it book after book. But we must admit that preaching would be quite another thing if preachers, following the ancient custom, explained to the people the holy books one after the other. Calculate for yourself what authority a man would have if he said nothing of his own devising and did nothing but follow and explain the thought and the word of God. Moreover, he would be doing two things at once: in explaining the truths of the Scripture, he would be interpreting its text, and would be habituating Christians always to see the relation between the meaning and the letter. What more is needed to accustom them to nourish themselves upon this sacred bread![49]

This kind of commitment to lectio continua preaching is illustrated by John Calvin when he was evicted from Geneva on Easter of 1538 and upon his return to Geneva in September of 1541 he returned to the precise place where he was stopped three and a half years earlier.[50] Now that's commitment to verse-by-verse exposition!

SCRIPTURE AS PROPOSITIONAL TRUTH

To assert that Scripture is propositional truth is not a claim that the Bible is composed of nothing but propositions. To assert that Scripture is propositional truth is not a denial of the obvious fact that Scripture includes many genres. The assertion that Scripture is propositional truth means that from all the genres of the Bible, objective meaning is discernable. Furthermore, meaning that has been discerned can be stated.

The Discovered Meaning of a Text Declared

A preacher, having studied any portion of Scripture and from the fruit of his study having derived an accurate understanding of the contents of the biblical passage, can communicate the discovered truths to others. The declaration of the discovered truths can be proclaimed with certainty, as factual statements of truth from God to man. These are indeed statements of truth from God to man because the meaning of a biblical text is discernable, it can be grasped, and it can be articulated. "It is written" and "Thus saith the Lord" and "The Bible says" are not assertions that can be made in some sermons only. These are the unyielding claims of an expository preacher in every message preached, regardless of the genre of the biblical text.

Preaching, because it deals with what God has done and spoken and intends to do, must rest solidly in the indicative mood or as it is sometimes referred to as the declarative mood, which is the fundamental mood of language. The indicative mood indicates, it states, it declares, it announces, it asserts, it explains. The indicative mood operates with declarative sentences and deals with objective facts.[51] The indicative mood establishes and is suited well for the declarative mode of address for expository preaching. Broadus writes:

> There is in preaching very frequent need of explanation ... To explain the Scriptures would seem to be among the primary functions of the preacher. And there will often be occasion to explain, not merely the text of the sermon, but various other passages of Scripture which may be introduced into the discussion. What nobler work than that of "opening" the Scriptures, as Paul did at Thessalonica? (Acts 17:3)[52]

Fenelon ended his book *Dialogues on Eloquence* with a challenge to preachers that is honored by every preacher who is a faithful expositor of God's Word. "The discourses of a preacher must be full of the sacred Scripture. Don't be a declaimer, but a true teacher of the mysteries of your God."[53]

Scripture as a Guide for Faith and Practice

Such a stance for preaching, the stance to explain the Scriptures, comes from the fact that the Word of God is given to us as our guide for faith and practice—what we are to believe and how we are to live.

> *It is written.* This is the belief that in his revelation in history God also preserved his words for future generations. It is on this basis that our teaching and preaching are based on the Bible. On many occasions when God spoke, his intention was not only that his words would constitute revelation to the original audience, but that they would also serve as revelation for future generations.
>
> Other language which is used to describe the activity of God is that of "inscripturation" and "fixation." It is the simple idea that when God spoke he had two audiences in mind, the generation that was present, and future generations (cf. Rom. 15:4; 2 Tim. 3:15–16). The fundamental idea is that of preservation: "inscripturation" describes the method that was either immediately or eventually employed to preserve the words for future generations, and "fixation" describes the belief that God's revelation is fixed or settled at a particular time for the future.[54]
>
> The New Testament not only assumes the inscripturation of the cumulative revelation, it also believes that because the Old Testament Scriptures point forward to Christ, it is those who believe in the Lord Jesus who are now addressed by God through those same Scriptures. For example: "These things happened to them to serve as an example, and they were written down to instruct us, on whom the ends of the ages have come" (1 Cor. 10:11). "For whatever was written in former days was written for our instruction, so that by steadfastness and by the encouragement of the scriptures we might have hope" (Rom. 15:4).[55]

If God has spoken, and he has; if the Bible is the Word of God rather than man's word, and it is; then it is only consistent to study and explain that which he has given to us for our instruction!

The explanation of the passage, that is, the exposition of the biblical text is not to be viewed as an optional approach in preaching. If the Word of God is given to us as a guide for faith and practice then it must be known and understood. Derek Thomas writes:

> Expository preaching is a necessary corollary of the doctrine of the God-breathed nature of Scripture. The idea is not so much that God breathed into the Scriptures, but that the Scriptures are the product of His breathing out. Scripture maintains a "breath

of God" quality. The preacher is to make God's Word known and to make it understandable. He is to limit himself to it without adding or subtracting.[56]

Expository preaching then takes seriously the nature and purpose of Scripture for our lives as the expositor seeks to explain God's Word rather than preach his sermon. The French preacher Bossuet said, "Any preacher who from the pulpit gives to the faithful, not the word of God, but his own speculations, is guilty of nothing less than sacrilege."[57]

The explanation of the passage, as important as that is, however, is not enough. Explanation must pave the way for application, what the text means for us, in the circumstances we find ourselves in everyday life. The fundamental task of expository preaching is "the explanation of the text in its context, the unfolding of its principles, and only then their application to the world of the hearers."[58] This means that expository preaching will operate primarily, although not exclusively, in the indicative mood but must include the imperative mood as well. The very thought of imperatival preaching is not a welcomed thought for some people. However, John Wood provides the needed corrective as he writes: "No doubt many of us have suffered at the hands of those pastors and evangelists whose sermons consist of nothing but exhortation and persuasion. But the answer to such a travesty of preaching is not to exclude the appeal element altogether, but to improve the appeal by basing it squarely on sound exposition."[59]

Any and every accurate assessment of the purposes for preaching or the role of preaching will include the explanation and application of Scripture. Sinclair B. Ferguson for example says preaching "will give expression to four things: instruction in the truth, conviction of the conscience, restoration and transformation of life, and equipping for service."[60]

What good is it to assert the truth of Scripture when we preach it without the accompanying injunction to live by it? Certainly we expound the Scriptures so that lives can be lived conforming to the truth of God's Word. But in a holistic sense, an expository preacher expounds the Scriptures so that the hearer's conception of truth may be corrected, their consciences toward the truth may be sensitized, their conduct in the world may be commensurate with the truth, and their character may be above reproach as they establish a proven track record of abiding in the truth of God's Word. Therefore, any discussion of the supremacy of explanation over application or application over explanation may reveal a reticence to incorporate one as sufficiently as the other. This will not do! Both have their place in expository preaching and both must take their place in order that excellence in expository preaching may be achieved. Without trying to assert that one is more important than the other, I want to affirm that both are absolutely necessary for excellent expository preaching.

Be assured of this—Explanation with little or no application is nearsighted, and application with little or no explanation is blind! There must be thorough explanation of the passage before any application should be made. After all, how can you apply what you do not know or do not understand? So the expositor will start with explanation before moving to application and he will stay with explanation longer than he will stay with application.

Does this mean that explanation is unjustly favored over application? Not at all! If the expositor does not spend time thoroughly explaining God's Word, he has nothing to say to the people about their lives anyway. I mean, who does a preacher think he is telling people what to do and how to live based upon his own authority? If a man purportedly speaks to people about their lives on behalf of God, should he not speak to them what God has spoken? Temporal, personal, subjective truth can only be derived as timeless, universal, objective truth is known. If, therefore, more time is devoted to establishing an understanding of the text than applying the truth to life once the truth has been established, this is to be viewed as necessary but impartial treatment regarding explanation and application.

A balanced treatment between explanation and application will not require a balance of time between explanation and application. For example, I have a son who was a baseball player and a daughter who was a runner. I participated with each of them in their athletic endeavors. A typical baseball practice time with my son was two and a half hours and a typical running time with my daughter was one hour. This certainly was not a balance of time spent with each of my children but it was a balanced treatment with each of my children in their differing pursuits. The balanced treatment was one of sufficiency. My daughter had no misgivings about the fact that we did not run for two and a half hours. Such time never became a daily necessity. She never felt slighted in running for an hour because we ran as much as she cared to run. My son and I practiced baseball sufficiently and my daughter and I ran sufficiently. Sufficiency for both was based upon the equal effect of the time invested for each one, not the unequal time spent in achieving the effect for each one. An unequal time was devoted to each in order to effect an equal result for each—sufficiency. Baseball required more time than running. So it is in expository preaching. Explanation commonly requires more time than application. This will certainly be the case for the expository preacher. For preachers whose sermons may be good, but they are not a good exposition of a text of Scripture, they will spend more time in application since they are not trying to explain Scripture in the first place.

Each preacher must determine sufficiency of explanation and application in his preaching. This will be a subjective sufficiency for sure, but each man must provide both in a way that is comfortable to him and rightly represents his view of appropriate explanation and application of Scripture in preaching. How he determines his own subjective balance between explanation and application will determine if he is an expository preacher and how good of an expositor he is.

For example, consider two preachers—preacher 1 who is great at dealing with the text and providing some application, and preacher 2, who is great at dealing with application and provides some explanation of the text. Now, consider two questions about these preachers. Which preacher is an expository preacher? Which preacher is the better preacher of the two?

In reference to which is an expositor, some would say "only preacher 1 is an expositor" while others would say that "both are expositors but preacher 1 is a better expositor than preacher 2," yet others would say "both are expositors, however, preacher 2 is a more relevant expositor than preacher 1." If you and I were considering which one of the two preachers is an expositor, you might hold to one of the three views above while I might hold to one of the other two views, but my answer might be different from yours and yours might be different from mine. And, of course, your answer would be right according to your frame of reference just as my view would be right according to my frame of reference. But you and I might agree completely, having the same view of what constitutes expository preaching.

In reference to which is the better preacher, some people would say that "preacher 1 is the better of the two" because they desire a thorough consideration and detailed explanation of the text for preaching to be "good." Others, believing that preaching is ultimately about what the truth means to us, would think "preacher 2 is a much better preacher than preacher 1."

In the examples of preacher 1 and preacher 2, both men are equally comfortable with their treatment of Scripture. But potential hearers would not be equally comfortable with their treatment of Scripture. Some hearers, prioritizing application, would be disappointed with preacher 1 just as some hearers, prioritizing detailed exposition, would be disappointed with preacher 2. The truth is every preacher is as expositional as he cares to be and he is as relevant as he cares to be. If a preacher is not relevant enough in his preaching, as viewed by his hearers, it is because his desire for relevance is not as great as their demand for relevance. And conversely, if a preacher is not expositional enough in his preaching, as viewed by his hearers, it is because his desire for exposition is not as great as their demand for exposition. In other words, a great expository preacher would be a flop when preaching at the First Baptist Church of Tremendous Application just as a great relevant preacher would be a flop when preaching at the Jot and Tittle Bible Church of Detailed Exposition! The pleasure of preaching is found primarily in sufficient balance between explanation and application just as the displeasure of preaching is found primarily in insufficient balance between explanation and application.

The subjective reality is that sufficient balance between explanation and application will be arrived at variously in preaching. The objective reality is that both explanation and application have their place in preaching if the Bible is our guide for faith and practice. What we believe must shape how we live. How we live and what we believe must be determined by an understanding of the content of the Scriptures. The content of the Scriptures is understood through biblical exposition which seeks to explain and apply the meaning of scriptural texts. John Stott rightly asserts that there is no appeal without proclamation just as there is no proclamation without an appeal. He writes, "First, we must never issue an appeal without first making the proclamation." And, "we must never make the proclamation without then issuing an appeal."[61]

Since Scripture is an actual guide for faith and practice for the Church of the Lord Jesus Christ, Scripture must be explained and applied. Fidelity to this straightforward approach to preaching will not only prevent a preacher from being monotonous but it will be the grounds for continued refreshment through many years of preaching, as Charles E. Jefferson suggests: "A preacher who is content to speak in everyday language to his people Sunday after Sunday about Jesus Christ and the application of Christian ideas to their personal experiences and to the problems of their generation can be interesting and fresh at the end of thirty years."[62]

Implications of Scripture as Propositional Truth

Allows for Responsible Fulfillment of One's Calling

I think it is both an outright disgrace and contradiction to think of the Bible as revelation from God, yet within that revelation from God, He really didn't mean much of anything by it! A preacher has not only the possibility but even more so, the responsibility to assert strongly, clearly, and confidently—"This is what this passage means and you must comply with God's truth and conform your life to his truth!" A preacher has this possibility and responsibility when he preaches from any portion of Scripture, from Genesis 1:1 to Revelation 22:21. This is so simply because Scripture is propositional truth.

If meaning of God's truth found in the Scriptures is able to be grasped—and it is—then it must be proclaimed. And if it is proclaimed with clarity and certainty of the highest order, it will be done so through statements of propositional truth, that is, statements of theological principle. What is said concerning the propositional nature of the Bible is equally true of the propositional preaching of the Bible from all genres— "And because a propositional statement affirms or denies something, propositional revelation is the form of revelation in which the content is clear and brief."[63]

The meaning of any passage of Scripture, regardless of its genre, can and must be understood. The derived understanding of a text must be explained. This is expository preaching. Expository preaching is not an approach to preaching that is limited to some portions of Scripture and some genres of Scripture. Expository preaching should be the end-product of the study and understanding of all of God's Word. Earlier we discussed sufficient balance between explanation and application in preaching. Certainly expository preaching must contain application of the truth that is explained. But, beyond this, we must recognize that the essence of expository preaching is not only an emphasis on explaining the text but the declaration of what the explanation codifies in terms of propositions, or propositional statements, or statements of theological principle. The propositional statements act to clarify all of the detailed explanation provided in the effort to interpret a passage.

The following declaration and questions are included in order to solidify the role of textual exposition in preaching to fulfill one's calling to preach the Word. A preacher cannot fulfill his calling by God to preach the Word if he does not consistently explain whatever passage he purposes to preach. If a preacher is not explaining the passage, what is he doing with it? If a preacher is not explaining the passage, is he really preaching the passage? If a preacher is not preaching the passage, is he really preaching the Word?

A responsible fulfillment of one's calling to preach God's Word means one gives earnest effort to explain the Word of God and, from the explanation of the truth, an intentional transition to confront the hearers with the personal relevance of God's Word for their lives. When the main points of the sermon are cast in statements of propositional truth or statements of theological principle, the preacher fulfills his calling most honorably since his structure helps his hearers understand the text and comprehend the meaning it has for them.

SUPPLIES THE NEEDS OF HEARERS

I think Peter Adam raised and answered very well a fundamental question in reference to the nature of the Bible and the nature of preaching. He wrote:

> Since the idea of God speaking is so fundamental to the Bible, why are we so reluctant to accept it? ... People prefer a God who does not speak because he makes less clear demands, asks no questions, makes no promises, and threatens no punishment. One reason people prefer the company of dumb animals to that of humans is that dumb animals make fewer demands, ask no questions and make no promises. Nowadays this rejection of the meaning and purpose of God goes even deeper. The postmodern move against meaning in words, and against words themselves, is part of an attempt to create not only a world without God but a universe without meaning.[64]

With the understanding that Scripture is propositional truth, what is the minimal claim we can make about the purpose, or the goal, of the exposition of any text of the Bible? The most basic purpose, the most general goal, the most principal reality of expository preaching is simply this—*any attempt to teach or preach from a biblical text must surface the truth claims of that passage.* Spurgeon wrote, "Sermons should have real teaching in them, and their doctrine should be solid, substantial, and abundant. We do not enter the pulpit to talk for talk's sake; we have instructions to convey important to the last degree, and we cannot afford to utter pretty nothings."[65]

This view is predicated upon the basic presuppositions that Scripture is propositional truth and as propositional truth it can and should be understood and expressed propositionally. The sermon proposition is a general statement of propositional truth of the scriptural text while the individual points of the sermon structure are more specific statements of propositional truth. Simply put, sermon points should be statements of theological truth which have been principlized from the text to be preached upon. In other words, the meaning of a scriptural text can be ascertained in the process of study and then explained in the pulpit! As Warren Wiersbe phrased it:

> If we're adequately prepared and the Spirit is at work, we don't preach the Bible so much as allow the Bible to preach through us. Not that we're passive channels, for the personality of the preacher is an important part of the message; but the preacher is the "distributor" rather than a "manufacturer." For this reason, we must be devoted to the Word of God, meditating on it daily, studying it systematically, reading it continually, and always feeding our own souls and preparing to feed our people.[66]

To the degree we are expounding the Bible, we are distributing his Word. To the degree we are doing other than expounding the Word, we are manufacturing something that takes the place of the Word of God in our preaching. The acid test for a preacher in his preaching is his ability to communicate accurately what God has committed to mankind through his Word. A preacher will fail in this regard to the extent that he loses sight of the fact that he is called by God to be a herald, a faithful deliverer of what the King has declared. Therefore, it is crucial that a preacher exhibit textual fidelity, that is, "sticking to the text" in order to provide an accurate communication of what God has declared as he provides a thorough discussion of the subject-matter and teachings of the text.[67] The very fact that a preacher understands that he is to be nothing other than a herald in his preaching should cause him to preach expositionally.

A thorough dealing with a text means that the text has been explained and applied. As previously discussed, the indicative mood and the imperative mood are crucial for expository preaching. The imperative mood is essentially directive, in that, it is used to express a request, command, order, exhortation, etc.[68] As one renown expository preacher affirmed, indicatives lead to imperatives in preaching as they do in Scripture so that expository preaching is not limited to furnishing information but to produce action as well as impart instruction.[69] Yet, the indicative mood of expository preaching which declares what the truth is, as well as the imperative mood of demanding compliance with the truth, are what spearhead the common opposition to expository preaching. Here is the basis for the common opposition to expository preaching—the authoritative, propositional reality of such an approach to preaching. The authoritative nature of an indicative/imperative stance for preaching is just too propositional for many people today, including both parishioners and preachers. But this is only so because the propositional nature of an indicative/imperative stance for preaching is just too authoritative for many people today, including both parishioners and preachers. Unfortunately, many people do not want to hear from an authoritative God who speaks through Scripture which is made clear through propositional preaching.

CONSIDER THE FOLLOWING QUESTIONS

1. Why is clear sermon structure needed in expository preaching, especially?
2. What does sermon structure provide that is indispensable for good preaching?
3. What is the rationale for a good exegete needing a good sermon outline in order to preach a good expository sermon?
4. What fact of the learning process is overlooked by those who advocate preaching that is unorganized and without structure?
5. How does an unstructured sermon affect the patience of the hearers?
6. How does the fact that the canon of arrangement, one of five canons of rhetoric, has been advocated for over two millennia provide support for sermon structure in preaching?

7. What are four abuses of sermon structure in terms of "excess"?
8. How does structure help a sermon become a good sermon?
9. What are the five benefits of "interested comprehension" through using an outline in a sermon?
10. Beyond interested comprehension, what results are achieved by the use of sound sermon structure?
11. How might sermon structure help the hearers to respond to the truth of a sermon to their lives?
12. What is the result of one's preaching who cannot understand the passage well enough to provide an outline of the passage versus the result of one's preaching who will not provide an outline in his preaching?
13. How does a structured sermon aid in the interest of the sermon?
14. In what way does a preacher shirk his responsibility by not using an outline?
15. What are the three precepts that establish the basis of integrity between the text, the sermon, and the sermon structure?
16. What does appropriate sermon structure help the preacher to clarify?
17. What is the result of a clear discussion of a text, understood point by point?
18. How does macroscopic integrity compare with microscopic integrity in regards to sermon structure?
19. What assurance does the microscopic organic unity between the sermon proposition and the sermon structure provide for the hearers?
20. How does communicative disunity contrast with cognitive disunity?
21. What is the rationale for linking running commentary approach to preaching with men of conservative theology?
22. How does John Killinger provide correct and incorrect assessments of expository preaching?

23. In the view of Fenelon, why isn't expository preaching done more commonly?
24. What are the two things one accomplishes by preaching verse-by-verse through books of the Bible?
25. What is meant and not meant in the assertion that Scripture is propositional truth?
26. Why is the indicative mood well-suited for expository preaching?
27. What is the reason for the imperative mood in expository preaching?
28. What is the needed corrective for imperatival preaching?
29. What is it that expository preaching provides in a holistic sense?
30. How can explanation without application and application without explanation be described analogically?
31. What constitutes the framework for assessing whether a preacher is an expositor or not an expositor as well as how good of an expositor he is?
32. What is the subjective reality versus the objective reality regarding explanation and application in preaching?
33. How can one argue in favor of textual exposition in preaching? In other words, what declaration and questions can be included in an effort to solidify the role of textual exposition in preaching to fulfill one's calling to preach the Word?
34. What is the most principial reality of expository preaching and what results when this principial reality is given propositional expression in preaching?
35. How should the understanding that a preacher is to be a herald of God direct him to preach expositionally?
36. What is the basis for the common opposition to expository preaching today?

ENDNOTES

1. Luccock, *Workshop*, 118.
2. McDill, *Skills*, 137.
3. Evans, *Prepare*, 73.
4. Davies, *Papers*, 209.
5. Vines and Shaddix, *Power*, 143.
6. Holland, *Structure*, 13.
7. Halvorson, *Authentic*, 83–84.
8. Larsen, *Anatomy*, 61.
9. Ibid., 62.
10. Ibid., 64.
11. Davies, *Papers*, 207.
12. Brown, *Art*, 104.
13. Ibid., 105.
14. Wiersbe and Perry, *Wycliffe Handbook*, 115.
15. Dargan, *Light*, 111.
16. Wiersbe and Perry, *Wycliffe Handbook*, 47.
17. Ibid., 99.
18. Vines and Shaddix, *Power*, 144.
19. Wiersbe and Perry, *Wycliffe Handbook*, 264.
20. Vines and Shaddix, *Power*, 144.
21. Clowney, *Biblical Theology*, 121.
22. Davies, *Papers*, 233.
23. Skinner, *Teaching Ministry*, 161.
24. Lloyd-Jones, *Preaching*, 206–7.
25. Ibid., 208.
26. Scherer, *Treasure*, 167.
27. Lloyd-Jones, *Preaching*, 72–73.
28. "Interested comprehension" is not a term used by White. I have suggested this term to summarize the results of his five benefits of using sermon structure. The benefits effectiveness analysis, from early in the sermon to the completion of the sermon as well as the rearrangement of his five benefits to reflect the duration of these benefits, goes beyond White's discussion of the subject.
29. White, *Guide*, 82–84.
30. Demaray, *Proclaiming*, 85.
31. Fenelon, *Dialogues*, 58.
32. Lloyd-Jones, *Preaching*, 209–10.

33. Hendricks, *Teaching*, 108.
34. Lloyd-Jones, *Preaching*, 211.
35. Spurgeon, *Lectures*, 72.
36. Ibid., 73.
37. Lenski, *Sermon*, 76.
38. Davis, *Design*, 25.
39. Lenski, *Sermon*, 79.
40. Hamilton, *Handbook*, 48.
41. Lenski, *Sermon*, 80.
42. McComb, *Theory and Practice*, 55.
43. Allen and Bartholomew, *Verse by Verse*, 7.
44. Killinger, *Fundamentals*, 57.
45. Ibid., 58.
46. Ibid., 60.
47. Mohler "Primacy of Preaching," 31.
48. Fenelon, *Dialogues*, 134–35.
49. Ibid., 134.
50. Thomas, "Expository Preaching," 68.
51. Carrick, *Imperative*, 8–9.
52. Broadus, *Treatise*, 144, 146.
53. Fenelon, *Dialogues*, 153.
54. Adam, *Speaking*, 27.
55. Ibid., 31.
56. Thomas, "Expository Preaching," 63.
57. Kerr, *Early Church*, 70.
58. Ferguson, "Exegesis," 193.
59. Wood, *Workshop*, 24.
60. Ferguson, "Heart," 200.
61. Stott, *Portrait*, 55, 57.
62. Quote from Charles E. Jefferson, cited by Kerr, *Early Church*, 48.
63. Adam, *Speaking*, 19.
64. Ibid., 23–24.
65. Spurgeon, *Lectures*, 70.
66. Wiersbe, *Dynamics*, 24–25.
67. Dabney, *Sacred*, 105.
68. Carrick, *Imperative*, 83.
69. Ferguson, "Exegesis," 193.

Words to Live and Preach By

The Destructive Deception of the Unfaithful Messenger

*Put away from you a deceitful mouth
and put devious lips far from you.*
Proverbs 4:24

*The mouth of the righteous is a fountain of life,
but the mouth of the wicked conceals violence.*
Proverbs 10:11

*Where there is no guidance, the people fall,
but in abundance of counselors there is deliverance.*
Proverbs 11:14

*There is one who speaks rashly like the thrusts of a sword,
but the tongue of the wise brings healing.*
Proverbs 12:18

*Lying lips are an abomination to the Lord,
but those who deal faithfully are His delight.*
Proverbs 12:22

*A worthless man digs up evil,
while his words are like scorching fire.*
Proverbs 16:27

*He who justifies the wicked and he who condemns the righteous,
both of them alike are an abomination to the Lord.*
Proverbs 17:15

*Better is a poor man who walks in his integrity
than he who is perverse in speech and is a fool.*
Proverbs 19:1

*A false witness will not go unpunished,
and he who tells lies will not escape.*
Proverbs 19:5

*A false witness will not go unpunished,
and he who tells lies will perish.*
Proverbs 19:9

*Do you see a man who is hasty in his words?
There is more hope for a fool than for him.*
Proverbs 29:20

4

Sermon Structure as a Necessity, Not a Liability

OPPOSITION TO PROPOSITIONAL PREACHING

IN PREACHING WE ARE called to deliver, not create truth. We are to disseminate the truth that God has given to us. We can understand it, explain it, and clarify the explanation most clearly through propositional statements. However, I am well aware that many do not believe that this is true. For example, consider the following quotation from an award winning book in homiletics.

> Thus we have deliberately bypassed the rationalistic definitions of preaching found in didactic homiletics. Preachers do not explicate teachings; they explore symbols. Faith does have content, but not a content that can be spelled out in propositional statements for instruction.[1]

I could not disagree more! Such a sulphuric sentiment could arise only from the pit of a homiletical Hell! Biblical truth can be spelled out in propositional statements of instruction! By all means, when one is preaching he should spell out biblical truths found in the preaching passage and they should be spelled out in statements of theological principle, which definitely are propositional statements for instruction.

However, it is the clear, straight forward declaration of timeless truths from the Bible that is so repulsive to those who do not wish to have their holy of holies, the space between their ears, encroached upon by the truth of the Bible! This is expressed clearly by the modern pointman for inductive preaching, Fred Craddock, in his book *Overhearing the Gospel*. Craddock contends,

> The church has a long history of *using the Bible* to prove the existence of God and a history almost as long of *using the Bible* to legislate for society as a whole the convictions of the Christian

> community. I do not wish here to argue pro or con the merits of such use, although you probably sense my drift away from these exercises. Both distance and appropriation are violated by such arbitrary applications.²

Even more specifically Craddock bemoans the assertive nature of direct declaration to hearers regarding the truth claims of the Bible as these threaten the much coveted foci of overhearing the Gospel: distance between the hearers and the truth of Scripture, and the opportunity of the hearers to participate in determining the truth of Scripture.

> As a listener who is also a teacher and preacher, I am aware that being armed with Holy Writ and the Word of God tempts the communicator to think the urgency and weight of the message call for pressing in and pressing down, leaving the hearer no room for lateral movement. But the listener worth his salt will soon, against this assault, launch a silent but effective counter-attack: find flaws in the speaker's grammar or voice or logic or dress; raise questions about the speaker's real motives; wonder imaginatively if the speaker has a dark past or even at this moment is entangled in affairs illicit; make distracting body movements; count things, such as light bulbs, knots in wood, number of persons present wearing glasses, etc. I need go no further; your list of things to do when surrounded by such a speaker probably is longer than mine.
>
> The other element in the experience of overhearing is participation; free participation on the part of the hearer in the issues, the crises, the decisions, the judgment, and the promise of the message. Participation means the listener overcomes the distance, not because the speaker "applied" everything, but because the listener identified with experiences and thoughts related in the message that were analogous to his own.³

Such psycho-babble is unfit instruction for an authentic proclamation of God's truth! Such hearers do exist today, in greater numbers than ever before, but they have always existed. They existed in the form of Aaron and Miriam in regards to Moses, the nation of Israel and the ten spies in regards to Joshua and Caleb, the people of the Nazareth Synagogue in regards to Jesus Christ, and most of the Mars Hill crowd in regards to the Apostle Paul. The response of Moses, Joshua and Caleb, Jesus Christ, and Paul was not to curb, hedge, cut back, tone down the truth because the people before them desired to live in the absence of truth rather than in the light of the truth!

Is this tact of not declaring the explanation and application of God's Word simply the capitulation of a *religious communicator* (who is not a preacher) to people who have been so influenced by, and conformed to, their culture that they have become arrogant, and anti-authoritarian? And are these traits of anti-authoritarian arrogance demonstrated to such a degree that they do not want to be told what the truth is and how it must be complied with even when the author of the truth is God, the substance of the truth is God's Word, and the messenger of the truth is God's ambassador? Is such a cultural milieu grounds for the messenger of God to play hide and seek with the truth? Is it grounds for the messenger of God to say that which may please but certainly will not displease the hearers? Is it grounds to say, in effect—"Let's coauthor truth! I'll provide some thoughts and you determine the meaning of truth!"? This deplorable state of confusion stemming from man's arrogant unwillingness to hear from God was aptly illustrated by Howard Hendricks as he writes: A Time magazine reporter asked novelist Ayn Rand, "Miss Rand, what's wrong with the modern world?" Without hesitation she replied, "Never before has the world been so desperately asking for answers to crucial questions, and never before has the world been so frantically committed to the idea that no answers are possible. To paraphrase the Bible," she continued, "the modern attitude is, 'Father, forgive us, for we know not what we are doing—and please don't tell us!'"[4]

Let's clarify two assertions about the prospect of preaching expositionally in a culture such as the one in which we live. First, *arrogance in the pews will never accept, nor even tolerate, God's truth without the intervention of God's grace upon the hearer!* Second, *cowardice in the pulpit will prevent much of the truth of the Bible from ever being spoken to the hearers so that it cannot even be rejected by them!*

People who are not inclined to accept God's truth need nothing more than God's truth clearly explained and forcefully applied to them. Not declaring God's truth but rather substituting God's truth can only further establish them in their resistance to the truth. What they need, though it is not wanted, is still, none-the-less, needed. Sin regarded in the heart of an individual puts one in a disposition to not be open to God's Word, not to be receptive of it. But, God works through his Word to open the heart and grant repentance from sin. Therefore, preaching God's Word cannot be the problem! However, preaching God's Word is *the only solution* to this problem! Any attempt to withhold, curtail, tone down God's Word becomes an extension of the problem. When this is the case, the sinfulness of the pew—not being willing to receive God's Word, has now been joined to the sinfulness of the pulpit—not being willing to provide God's Word. Our duty is to proclaim God's truth, not spare people from God's truth. "William Ernest Hocking is reported as having asked C. F. Andrews, 'How do you preach the gospel to a Hindu?' to which Andrews replied, 'I don't. I preach the gospel to a man.' That is a profound answer."[5] Simply preaching God's truth is a profound thing, always! Unfortunately, such profundity is becoming an increasingly rare thing.

Let's be clear about a non-negotiable reality of preaching in a culture that in not inclined to accept God's Word when it is explained accurately and enforced boldly—*the character and the integrity of the preacher will be demonstrated in how he preaches God's Word!* So the issue for the preacher is this, will he be God's spokesman or man's puppet? Does he desire to see people transformed by God's Word or does he desire to see them placated by his less-than-God's-Word sermon? Will he dare to be a prophet, a spiritual prophet, before them or will he be content to profit, financially profit, from them? Will he seek to secure the spiritual advancement of his hearers by explaining God's Word to them and demanding their compliance to it, or will he settle to secure the approval of his hearers by offering his sermon to them for their consideration or commendation?

Let's be clear about another non-negotiable reality of preaching in a culture that in not inclined to accept God's Word when it is explained accurately and enforced boldly—*the preacher does not have to garner man's approval in order to achieve God's approval but he may forfeit God's approval by achieving the approval of man!*

What people need is to understand God's Word and align their lives with its instruction. Again, this need is only heightened for those who are not inclined to hear God's Word explained to them and enforced upon them. For example, King David was in a non-hearing inclination after his sin with Bathsheba and his sin against Uriah. He was corrected only after Nathan the prophet came to him and, through his story, illustrated to him how sinful and deserving of death he was. That David understood Nathan's message is exemplified by the following propositional statements. David said, "As the Lord lives, surely the man who has done this deserves to die" which is truth propositionally stated. David continued, "He must make restitution for the lamb fourfold, because he did this thing and had no compassion" which is another propositional statement of truth accurately understood. Nathan declared, "You are the man!" a statement that could not be more propositional, confrontational, and indicting. David said to Nathan, "I have sinned against the Lord" which is obviously a statement of propositional truth. The result of Nathan's story was that God's truth was understood propositionally by the hearer, David. The extent of his culpability was expressed propositionally. The measure of his restitution was announced propositionally. His sinful state was declared propositionally. His sinful state was understood and confessed propositionally. The telling of a story was only the initial vehicle for the needed truth to be perceived. But perceived truth is always truth that can be stated propositionally when exact understanding has been achieved. The purpose of the story served as a means to clearly and forcefully establish propositional truth! Propositional truth was the end whereas the story was simply the means to the end. Without the end— the establishment of propositional truth—the means are meaningless. God's Word must be explained and enforced propositionally!

Certainly illustrations have a great place and purpose in the process of preaching. I am not about to devalue the role of illustrations in preaching since the greatest need for illustrations is found in expository preaching. My contention is not with the use of illustrations in preaching. My contention is with the idea that preaching is to be devoid of propositional truth.

I don't think it is even an option for the truth not to be declared propositionally. Propositional truth may be rejected but it must not be silenced, substituted, or soft-peddled by men who do not have the courage or the integrity to explain what God has spoken! We must understand the significant place that the pulpit must have in the Church. Let's clarify the significant place the pulpit must have in the Church with two final assertions. *The pulpit is no place for a man who is suffering from cowardice and is reticent to proclaim God's Word!* On the other hand, *the pulpit is no place for a man who is suffering from hubris and is quick to establish his word instead of exposing God's Word to the heads and the hearts of the hearers!* The solution for both extremes is to expound the Scriptures through the means of statements of theological principle.

INDUCTIVE THINKING AND PROPOSITIONAL TRUTH

Statements of theological principle are the products of inductive thinking. Inductive thinking is the thought process of deriving a general assertion from particular details. The inductive thought process is no insignificant matter in the process of comprehending God's Word. The power to make generalizations is one of the most astounding faculties of the mind and is of invaluable service in preparing to preach generally, and specifically, in preparing sermon structure that consists of statements of theological principle.

The ability to make significant generalizations is the true test of intellectual power and a most determinative factor in preaching effectiveness. The time and energy spent to make significant generalizations are part of the constructive but necessary mental discipline involved in preaching expository sermons.

One of the essential characteristics of expository preaching is the objectivity of the sermon. The sermon's objectivity is due to the fact that the sermon was produced inductively, that is, "the biblical passage itself should provide all the components of the message."[6] The ability to think in terms of generalities, that is, to synthesize general principles, from a host of particular details is an incredibly significant issue for preaching. A generalization, then, has its own proper function to perform. It condenses a broad area of experience into a single statement, sees a large truth in a single glance. Its purpose is to pull together and unify a multitude of concrete but otherwise unrelated facts, incidents, fragments of life, and to hold them together in a unit of meaning. Its result is to achieve understanding, breadth and grasp of thought, to reveal and illuminate perspective from a vast field of data. Without clearly apprehended generalizations, a sermon will always seem to be dealing with an assortment of disjointed trivialities, minutia, fragments of insight, and scraps of information. That is what has happened when we wonder what a preacher is driving at when he is going on and on, talking about everything and making sense of nothing. He has failed to pull his material together and make a general statement about it. It is the generalizations that organize the material of a sermon.[7]

The propositional nature of Scripture, as processed through inductive thinking, will yield a decidedly deductive preaching event where statements of theological principle are emphasized. According to Spurgeon, "The word 'sermon' is said to signify a thrust, and therefore, in sermonizing it must be our aim to use the subject in hand with energy and effect, and the subject must be capable of such employment. To choose mere moral themes will be to use a wooden dagger; but the great truths of revelation are as sharp swords."[8] Still, in the view of some, and increasingly more in our day, Scripture as propositional truth and preaching as a deductive enterprise are co-conspirators in an attempt to exterminate effective preaching.

David L. Larsen rightly rebuts Clark Pinnock's claim against theological conservatives that their problem and plague is that they are "deductive and exegetical." Larsen asks, "Where will we go if we surrender logic and exegesis? Are propositional revelation and propositional theology really our chief nemesis as Pinnock argues? ... Is not Pinnock himself vulnerable to a dangerous cutting loose from the conscientious exegesis of propositional revelation and normative theology?"[9] Propositional declaration of God's Word is not the nemesis to the Church. The nemesis to the Church, regarding the enterprise of preaching, is the surreptitious replacement of, and overt lack of faith in, the Word of God as a sufficient foundation for preaching in which propositional truth is declared through statements of theological principle expressed to provide understanding of a biblical text, to provide a framework for theological thinking, and to provide insight into true wisdom which is the practicing of the truth in life.

THE PROPOSITIONAL NATURE OF DEDUCTIVE PREACHING

Not all inductive homileticians would possess the same view of Scripture. However, they still advocate an approach, the inductive approach to preaching, that purposely steers clear of any declaration of propositional statements of truth deduced from Scripture. According to inductive homileticians, the methodology to articulate principlized statements of truth found in a passage, the deductive approach to preaching, is to be avoided strenuously. Consider a small sampling of inductive homiletical sentiment from only one among many other adherents as he seeks to contrast deductive and inductive preaching.

> Deductive preaching starts with a declaration of intent and proceeds to prove the validity of what the preacher says is already determined to be true.[10]

> He (the inductive preacher) doesn't cling to any elevated position of authority, but by the attitude evident in the inductive process he descends to become one among his listeners. He puts aside pride to be a worker together with his hearers. He serves as a player-coach, not as a loud voice admonishing from a platform above the field. He sits not as a sovereign monarch, or even as the king's representative looking down on a vast domain, but rather carves out a common niche, a place to stand among the people.[11]
>
> Deduction exerts a strong sense of authority in its propositional dictums. On the contrary, induction allows a listener to assume a measure of authority in the process of reaching conclusions. Deduction stands on traditions and the authorities of the past. Induction accounts for the pressures of the present.[12]
>
> Deduction defines, delimits, diminishes, dissects or defends its first premise. Inductive examples precede and lead to assertions; deductive examples follow and bolster assertions already made.
>
> In an inductive format any propositions, assertions, declarations or exhortations follow or flow out of the illustrative material in the course of the sermon process. Deductive sermons begin with the preacher's conclusions that are a result of sermon preparation—conclusions offered as *givens* to listeners who may or may not be ready to accept them and go on from there.
>
> The difference may be summarized this way. The deductive preacher begins with truths and then sets out to prove them. The inductive preacher seeks to help listeners see the truth in such a way that they are ready to accept, agree with and respond to that truth at the end of the sermon.[13]

Such statements regarding deductive preaching in contrast to inductive preaching assert as fact that the deductive preacher is flawed not only in methodology but in character as well. Last but not least, the deductive methodology is seen by inductive homileticians as an ineffective, even detrimental activity.

This view of preaching, the inductive approach, I believe is not best for instructing people according to the teachings found in a passage of Scripture. Even William Willimon, one who has been a strong advocate of inductive preaching, has experienced a changed orientation toward expository preaching having admitted to an obvious weakness of the inductive methodology he has employed. He writes,

> Too much of my preaching begins at what I judge to be "where people are." I begin with their experience, their "felt need," then, in twenty minutes, I attempt to move them to the gospel. This renders the gospel into nothing more than a helpful resource to get us what we wanted before we met the gospel.[14]

A rather candid though regrettable account of one's injudicious handling of Scripture. Preaching God's Word through the deductive exposition of its contents is a certain correction to such a lamentable compromising of the gospel and many biblical texts.

To present statements of theological principle in the form of sermon points in one's preaching is deductive preaching and this is to be understood as the approach I will be advocating as I deal with sermon structure. While I concur with very much of what Donald Hamilton has to say in his *Homiletical Handbook* about the structuring of expository sermons, I think two assertions he makes are worthy disclosures regarding a statement of theological principle. He asserts that, "No apology is made or considered necessary" for the more traditional deductive approach to structuring sermons.[15] He also says that "Good structuring (of a sermon) confirms and solidifies the preacher's grasp of the material being presented in the sermon. Conversely, the lack of good structure may indicate that the preacher is still struggling to understand fully the relationship of the various concepts with which he is dealing."[16] These assertions are pivotal in the framework of preparing and preaching sermon structure as statements of theological principle.

Because Scripture is propositional truth, regardless of the varieties of genre for any specific passage, it can therefore be proclaimed to men as the truth from God to men through the agency of a servant of God. This constitutes deductive preaching.

Deductive preaching is declared for the purpose to change lives, knowing that lives can and should be changed because the preacher is not dispensing his own weak views, but rather, he is declaring God's truth—truth that is both timeless and life-changing. This is the objective of true preaching.

> When you undertake to preach a sermon you set yourself the task of convincing the judgment, of kindling the imagination, of moving the feelings, and of giving such a powerful impulse to the will that this finer quality of being may find expression in finer forms of action. And we know from experience that in

securing this high end the divine energy operates habitually and most powerfully through those vital truths which bear upon the development of spiritual life. The sermon embodying in living form some important portion of this truth is therefore designed to make men feel, and feel so deeply that they will resolve. It is designed to make men resolve and resolve so strongly that they will act . . . We sometimes hear light-hearted and light-headed people who have not learned their way about, remarking in this strain, "We do not want our preachers to give us theology—let them give us the simple gospel." But "the simple gospel," as men sometimes call it, not knowing what they say, is brimful of theology. It is a presentation of truths, deep, broad, high, stretching on endlessly in their abiding significance.[17]

Deductive preaching, because it delineates timeless truths from God's Word, is preaching that changes lives according to the understanding of the God-ordained means of changing the lives of men, God's Word. The deductive preaching of God's Word is carried out best when the truths are presented clearly to the hearers. The clearest presentation of God's truth is made through the means of organization, so that there is sequential progression of the content to be presented. The strongest organization of content is demonstrated by a sermon outline. The sermon outline which organizes the clearest presentation of the timeless meaning of a biblical text is composed of statements of theological principle.

EXPOSITORY PREACHING AS DEDUCTIVE PREACHING

Expository preaching is deductive preaching at its best. In expository preaching, not only are there clear truth-claims of the text being given, but these statements of theological principle rise out of the text and are understood and clarified as the text is explained. The expository preacher then, is not one who is involved in the process of preaching sermons so much as he is explaining what God has given to the church for its spiritual wellbeing. James W. Thompson writes:

> As 1 and 2 Corinthians indicate, Pauline preaching is the authoritative preaching of the prophetic tradition . . . If Paul is a model for preaching, he is the reminder that Christian speech rests ultimately on the apostolic authority that is mediated by the apostolic witness. The preacher, therefore, is not "one without authority," but one who mediates authoritative instruction to the church. The preacher is the heir of the prophetic tradition,

recalling the words of those who spoke only the words of God. Preachers do not speak for themselves, but they act as "stewards" whose task is to be faithful in upholding what has been given to them. The preacher functions as the emissary of the apostle, "explaining his ways" to the believing community.[18]

Though Thompson does not write in advocacy of expository preaching, his words are uniquely true for one who is an expository preacher.

Deductive preaching and especially expository preaching are aided immeasurably by good sermon structure. In his book *Christ-centered Preaching*, Bryan Chapell provides one of the better accounts of expository preaching as he links biblical exposition with sermon structure. "An expository sermon takes its topic, main points, and sub points from the text. In expository preaching the expositor is committed to explain what a specific biblical passage means. The goal of the expository preacher is simple: to have listeners personally understand what the passage under consideration means before the leave the service."[19] Expository preaching, as it is most commonly done, is the focus of one passage of Scripture.

Though references to other passages should occur, they should occur only as the preacher attempts to confirm, corroborate, or elaborate matters that are evident in the immediate text. Merely because a thing is true, because it has a biblical foundation, or because it comes to the preacher's mind does not mean it has a place in an expository sermon. The main idea of an expository sermon—the sermon proposition; the divisions of that idea—the main points; and the development of those divisions—the sub points; all come from the truths the text itself contains. No portion of the text is ignored. In other words, expositors willingly stay within the boundaries of a text and do not leave until they have surveyed its entirety with their listeners.[20]

An expository sermon, in regards to its sermon structure, expounds Scripture by deriving from a specific text main points and sub points that disclose the thought of the author, cover the scope of the passage, and apply the truth of the text to the lives of the listeners.[21] In any valid assessment of expository preaching, sermon structure is a crucial issue. And as everything else is of equal quality in two different expository sermons, the one with the better structure will be the better sermon.

GOOD SERMON STRUCTURE IN EXPOSITORY PREACHING

In dealing with the matter of sermon structure, I want to repeatedly raise the question, what makes for "good" sermon structure? Trying to establish the criteria for sermon structure that may be viewed as "good" is the objective to be achieved from this point forward. Before discussing both general and specific criteria which will enhance the quality of a sermon outline, Don McDougall has listed three inviolable imperatives that must be honored as one seeks to establish an outline for an expository sermon—Let the passage dictate to you; don't dictate to it: Find the outline; don't create it: Communicate the message; don't just outline it.[22] As long as these basic principles are adhered to methodologically, then we can concern ourselves with incorporating general and specific criteria for enhancing the overall quality of our sermon outlines.

Before sermon structure can be good, or otherwise, there must be structure. So the question is, how do we get structure for a sermon, sermon structure that we have discovered rather than borrowing the structure that someone else has already discovered? This was a question that haunted me many years ago and drove me to seek a satisfactory answer. The answer came by way of a chapter entitled "The Analytical Method" in a book by Howard F. Vos, *Effective Bible Study*,[23] written to provide various methodologies for Bible study. In reference to an overview of the analytical method Vos writes, "The analytical method, then, will begin with a grammatical diagram of the text, will proceed with a careful outline based upon the diagram . . . Grammatical analysis involves rewriting the text."[24] Subsequently, I found helpful variation and modification of this basic approach through Walter Kaiser's discussion of block diagramming in his book *Toward an Exegetical Theology*,[25] Lee Kantenwein's book on *Diagrammatical Analysis*,[26] and Donald W. Emery's book on *Sentence Analysis*.[27] But since 1980, with the helpful instruction provided by Vos, the only way I know to derive my own outline of a biblical text is to diagram the passage from which I will preach. Diagramming has been of invaluable service to me and I wholeheartedly commend it to others.

DIAGRAMMING A TEXT—DISCOVERING HOW THE PARTS OF THE TEXT RELATE

The purpose for diagramming a passage is to discover the internal relationship of the parts of the biblical text to be outlined and preached. This is a very important goal but the process of diagramming may become needlessly difficult. Since the purpose of diagramming a text is to preach from it rather than identifying and labeling the parts of speech of each word in a sentence, there is no premium to be obtained by making the process difficult. What is minimally necessary is to rewrite every word of the passage (sentence diagramming) in a new configuration that will establish the major and minor assertions of the text in order to see how the minor assertions of the passage modify the major assertions. In sentence diagramming, the core of each sentence is placed on the left side of a page and every word of the sentence is indented and placed under the word or phrase being modified.

When dealing with a text that is reasonably short, sentence diagramming is appropriate. If the passage is lengthy, such as many narrative texts are inclined to be, then block diagramming is in order. In block diagramming, the major assertions of each paragraph are represented by placing them to the left margin of a page. The modifying sentences within that paragraph are indented showing how each one relates to the main statement or other modifying statements of the paragraph. Every word does not have to be plotted on the block diagram.

An example of sentence diagramming and block diagramming are provided for a short and long passage of Scripture. The complete outlines generated from the diagrams, as well as the diagrams, are given below.

The sermonic designations of the sermon outline are placed on the diagram to show what portion of the text was responsible for the specific major or minor assertions found on the sermon outline. Again, it is crucial that each point of main and substructure come from the text. Therefore, every point and sub point of the sermon outline must be found on the diagram. This will assure that the outline of the sermon has been generated from the text that will be preached.

Sentence Diagram and Outline—Matthew 5:10–12

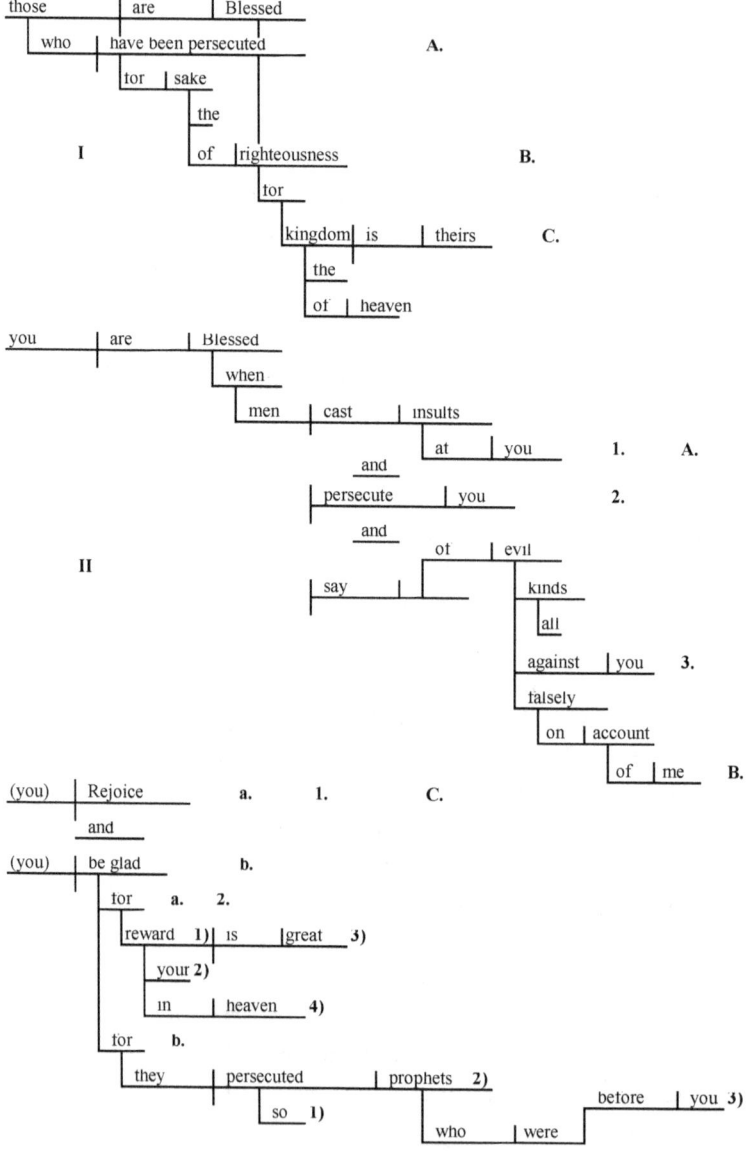

Sermon Structure as a Necessity, Not a Liability

In his Sermon on the Mount, Jesus affirms that those who suffer persecution are doubly blessed as persecution brings to them 2 <u>benefits</u>.

I. Persecution Bears a Proof of Citizenship in the Kingdom of Heaven
   A. Persecution Has Always Been a Mark of God's People (10a)
   B. Righteousness Has Always Been the Cause of Persecution (10b)
   C. Inclusion in the Kingdom Has Always Been an Exclusive Reality (10c)

IV. Persecution Brings a Promise of Reward in the Kingdom of Heaven
   A. The Forms of Persecution
      1. Direct verbal abuse (11a)
      2. Direct physical abuse (11b)
      3. Indirect verbal abuse (11c)
   B. The Reason for Persecution (11d)
   C. The Response to Persecution
      1. A 2-fold requirement for our response (12a)
         a. rejoice
         b. be glad
      1. A 2-fold reason for our response
         a. heavenly reward (12b)
            1) its reality
            2) its significance
            3) its character
            4) its reception
         b. prestigious accompaniment (12c)
            1) regarding treatment
            2) regarding identification
            3) regarding legacy

Block Diagram and Outline—1 Samuel 1:1-28

There was a man, Elkanah, an Ephramite		**A.**
He had two wives **B.**		
Peninnah had children		
Hannah had not children		
He would go to Shiloh		

<pre>
There was a man, Elkanah, an Ephramite   A.
   He had two wives   B.
      Peninnah had children
      Hannah had not children
   He would go to Shiloh
      Yearly
         To worship and to sacrifice to the Lord   A.
         Hophni and Phinehas were priests there
I.   When he sacrificed
         He would give portions to Peninnah
         He would give double portions to Hannah   A.
            For he loved Hannah
            But
            The Lord had closed her womb   1.
            However, her rival would provoke her bitterly   C.
               Year after year she would provoke her
                  So that she wept and would not eat   2.
      Then Elkanah said, why … why … why … ?
         Am I not … ?

   Then Hannah, greatly distressed
         prayed to the Lord and wept bitterly   A.
         And she made a vow and said
            If you will Thy maidservant a son
            I will give him to the Lord
               All the days of his life
                  And a razor shall never come on his head
            As she continued to pray, Eli thought she was drunk
               He said to her, How long … ?
                  Put away …
II.   But Hannah said, No my Lord …
               Do not consider your maidservant …
                  Then Eli answered and said …
         And she said, Let your maidservant …
         So the woman went her way and ate
               and her face was not longer sad
</pre>

Then they arose and worshiped and returned to their house   **B.**
And Elkanah had relations with Hannah
        And the Lord remembered her
        And she had a son
        And she named him Samuel
                Saying, Because I have asked him of the Lord

Then Elkanah went up to offer the yearly sacrifice   **A.**
        But Hannah did not go up
                For she said
                      Until the child is weaned
                      Then I will bring him
                      That he may stay there forever
        And Elkanah said to her,
                Do what seems best to you
                Remain until you have weaned him
                Only may the Lord confirm His word
        And Hannah nursed her son until she weaned him

III.
Now when she had weaned him   **B.**
        She took him up with her
                With a three year old bull
                And one ephah of flour
                And a jug of wine
        And brought him to the house of the Lord
        Then they
                slaughtered the bull
                And brought the boy to Eli
        And she said, I am the woman
                who stood beside you
                praying to the Lord
                For this boy I prayed
                And the Lord has given me my petition
                So I have dedicated him to the Lord
                      As long as he lives
                      He is dedicated to the Lord

And he worshiped the Lord there

In this chapter we discover 3 <u>qualities</u> of parents who are pleasing to God in the raising of their children.

Parents Who Are Pleasing To God In The Raising Of Their Children...

I. Are Devoted To God In Spite Of Their Imperfections
   A. Their Permanent Devotion (1,3–5a)
   B. Their Past Mistakes (2)
   C. Their Present Afflictions
      1. Inner misfortune (5b, 6)
      2. Outer misfortune (7–8)
II. Are Dependent Upon God To Accomplish Their Purpose In Life
   A. In Fervent Prayer (9–18)
   B. In Personal Worship (19–20)
III. Are Dedicated To God In The Raising Of Their Children
   A. By Establishing Priorities For The Home (21–23)
   B. By Fulfilling Duties Toward God (24–28)

CONSIDER THE FOLLOWING QUESTIONS

1. What are the two foci of inductive preaching that are threatened by expository preaching?
2. What five questions suggest the case for the tact of "capitulation by a religious communicator" who refuses to declare the explanation and application of God's Word?
3. How did Ayn Rand assess and paraphrase the deplorable state of our modern attitude of not wanting to hear from God?
4. What are the two assertions regarding the prospect of preaching expositionally in a culture such as ours?
5. In the instance of preaching to people who are not inclined to accept God's truth, how can declaring God's truth clearly and forcefully be viewed as needed, be viewed as not problematic, and be viewed as the preacher's duty?

Sermon Structure as a Necessity, Not a Liability

6. What are the two non-negotiable realities of preaching in a culture that is not inclined to accept God's Word when it is explained accurately and enforced boldly?
7. What three questions clarify the issue about the preacher's character as demonstrated by his preaching?
8. How does Nathan's parable to David represent in fourfold fashion that truth, when understood, must be expressed and applied propositionally? Identify the four propositional understandings along with the four statements of propositional truth.
9. What role did the telling of the story fulfill and how does it finally achieve a meaningful purpose in reference to propositional truth?
10. What kind of man is to occupy the pulpit if the pulpit is to have a significant place in the Church?
11. What two assertions about the man who has a place in the pulpit clarify the significant place the pulpit must have in the Church?
12. How is the inductive thinking process defined?
13. How does the ability to make generalizations impact expository preaching?
14. How is the proper function performed by generalizations described?
15. What is the nemesis of the Church in regards to the enterprise of preaching?
16. Why is expository preaching deductive preaching at its best?
17. What three basic principles should be honored as one seeks to establish an outline for expository preaching?
18. What is the purpose of diagramming a passage for preaching?
19. Why is it crucial to place the sermon designations representing the main points and sub points of one's outline on the diagram?

ENDNOTES

1. Buttrick, *Moves*, 41.
2. Craddock, *Overhearing*, 66.
3. Ibid., 122–23.
4. Hendricks, *Say*, 23.
5. Niles, *Stumbling*, 89.
6. Zemek, "Grammatical Analysis," 158.
7. Davis, *Design*, 245.
8. Spurgeon, *Lectures*, 79.
9. Larsen, *Telling*, 76.
10. Lewis and Lewis, *Inductive*, 43.
11. Ibid., 45.
12. Ibid., 54.
13. Ibid., 81.
14. As quoted in Elliott, *Creative*, 133.
15. Hamilton, *Handbook*, 28.
16. Ibid., 22.
17. Brown, *Art*, 2–3.
18. Thompson, *Paul*, 79.
19. Chapell, *Christ-centered*, 128.
20. Ibid., 128.
21. Ibid., 129.
22. Mc Dougall, "Central Ideas," 233.
23. Vos, *Effective*, 33–38.
24. Ibid., 34.
25. Kaiser Jr., *Exegetical*, 99–104, 165–81.
26. Kantenwein, *Diagrammatical*, 7–107.
27. Emery, *Sentence*, 1–98.

Words to Live and Preach By

The Foolish Ways of a Fool

*The fear of the Lord is the beginning of knowledge;
Fools despise wisdom and instruction.*
PROVERBS 1:7

*His own iniquities will capture the wicked, and he will be held
with the cords of his sin. He will die for lack of instruction,
and in the greatness of his folly he will go astray.*
PROVERBS 5:22–23

*Go to the ant, O sluggard, observe her ways and be wise, which,
having no chief, officer or ruler, prepares her food in the summer,
and gathers her provision in the harvest. How long will you lie down,
O sluggard? When will you arise from your sleep? "A little sleep, a little
slumber, a little folding of the hands to rest"—And your poverty will come
in like a vagabond, and your need like an armed man.*
PROVERBS 6:6–11

*The way of the Lord is a stronghold to the upright,
but ruin to the workers of iniquity.*
PROVERBS 10:29

*From the fruit of a man's mouth he enjoys good,
but the desire of the treacherous is violence.*
PROVERBS 13:2

The one who despises the word will be in debt to it, but the one who fears the commandment will be rewarded. The teaching of the wise is a fountain of life, to turn aside the snares of death. Good understanding produces favor, but the way of the treacherous is hard.
Proverbs 13:13–15

A rebuke goes deeper into one who has understanding than a hundred blows into a fool.
Proverbs 17:10

He who is slack in his work is brother to him who destroys.
Proverbs 18:9

The sluggard does not plow after the autumn, so he begs during the harvest and has nothing.
Proverbs 20:4

He who turns away his ear from listening to the law, even his prayer is an abomination.
Proverbs 28:9

5

Sermon Structure as Statements of Theological Principle

GENERAL CRITERIA FOR QUALITATIVE DEDUCTIVE PREACHING SERMON STRUCTURE

IF SERMON STRUCTURE IS to be used in preaching then, like everything else in a sermon, it must be qualitative. The question is—what criteria establish good sermon structure from poor sermon structure? In this chapter and the ones to follow we will establish general and specific criteria for good deductive preaching sermon structure. General criteria for qualitative deductive sermon structure include; clear arrangement, statements of theological principle, and textual congruity. Specific criteria for qualitative deductive sermon structure includes; relevance, parallelism, repetition, alliteration, assonance, progression, advancement of thought, and substructure.

THE GENERAL CRITERION OF CLEAR ARRANGEMENT

Structured Sermons versus Running Commentary

As we have already determined, expository preaching is not simply a running commentary on a text of Scripture. However, many equate expository preaching as nothing other than a simple running commentary of a passage of Scripture. In the book *Preaching Verse by Verse* its coauthors equate expository preaching with the running commentary. Though the coauthors make a laudable effort to defend an approach to preaching which actually attempts to concentrate upon the contents of a biblical text rather than dismissing the text, they freely admit that the running commentary "can become boring . . . When concentrating on the details of the text, the preacher can lose sight of the main message of the passage."[1] These comments are correct. These comments cry out for what is actually required in true expository preaching—a structured sermon in which the contents of the biblical text are expounded through the significant means of inductively derived statements of theological principle which provide the essential understanding of the unifying message of the text. Again, Lloyd-Jones is incredibly astute as he concludes:

> There are many today who have become interested in what they regard as expository preaching but who show very clearly that they do not know what is meant by expository preaching. They think that it just means making a series of comments, or a running commentary, on a paragraph or a passage or a statement. They take a passage verse by verse; and they make their comments on the first, then they go on to the next verse, and do the same with that, then the next, and so on. When they have gone through the passage in this way they imagine they have preached a sermon. But they have not, all they have done is to make a series of comments on a passage. I would suggest that far from having preached a sermon such preachers have only preached the introduction to a sermon![2]

If expository preaching is by nature deductive preaching, and it is, then the propositional truths deduced from the passage must receive additional attention. They must constitute the most foundational, most important, truths to be understood regarding the preaching portion. In other words, there must be a hierarchy of thought advanced in the sermon. Simply put, major assertions must receive major attention but the attention they receive must come through a combination of minor assertions related to them. The necessity of understanding major and minor assertions of a passage and seeking to communicate them as such requires organization and clear arrangement.

It is significant to understand expository preaching as preaching that must incorporate clear sermon structure. Charles Reynolds Brown is helpful in establishing the necessary link between sermon structure and expository preaching. He wrote:

> I am a firm believer in the value of expository preaching. There is a good deal of counterfeit money in circulation at this point. There is that which is called "expository preaching" but in reality it is another sort of thing altogether; and the discredit which attaches to the spurious article has shaken the faith of many preachers in the utility of expository sermons. It has also repelled the interest of the people in advance of any fair trial of its merits.

> By expository preaching, I do not mean a running, skittering comment, suited to a Sunday School class. The man who lumps out on his congregation a lot of undigested information … with "the drawing of lessons," apt and inapt, is not in any sense an expository preacher. He has no unity in his message, no sense of progress, no real organization of his material, no definite aiming at a particular goal, to confer upon his effort the honor of being a sermon.
>
> By expository preaching I do not mean a prayer meeting style of comment, full of pious homily, and with a certain amount of exegesis of a loose type … The slovenly comments on some passage which become "a kind of weak and watery paraphrase of the original" is not expository preaching—it is just an exhibition of plain unregenerate laziness, on the part of a man who had not energy enough to prepare a real sermon.
>
> The expository preacher organizes the material in his passage so that he secures the sense of unity and of progress. He also aims at the end and arrives at some definite goal.[3]

Brown's comments are a worthy means to clarify supposed expository preaching from actual expository preaching.

Clear Arrangement and Clear Communication

In dealing with the structure of a sermon we once again must return to the subject of clarity. In effect, preaching is an unending struggle to be clear in one's communication of the truth. First and foremost in preaching clarity is required. Therefore, it must be relentlessly and ruthlessly pursued. Obviously, then, clarity is not achieved easily. It is a daunting challenge to be clear in one's preaching. The noted Puritan preacher, Richard Baxter, thought it no small matter to stand up in the face of a congregation and deliver a message as from the living God. He expressed this as he wrote, "*It is no easy matter to speak so plain, that the ignorant may understand us*; and so seriously that the deadest hearts may feel us, and so convincingly, that contradicting cavilers may be silenced." (Italics added)[4]

This kind of clarity will not be the product of good sermon structure alone but it cannot result without the benefit of good sermon structure. Whether we are dealing with clarity in the structure of the sermon or clarity regarding the exposition of the text which fleshes out the structure of the sermon, the expository preacher is engaged in an ongoing battle for communicative clarity.

The expository preacher's difficulty to be clear to those who hear him preach is increased since he must be faithful to the biblical text which means, among other things, that he cannot skip or gloss over any portion of the passage. Augustine's insights are especially fitting and descriptive of the expository preacher.

> There are some things which are not understood, or barely understood, in themselves, no matter how carefully they are expressed or how many times they are repeated by even the plainest of speakers . . . We should not shirk the duty of making plain to the minds of others the truths which we ourselves perceived, however hard they may be to comprehend, with as much effort and argument as may be necessary . . . in whatever way they are presented by a teacher concerned not for the eloquence of his teaching but its clarity.[5]

Many times the fiercest battle fought by the expositor is on the battleground of clear sermon structure. This is a battle, regardless of its ferocity, which must be won.

Organization

Ultimately, good sermon structure is a matter of organization. Organization entails much more than mere order. In true organization there must be a controlling principle. The proposition is a controlling principle of organization for a sermon. The sermon proposition dominates all the parts of the sermon.[6]

However, in expository preaching there is *a* controlling principle and *the* controlling principle. *The* controlling principle is not the sermon proposition but the biblical text. A sermon proposition and its related sermon structure is *a* controlling principle for the organization of the sermon but the proposition and structure have a right of existence only as they relate to and accurately depict the text.

If the controlling principle of sermon organization is the proposition then all sorts of material, even very good material, can rightly find its way into the sermon, although it has nothing to do with the biblical text, simply because the highest court of appeal is this—does this material relate to the sermon proposition and its structure?

However, in expository preaching the controlling principle is always the biblical text. The text controls the structure of the sermon—the proposition, main points, sub points as well as the supporting material that fleshes out the structure because the purpose for everything contained in an expository sermon is to clarify the understanding of the biblical passage. When the controlling principle of organization is the text the highest court of appeal is this—does this material relate to the clear understanding of the biblical passage?

Sermon structure must help to make the actual meaning of the passage clear. If this is not the case then sermon structure is of little value. Fenelon took exception to divisions in a discourse when they were more apparent than they were real, providing no genuine unity but only stringing together distinct discourses unified only by arbitrary interconnection.[7] According to Fenelon, partitioning assists the speaker's mind and those who have studied and whom school has accustomed to the method, but actual connections guides the mind.[8] Great effort is required to assure that the points of main structure arise from the text and accurately reflect the meaning of the passage. Lloyd-Jones writes:

> The important thing about these "heads" is that they must be there in your text, and that they must arise naturally out of it. This is vital. The actual division into heads is not as easy as it sound. Some people seem to be gifted with an unusual facility in this respect ... However, we must always make sure that these divisions arise naturally out of the text. Let me first put this negatively; because it is so important. Never force a division. And do not add to the number of divisions for the sake of some kind of completeness that you have in your mind or in order to make it conform to your usual practice. The headings should be natural and appear to be inevitable.[9]

So, if sermon structure reflects the genuine unity of the text, the divisions of the sermon must actually arise from the passage.

The controlling principle of organization, the text of Scripture to be expounded, determines the material incorporated into the sermon as well as the placement or position of the material within the sermon. In expository preaching, as controlled by the biblical text, the substance and sequence of material is determined by its usefulness to expound the meaning of the passage.

Both general and specific organization is needed for good sermon structure. Without general organization of material and specific organization of concise statements of theological principle, good sermon structure cannot result. In regards to the specific organization of constructing concise statements of theological principle, reflect upon Christ's Sermon on the Mount. In this sermon one will find the genius of organized thought that yielded theological insight that was profound in style and substance. He was able to articulate weighty statements of profundity in clear concise sentences. Long involved sentences will cause any man to stumble in his delivery, thereby, making his sermon less effective.[10]

In regards to general organization, or the lack thereof, a sermon is like a voyage without a set destination. General organization, or sermon structure, becomes the road-map for a sermon providing direction for the course when preaching. Organization establishes one's starting place, the intermediate stops, and the final destination for the sermon. Because of organization, the preacher and the congregation always know where they have been, where they are, and where they are going. A sermon is "crippled and loose-jointed without it."[11]

The sermon structure, or the organization or arrangement of the substance of the sermon is indeed a crucial element for a preacher to be able to preach effectively. Woodrow Kroll argued for the absolute necessity of sermon structure for effective preaching.

> Many times the only difference between a good sermon, one with great persuasiveness, and a sermon lacking in such power is a difference in arrangement. Lack of arrangement is probably the single most common fault of preaching today. Some sermons remind the congregation of the beginnings of creation; they are like the early earth, "without form and void."[12]

The wise preacher will supply structure to his sermon just as certainly as a builder would supply structure to a building. And, by the way, do you think you could even have a building without structure? Certainly not, but there are preachers who think they have put together a sermon though it has no structure. In arguing the case for the necessity for outlines in preaching, R. E. O. White stated that the "outpouring of a well-stored mind in eloquent freedom and spontaneity may be very enjoyable to the trained listener, most hearers will find the total fare somewhat undigestible."[13]

No preacher has completed his task of constructing a sermon until he has "several divisions, each with subdivisions, but ends up with but one unified sermon."[14] The final product of a unified sermon, unified by the means of sermon structure, is beneficial to the preacher and his congregation.

When a preacher has a well-arranged sermon it assists him in working out the little details of the message. They fall naturally into place. He will also have far less difficulty in delivering his sermon if the preacher outlines it properly. If he is to use the memorization method, he will be aided by arrangement. If he is to preach extemporaneously without notes, arrangement aids him. Whatever is logically and clearly outlined will be easier to memorize and retain.

Arrangement adds to the beauty of the sermon. Harmony in arrangement turns a dull sermon into an interesting one.

Again, good arrangement makes a sermon more persuasive. Progressive arrangement is the key to persuasion.

It is absolutely essential that the preacher arrange his sermon so that the congregation can follow him. Good arrangement will help keep the audience with you. If a good outline makes it easier for the preacher to remember his sermon, it will certainly make it easier for the audience to remember it. To accomplish this demands clear arrangement. Clear arrangement will engender a remembering congregation. Without specific arrangement the congregation will soon forget the message and the sermon will be of little value.[15]

The Unity and Diversity of Clear Arrangement

It is never sufficient to preach about a subject or to expound a biblical text without presenting distinct but related concepts of the passage's subject-matter. These distinct but related concepts form the main points of the sermon structure. For good sermon structure, it is essential to have each main point distinct from the other sermon points and yet related to each of the other points of the sermon to establish continuity of thought and development of the passage's subject-matter. The main points "help understanding by viewing the truth from a variety of perspectives."[16]

Clear arrangement must be understood as a result of unity and diversity. As was discussed earlier, a sermon must always be about one thing. The one thing the sermon is about provides the unity for the sermon and the sermon's structure. But the one thing the sermon is about will be discussed, clarified, and understood as several truths of the subject-matter are made known. This provides the diversity of the sermon and the sermon's structure. Unity refers to the sermon structure as a whole; diversity concerns the various parts in relation to the whole and to each other.

When a preacher preaches with good, clear arrangement that means he preaches a unified sermon. According to A. W. Blackwood, sermonic unity means that a preacher "delivers only one message at a time" asserting as fact that "Nothing is so fatal to the effect of a sermon as the habit of preaching on three or four subjects at once."[17] The orderly arrangement of the diverse points of the sermon, all having to do with the unified subject of the sermon, clarify and deepen understanding of the subject-matter in each of its parts, one after another.

A unified subject sustaining a diversity of related but distinct clarification yields progress, and advancement of thought in regards to the sermon and the text from which the sermon is preached. The combination of clear arrangement, containing unity and diversity, means that "a sermon ought to keep moving forward to its destination, much as a stream flows towards the ocean. Everywhere a sermon calls for onward motion, with never a break." Without unity and diversity the work of preaching resembles "a merry-go-round, the sermon as a whole would lead to no sense of arrival. Such entertainment may seem harmless, but why call it a sermon?"[18]

Beyond the significant help sermon structure provides for the hearers and the preacher to process the biblical text with understanding, good sermon structure casts a positive reflection upon the preacher as a man who is well organized. Chapell writes,

> Organization not only promotes the communication of the message's content (logos), but also is a vital indicator of the pastor's competence and character (ethos). "He's so disorganized" is a deadly assessment of any preacher's efforts. Such a characterization means the listeners have concluded that the preacher is either intellectually incapable of ordering thought or is too lazy to do so. The first conclusion frustrates listeners, the latter angers them, and either removes their reason for listening.[19]

In light of the credibility afforded an organized preacher who wields good sermon structure and the discredit passed on to a disorganized preacher, who would care to preach without the benefit of sermon structure?

But sermon structure, just because it exists, is not necessarily good sermon structure. All sermon outlines are not created equal. What constitutes sermon structure that may be considered a truly good outline? We have discussed the need for clear arrangement in sermon structure. Clear arrangement is vital for any outline that might be a good outline.

Sermon Structure as Statements of Theological Principle

The substance that is clearly arranged is crucial as well. An outline that is truly a good one must consist of statements of theological principle.

THE GENERAL CRITERION OF STATEMENTS OF THEOLOGICAL PRINCIPLE

The Bible is substantial truth. Expository preaching, if it is indeed preaching that expounds a scriptural passage, should not fail to reflect this fact. Therefore, the main points of the sermon should be statements of truth, timeless truths, which are far more than organizational memory pegs offered to the hearers to help them hang thoughts germane to the passage. No passage of the Bible is atheological—without theology. The main points of an exposition of a biblical passage must reflect the theology of the text. The operative word here is *reflect*. The main points are not to be pure statements of theology without bearing any semblance of practical worth. Likewise, the main points are not to be pure statements of practical instruction devoid of a theological basis. James W. Thompson addressed well the inadequacy of preaching that is not moored tightly to theology. He writes:

> Without critical theological reflection, the church mistakes the gospel for the reigning ideologies and popular special interest causes, thus failing to bring listeners to consider what really matters. Sermons that "baptize" nationalism, the pursuit of personal happiness, or the cult of self-esteem have lost the capacity for theological critique. Thus in the absence of theological preaching, the church's message is reduced to trivia.[20]

This simply cannot be the case for expository preaching. The main organizational statements, representing the essence of a passage of Scripture, cannot be trivial. Walter Kaiser pondered the plight of the present-day pulpit as he remarked:

> It is no secret that Christ's Church is not at all in good health in many places of the world. She has been languishing because she has been fed "junk food"; all kinds of artificial preservatives and all sorts of unnatural substitutes have been served up to her. As a result, theological and Biblical malnutrition has afflicted the very generation that has taken such giant steps to make sure its physical health is not damaged by using foods or products that are carcinogenic or otherwise harmful to their physical bodies ... The Biblical text is often no more than a slogan or refrain in

> the message ... Biblical exposition has become a lost art in contemporary preaching ... Motto preaching may please the masses in that it is filled with a lot of epigrammatic or proverbial slogans and interesting anecdotes, but it will always be a powerless word lacking the authority and validation of Scripture ... American parishioners ... are often rewarded with more or less the same treatment: repetitious arrangements of the most elementary truths of the faith, constant harangues which are popular with local audiences, or witty and clever messages interspersed with catchy and humorous anecdotes geared to cater to the interests of those who are spiritually lazy and do not wish to be stirred beyond the pleasantries of hearing another good joke or story. Where has the prophetic note in preaching gone? Where is that sense of authority and mission previously associated with the Biblical Word?[21]

Unfortunately, Kaiser is absolutely correct in his indictment. The pulpit is too often filled with men who resemble a blend of comedian, politician, news-anchorman, psychologist, cheerleader, success consultant, and public relations expert. In his book, *Between Two Worlds*, John Stott depicts the problem that exists for the preacher—bridging the gap between the biblical world and present world. Failure in preaching is marked by being biblical but not contemporary or contemporary without being biblical. He seeks to hear preachers who can bridge the chasm that exists between two worlds; preachers "who struggle to relate God's unchanging Word to our ever-changing world; who refuse to sacrifice truth to relevance or relevance to truth; but who resolve instead in equal measure to be faithful to Scripture and pertinent to today."[22]

Scriptural faithfulness is not only the sure way in which a preacher can truly be pertinent in his preaching, but scriptural faithfulness constitutes his only basis of preaching with authority. In his book, *The Preacher's Portrait*, Stott relegates the preacher's authority to the truth of the text being preached. He writes:

> Here, then, is the preacher's authority. It depends on the closeness of his adherence to the text he is handling, that is, on the accuracy with which he has understood it and on the forcefulness with which it has spoken to his own soul. In the ideal sermon it is the Word itself which speaks, or rather, God in and through his Word. The less the preacher comes between the Word and its hearers, the better. What really feeds the household is the food which the householder supplies, not the steward who dispenses

> it. The Christian preacher is best satisfied when his person is eclipsed by the light which shines from the Scripture and when his voice is drowned by the Voice of God.[23]

The closeness of the sermon to the biblical passage is reflected through a sermon structure that reflects the theology of the passage—in other words, a structure that codifies statements of theological principle.

Expository preaching, when rightly understood, will be recognized *not by the length of the passage being treated but by how the passage is treated in the preaching of it*. The careful and thorough examination of the text and the clearly arranged sermon structure consisting of statements of theological principle which summarize the text's meaning is determinative of expository preaching. Stott and many others writing in reference to expository preaching wisely and correctly mandate that expository preaching is recognized by the content of the sermon as opposed to the size or scope of the passage of Scripture that constitutes the sermon. He writes:

> The size of the text is immaterial. What matters is what we do with it. Whether it is long or short, our responsibility as expositors is to open it up in such a way that it speaks its message clearly, plainly, accurately, relevantly, without addition, subtraction or falsification. In expository preaching the biblical text is neither a conventional introduction to a sermon on a largely different theme, nor a convenient peg on which to hang a ragbag of miscellaneous thoughts, but a master which dictates and controls what is said.[24]

The most clear, plain, accurate, and relevant explanation of a passage is spearheaded by a sermon structure which depicts the essence of biblical text through a series of statements which are the timeless truths of the passage, or statements of theological principle.

It is essential in expository preaching that the meaning of the passage is passed on to the hearers. This dissemination of the text's meaning will occur through explanation of the passage generally and through declaration of the theological framework of the passage specifically. The declared theological framework of the passage will be the statements of theological principle—the appropriate content which must constitute the structure of an expository sermon.

In expository preaching the preacher must use the sermon structure to summarize the seminal assertions of theological importance. The sermon structure must always depict the main truths of the text. The expository sermon structure must depict the main truths of the text in statements that reflect the theology of the passage in timeless, principlized statements. It is the bearing of the truth-claims of a passage that provides expository preaching its distinguishing characteristic—an authoritative disclosure of God's truth to mankind as his Word is explained and applied. Sidney Greidanus writes:

> If preachers wish to preach with divine authority, they must proclaim the message of the inspired Scriptures, for the Scriptures alone are the word of God written; the Scriptures alone have divine authority. If preachers wish to preach with divine authority, they must echo the word of God. Preachers are literally to be ministers of the word. Thus preaching with authority is synonymous with true expository preaching.[25]

James Daane provides valuable insights for expository preaching in relation to sermon structure as he insists that the expository sermon is not so much of an attempt to prove or even argue for the truth of the proposition. It rather explains, exhibits, spells out what the proposition declares. The components of the sermon that do this, the sermon structure, "must come from the text and not from anywhere else inside or outside the Bible."[26] The sermon structure constitutes the theological affirmations of the text. The discussion of each of the main points of the sermon (the roman numerals in our outlines), is in turn an exposition of that particular aspect of the passage responsible for each of these major assertions. "Thus, the whole structure of the sermon outline is determined solely by the text. The Word articulated in a given text determines what the sermon asserts; and as such the sermon says what the Word says. It is thus an authentic homiletical effort" when the sermon clarifies what the text means.[27] Such an authentic homiletical effort is what constitutes an expository sermon.

Statements of theological principle used in expository preaching to assert the clarifying truths of a biblical text are helpful in the declaration of the truth by the preacher and the comprehension of the truth by the hearers. However, the process and the product of structuring an expository sermon will never be able to provide the perfect assessment of a passage of Scripture. It can and must provide for an adequate assessment of the biblical text. James Daane acknowledges this as he writes:

> The Word of God is larger than our power of comprehension. Its length and height and depth always exceed our grasp. It overflows our categories of thought, our logical structures, our definitions and explanations. The truth of the scriptural text will thus elude our best sermon outlines. Because of this transcendent dimension of the divine Word, the sermon always says more than the preacher knows and understands, and it may thus effect in the person in the pew changes and healing of the spirit of which the preacher is wholly unaware.
>
> Because the Word eludes and transcends our efforts at absorption of it, there are no perfect propositional statements, no perfect sermon outlines, and no perfect sermons. Outlining one text will give the preacher more difficulty than the next, but none will be perfect. This inevitable limitation of even our best efforts to structure the thought of the text in unity and rational integrity is, however, no excuse for not making the effort.
>
> We cannot exhaustively comprehend the Word of God, but this does not lead us to give up all knowledge of God. Similarly, we cannot capture the whole of the Word found in a single text in our outlines and sermons, but this should not lead us to give up on the effort to construct logical outlines and carefully worked out sermons . . . Therefore the truth the church proclaims cannot be wholly encapsulated in a system of theology, in a propositional statement, or in the structure of the best logical outline. Like a cup that runs over, the truth always overflows our logical constructs and conceptional thought.[28]

No outline will allow the expositor to fully declare the meaning of a passage, but then, neither will one's most thorough exposition of the passage be the definitive account of that text's meaning. This does not keep us from preaching, and it should not keep us from preaching. It also should not keep us from outlining the passage. The sermon structure as well as the expository sermon preached from it will never affect the exhaustive interpretation of the text but it must be a sufficient and accurate account of the text's meaning. Such principlized statements of truth are the nature of the main points of a sermon.

Principlization of Scripture

Sermon structure that may qualify as good must incorporate statements of theological principle. Statements of theological principle are what should constitute the main structure of a sermon. "The preacher's task is to find out what Scripture means and then to preach what it says. Ours is not to *decide* what it means but to *discover* what it means."[29] The discovery of the text's meaning is what the sermon is all about. The question arises regarding the meaning of the passage—do we discover what the text meant to the original audience or do we seek the meaning of the passage for the present time? The answer is both. For a text to have meaning at all, it must have had meaning for the original audience. This is the starting point for the meaning of the passage—what it meant to the original audience. However, that is just the starting point.

Having discovered what the text meant originally we can establish the meaning that the text should have for our present time, culture, and circumstances. What we intend to do in preaching is to codify the timeless truths of Scripture. In order to do this we must principlize the passage. In his book *Toward an Exegetical Theology*, Walter Kaiser does a fine job in establishing the necessity of principlization of Scripture in order to preach with accuracy and relevance. Kaiser defines principlization as follows: "To 'principlize' is to state the author's propositions, arguments, narrations, and illustrations in timeless abiding truths with special focus on the application of those truths to the current needs of the Church."[30]

Principlization of Scripture in Preaching

The text's meaning must be structured in such a way that the crucial statements, which collectively convey the meaning of the passage, receive priority. They are prioritized as they are given emphasis as becoming the main points of the sermon. Having statements that have been prioritized above others provides greater clarity regarding the essential meaning of the text. Sermon structure, achieved through principlizing the text, results in a two-fold benefit of prioritization and clarification. The main structure constitutes the necessary lines of demarcation. Such a demarcation of truth is significant for preaching. There is more to be said in favor for clearly stating main points than is to be said against it. Alvin C. Rueter calls clarity "the handle factor" to help people get a grip on the sermon. If the handle should be invisible it is nonfunctional. The statements of the main points supply for the listening audience what the heads in a newspaper article or book supply to the reader. These are indispensable for communication.[31] In expository preaching the basic objective is to clarify the text. Strategically emphasized statements of theological truth help the hearers to understand what the preacher is saying in the sermon he is preaching, but more importantly they help the hearers understand the passage of Scripture the preacher is attempting to explain.

David L. Larsen pointedly and persuasively argued the case for structure in preaching as he commented that,

> There is preaching which could be described as a maze without a plan . . . The result is like throwing an egg into an electric fan . . . If a sermon is to be more than a soufflé, the proper arrangement of form is important . . . There must be magnitude to organize, for the elaboration of the obvious makes no positive contribution. It makes the preacher resemble a hippopotamus chasing after a pea.[32]

When there is a clear and emphatic compiling of statements of theological principle in the process of expounding a text, the hearers will know that determinative truth is being proclaimed to them.

Clear communication is both an end product and a step by step process. Each step of the process plays an important role in order to achieve the desired result. The statements of theological principle represent the crucial steps necessary for the expository preacher's quest for communicative excellence. The expositor must regard the statements of theological principle composing sermon structure as the keys for unlocking the understanding of the passage in the minds of the hearers. Augustine's words are fitted well to the sermon structure as keys for unlocking the understanding of a biblical text. He writes:

> What use is a golden key, if it cannot unlock what we want to be unlocked, and what is wrong with a wooden one, if it can, since our sole aim is to open closed doors? . . . A speaker wishing to instruct should not think that he has communicated what he wishes to communicate to the person he wishes to instruct until he is understood. Even if he has said what he himself understands, he should not yet think he has communicated with the person who fails to understand him; but if he has been understood, then, no matter how he has spoken, he has communicated.[33]

The points of main structure are the essential keys which must be used to by the expositor to provide a base of communication and for the hearers a base of comprehension.

Requirements for Statements of Theological Principle

Full Sentence Form

If the main structure is statements of theological principle, then several requirements are in order for these statements composing the main structure. To begin with, they should be in full sentence form. The statements will be primarily declarative or imperative in nature, although they occasionally will be interrogative. Larsen says, "We establish a significant beachhead in our argument with a full, assertive sentence."[34]

There is certain advantage in using complete sentences for our main points. By using this form it is immediately obvious to the preacher whether he has anything that is clear and significant to say about the proposition from which he will preach. The full sentence form for the structuring of the statements of theological principle is important in developing a sermon in which reason and proof play a prominent role. Reason and proof cannot be established and validated by words or phrases. Reason and proof require carefully formulated statements containing both subject and predicate.[35]

Present or Future Tense

Most importantly, these declarative statements must be cast in the present tense but occasionally the future tense may be required by the passage. Except for the instance in which an act or statement of the Godhead becomes a part of the statement of theological principle, the past tense dooms a preacher to affect nothing more than a lecture. For example, later in this chapter we will deal with possible statements of theological principle that could come from Jesus' statement found in John 10:30 where he said, "I and the Father are one." Even though a portion of the essence of his expression will be stated in the past tense, the statement of theological principle coming from this verse must not be deprived of the present tense declaration that "Jesus is God." Other than such instances of theological, christological, or pneumatological past tense expression of the words or actions of the Godhead, the past tense is not appropriate for statements of theological principle. Even these instances are used to express something that was said or done which had unique importance in the past, even more than now. Otherwise, the present tense can be used and the understanding will be conveyed rightly that what is true now was equally true then.

Grady Davis is in excellent form as he advocates the present tense as a necessity in our preaching.

> One of the most frequently heard and most urgent demands is that preaching be contemporaneous. Rightly understood, that demand is reasonable and necessary. Great preaching is always in the present tense, always speaks to the concerns of the day in the thought-forms and language of the day. It is never antiquarian, never merely esthetic or nostalgic after the past, never neutral or detached in its attitude. Great preaching occurs when a man of compassionate discernment . . . stands up on his feet and lets his heart and head speak to his fellows.[36]

As a general rule, present tense, full sentence, assertions are needed for statements of theological principle. We will return to the significance of the present tense for our statements of theological principle later in this chapter as we consider "the priority of now over then."

Personal Pronouns

The usage of the pronoun "one" is acceptable terminology in statements of theological principle. However, the use of the first person singular "you" or the use of the first person plural "we" may be better terms to bring the truth to the hearers. Although the usages of God's names are always appropriate, other proper names of the Bible are not to be used since they create distance in time between the text and its hearers.[37]

Participative Action

The statements of theological principle must make reference to the thinking, attitudes, motivations, which precede and accompany the action the text requires. As Larsen rightly observed, "Performative discourse and participative action are at the heart of biblical communication.[38]

As noted above, it is not only possible to principlize Scripture but it is to be understood that Scripture must be principlized. Richard Mayhue very correctly placed great weight upon the current applicability of a biblical text if it indeed has been principlized. He wrote:

> Preaching does not stop with understanding ancient languages, history, culture, and customs. Unless the centuries can be bridged with contemporary relevance in the message, then the preaching experience differs little from a classroom encounter. One must first process the text for original meaning and then principlize

> the text for current applicability. One's study falls short of the goal if this step is omitted or slighted.[39]

Mayhue's assertion is significant. The relevancy of scriptural truth is based upon the principlization of the truth in Scripture.

The understanding that principlization of scriptural truth is both possible and significant is a crucial one. Moreover, it is just as crucial to understand the immediacy of principlization. The applicability of Scripture should be sensed in the sermon points. In other words, the sermon points, or statements of theological principle, reflect truths that were and still are relevant—truths that depict the meaning of a biblical text and its meaning for a believer's daily life.

Certainly, application will be a functional element of each sermon point as each of the points are explained and illustrated but the applicability of Scripture must be discernable before explanation and illustration are attempted. In other words, the points of the sermon must be statements of theological principle that are so clearly crafted that one may see immediately the relevance of the stated principle. This is both the great requirement and the great result of expository preaching.

> The expository form of preaching gradually develops both in the pulpit and in the pew the Scriptural point of view, than which there is none better ... The people are encouraged to put their trust in the general trend and drift of the Bible's teaching, to shape their belief and conduct by the main conclusions to which it brings them, and to develop their attitudes by the whole point of view which it gradually induces ... The people in a congregation accustomed to live in the presence of the sublime truths of Scripture become trained in eye and ear, in moral judgment and in conscience. They form their taste and they shape their action with reference to the classical ideals and principles of the Bible.[40]

Sermon points then must serve double-duty to express the theological understanding of the passage as well as the relevance of the passage.

The Priority of Now over Then

The outline of a sermon is to consist of sermon points that are both theological and relevant, therefore the sermon points will be characterized as statements of theological relevance and statements of relevant theology. If the points of a sermon are not principlized they will not be relevant. They may be accurate statements of theological understanding but they contain no bearing toward the practical impact that the theology is to have or how people are to live in light of the theology advanced in the unprinciplized statements. Again, Walter Kaiser is very helpful for our understanding the requirement that the main structure of an expository sermon is to be timeless statements of truth as well as providing insight as to how these timeless statements of truth are formulated. Kaiser writes:

> The main pitfall to avoid in formulating these main points of the message is that of using dated statements. The tendency is to merely transfer from the text all proper names, places, incidents, and descriptions. This of course immediately makes more difficult a modern audience's efforts to hear God's "new" word to their generation from an admittedly old text. Therefore, the teacher or preacher will be well advised to delete all proper names from his main points (except for God's names). Likewise, anything that would tend to focus the listeners' attention more on the "then-ness" of the text than on the "now" of God's new challenge must be studiously avoided. At the same time each proposition must be so worded as to preserve the abiding, permanent, and fixed teaching of the text.[41]

The understanding that the main points of a sermon are the critical statements of a text's meaning provides a great degree of importance to the enterprise of formulating sermon structure.

Theological Enrichment and Practical Insight

The structure of a sermon will not be as significant as it should be in a preacher's perception or practice of preaching until he understands that the points of the sermon are far more than just mile-markers in the sermonic journey so that he and his listeners may know at any time where they are, where they have been, and where they have yet to go. A preacher must not limit his perception of the main structure of a sermon to this functional benefit only. Beyond the beneficial value of having a map for the sermon, the outline provides the most salient precepts, distilled from the passage, which are serviceable for theological enrichment and practical insight.

The practical insights and the theological understanding that are codified as statements of theological principle to be expounded from a text are significant for the hearers and the preacher. The apostle Paul could truly say, "I did not shrink from declaring to you the whole counsel of God." He did not select his themes with calculated, consideration for those with itching ears who would welcome only that which accommodated and matched their own spiritual sloth. Because he had declared the whole counsel of God, he was able to count himself "pure from the blood" of those who might fall under the divine condemnation.[42] We like Paul must be certain that what we preach is not some of God's truth but all of it. Thoroughly explaining God's Word, passage after passage, one biblical book at a time, book after book, through the years of our preaching is how we may preach the whole counsel of God. Generally speaking, such a methodology will provide a wide coverage of theological enrichment and practical insight from God's Word. This does not necessitate that a pastor preach through bible books exclusively but that he will be devoted to this as the primary approach to preaching. Much theological and practical insight may result from doctrinal, topical, and biographical exposition.

More specifically, however, we must make sure that in every individual sermon we preach there is theological enrichment and practical insight. Therefore, the main structure must be statements of theological principle so that an accurate understanding of the passage can be achieved and the personal implications of the truth are brought out as well. In other words, the main points of a sermon's structure will evidence the fact that the sermon consists of significant substance. As one man wisely advised, "Take care that your deliverances are always weighty, and full of really important teaching. Build not with wood, hay, and stubble, but with gold, silver, and precious stones."[43] If the sermon indeed is composed of such valuable content, shouldn't the structure indicate this fact? I believe that the sermon structure certainly should indicate this fact. If the sermon structure is composed of statements of theological principle then the significant content of the sermon will be apparent.

Good sermon structure must have clear arrangement and contain statements of theological principle. These clearly arranged statements of theological principle must be congruous to the text being preached. They must be derived from the text and they must be true to the text. At this point, some questions reflecting an objection to the idea of preaching theologically must be raised and settled. The objection might be reflected by these questions: "Are you really saying that our preaching is to be theological?" "Are you saying that the main points of the sermon are to be theological statements?" "Are you kidding, preach theology in our culture?" Let's deal with the questions. Yes, our preaching is to be theological. Yes, the main points of the sermon are to be theological statements. Yes, we must preach theologically in an atheological culture. John Armstrong deals with this well as he writes:

> Truth is an inevitable expression of our concern with God—God who is the measure of all things, who reveals to us His mind. He reveals His mind to us in the words of sacred Scripture so that we might hear and understand the mind of God. Therefore, not to be driven by the question "What is truth?" is to fail to understand and to be properly God-centered. Thus all preaching that reaches the mind must be theological preaching. Yes, we must unabashedly, unashamedly say that preaching must be theological preaching. Not theology as an end in itself, but as an expression of our attempts to understand God's mind, to understand the revelation of God ... As the late Dr. John Gerstner used to say, every Christian is a theologian—a good one, a bad one or an indifferent one, but every Christian is a theologian.[44]

Preaching theologically is necessary for believers to be what we should be—good theologians or, at least, what we must be—the best theologians we can be.

The only reason such preaching could be called into question is because we live in a day, and have become victimized by an era, that is marked by a weak fidelity to the Bible, an anemic interest in the things of God, and an enfeebled will to proclaim what God has said to a culture who is convinced that they know better than God about almost everything! If there has ever been a time that needed to have theology hammered out through good and faithful exposition of Scripture it is our day!

The questions we must ask ourselves are these: Are our hearers convinced that the truth, God's truth, theological truth, matters to us? Do they perceive that what we are trying to do, what we absolutely are committed to do, is to help them think theologically, to help them to understand Scripture, and to help them live according to the truth of God's Word? If our preaching ministries are not portraying such commitments then we had better assess what we are doing and why these things are not being accomplished and repent of the practices and the product of our degenerate preaching! And by all means let's be clear about this—preaching must be understood to be degenerate when it proceeds without such commitments!

We live in a theologically degenerate culture to be sure, but this must cause our preaching to reform, not reflect, the days in which we live! You may not be able to correct the morass of our day but you must not add to it! As our culture is certain to continue to decay, it must do so despite your preaching, not because of it! Does your preaching reflect that you are a product of our day or does it reflect that you are a prophet in this day? Could your preaching be described best as providing a deluge of theological insight, or rather, a drizzle of theological thought, or perhaps even a drought of theological content?

Even when preaching is not degenerate because of the presence of sound and solid theological insight provided in the sermon, all is not necessarily well. In this case, preaching may not be degenerate but it may be, to use the term of Lloyd-Jones, defective. He wrote:

> What is preaching? Logic on fire! Eloquent reason! ... It is theology on fire. And a theology which does not take fire, I maintain, is a defective theology; or at least the man's understanding of it is defective. Preaching is theology coming through a man who is on fire. A true understanding and experience of the Truth must lead to this. I say again that a man who can speak about these things dispassionately has no right whatsoever to be in a pulpit; and should never be allowed to enter one.[45]

Is your preaching degenerate or defective? Much preaching today is degenerate because it is lacking in theological insight. Some preaching today is defective because it is not theology on fire. Worst of all, there is defective-degenerate preaching that has neither fire nor theology! The lack of fire stems from the lack of theology. The lack of theology stems from the lack of dealing with the text from which a preacher is supposedly preaching. In other words, such a sermon fails to reflect textual congruity. These are the starting points at which a defective-degenerate sermon begins.

CONSIDER THE FOLLOWING QUESTIONS

1. How does a structured sermon prevent the boredom associated with a running commentary in which the details of the text cause one to lose sight of the main message of the passage?
2. Why does expository preaching, since it is by nature deductive preaching, require organization and clear arrangement?

Sermon Structure as Statements of Theological Principle

3. How does Charles Reynolds Brown assess counterfeit expository preaching and what is required to turn the counterfeit variety into authentic expository preaching?

4. What is good sermon structure about, ultimately, and what is necessary for this to be achieved?

5. What is *a* controlling principle versus *the* controlling principle for organizing an expository sermon?

6. What question represents the highest court of appeal in reference to *the* controlling principle of organization?

7. What must one do to insure that genuine unity is provided by sermon structure?

8. How does general organization differ from specific organization?

9. How is it possible that a variety of distinct sermon points can provide continuity of thought and development of the subject-matter of a passage?

10. In what way does sermon structure contribute to a sermon being analogous to a stream flowing to the ocean and what is a sermon analogous to without unity and diversity?

11. What are the implications for the main structure of an expository sermon outline based upon the fact that no passage of Scripture is "atheological"?

12. What happens to a sermon whose message is devoid of theological instruction?

13. What is "the problem that exists for the preacher" and how is failure to correct the problem depicted and how is a successful correction of the problem depicted?

14. By what means is the closeness of the biblical text and the sermon reflected?

15. What criteria are determinative of expository preaching and by what criterion is expository preaching destined to be misunderstood?

16. How does the dissemination of the text's meaning occur generally and specifically?

17. What does an expository sermon outline depict and how does this relate to the distinguishing characteristic of an expository sermon?
18. What is the product that sermon structure is not able to provide, and what is the product that sermon structure must provide for an expository sermon?
19. What is the object of discovery for the meaning of a passage?
20. How does principlizing a text relate to what the preacher intends to do in preaching?
21. What two benefits result from sermon structure produced through principlization?
22. What two bases are provided through the use of sermon structure?
23. What advantages are attained by using complete sentences in sermon structure that make them a requirement?
24. Why is the past tense inappropriate for sermon structure?
25. What is it that the main points of sermon structure, as statements of theological principle, reflect?
26. What double-duty expression will be conveyed by statements of theological principle that have been clearly crafted?
27. The outline of a sermon is to consist of sermon points that are characterized in what way?
28. What will be true of sermon points if they are not principlized?
29. What is it that, according to Kaiser, must be studiously avoided in wording the propositions or the main points of a message?
30. To what perception of the main points of a sermon must a preacher not limit himself?
31. What benefit is derived for the hearers, and what benefit is derived for the preacher through the methodology of preaching passage after passage, through books of the Bible, throughout the years of one's ministry?
32. What is it that statements of theological principle are intended to help the hearers become, especially in an atheological culture?
33. What reason is responsible for questioning the legitimacy of theological preaching?

34. What commitments, when they are absent, cause preaching to be degenerate?
35. What is the basis for preaching that is defective?
36. What is the starting point from which defective-degenerate preaching begins?

ENDNOTES

1. Allen and Bartholomew, *Verse by Verse*, 11.
2. Lloyd-Jones, *Preaching*, 72.
3. Brown, *Art*, 42.
4. Baxter, *Reformed*, 183.
5. Augustine, *On Christian Teaching*, 115.
6. Lenski, *Sermon*, 80.
7. Fenelon, *Dialogues*, 111.
8. Ibid., 114.
9. Lloyd-Jones, *Preaching*, 207–8.
10. Brown, *Art*, 102.
11. Willingham, *Listen*, 39.
12. Kroll, *Prescription*, 153.
13. White, *Guide*, 81.
14. Kroll, *Prescription*, 153.
15. Ibid., 154–55.
16. Skinner, *Teaching Ministry*, 168.
17. Blackwood, *Preparation*, 130.
18. Ibid., 133.
19. Chapell, *Christ-centered*, 131.
20. Thompson, *Paul*, 123–24.
21. Kaiser Jr., *Exegetical*, 7–8, 19, 37, 191, 20.
22. Stott, *Between*, 144.
23. Stott, *Portrait*, 30.
24. Stott, *Between*, 126.
25. Greidanus, *Modern Preacher*, 12.
26. Daane, *Confidence*, 65.
27. Ibid., 66.
28. Ibid., 68–69.

29. Larsen, *Telling*, 81.
30. Kaiser Jr., *Exegetical*, 152.
31. Larsen, *Anatomy*, 63–64.
32. Ibid., 62–63.
33. Augustine, *On Christian Teaching*, 117–18.
34. Larsen, *Anatomy*, 68.
35. Cox, *Preaching*, 146.
36. Davis, *Design*, 203–4.
37. Larsen, *Anatomy*, 68–69.
38. Ibid., 69.
39. Mayhue, "Rediscovering," 16.
40. Brown, *Art*, 44–45.
41. Kaiser Jr., *Exegetical*, 157–58.
42. Brown, *Art*, 48–49.
43. Spurgeon, *Lectures*, 73.
44. Armstrong, "Mind," 169.
45. Lloyd-Jones, *Preaching*, 97.

Words to Live and Preach By

The Tests and Blessings of God

*The Lord by wisdom founded the earth; by understanding
He established the heavens. By His knowledge the deeps were broken up,
and the skies drip with dew. My son, let them not depart from your sight;
keep sound wisdom and discretion, so they will be life to your soul,
and adornment to your neck. Then you will walk in your way securely,
and you foot will not stumble. When you lie down, you will not be afraid;
when you lie down, your sleep will be sweet.*
PROVERBS 3:19–24

*Do not contend with a man without cause, if he has done you no harm.
Do not envy a man of violence, and do not choose any of his ways.
For the crooked man is an abomination to the Lord; but He is intimate
with the upright. The curse of the Lord is on the house of the wicked,
but He blesses the dwelling of the righteous.*
PROVERBS 3:31–33

*The backslider in heart will have his fill of his own ways,
but a good man will be satisfied with his.*
PROVERBS 14:14

The naïve inherit folly, but the prudent are crowned with knowledge.
PROVERBS 14:18

*The refining pot is for silver and the furnace for gold.
But the Lord tests hearts.*
PROVERBS 17:3

*With the fruit of a man's mouth his stomach will be satisfied;
He will be satisfied with the product of his lips.*
PROVERBS 18:20

*Every man's way is right in his own eyes, but the Lord weighs
the hearts. To do righteousness and justice is desired
by the Lord more than sacrifice.*
PROVERBS 21:2–3

*The crucible is for silver and the furnace for gold,
and a man is tested by the praise accorded to him.*
PROVERBS 27:21

6

Sermon Structure and Textual Congruity

IN THE LAST CHAPTER we considered two of the three general criteria for qualitative deductive preaching sermon structure: clear arrangement and statements of theological principle. This chapter will deal with the final criterion which is textual congruity.

THE GENERAL CRITERION OF TEXTUAL CONGRUITY

Good sermon structure is achieved initially by the terminology of the sermon points. Ultimately, good sermon structure results from sermon points that have been stated well because the statements composing the sermonic points express the meaning of the verse or verses to be explained for every sermon point. In other words, good sermon structure reflects textual congruity. Good sermon structure spearheads good expository preaching. "The wording of each main point will keep the preacher true to the dual expository task of exposing and applying the biblical truth."[1]

The explanation of a scriptural passage is neither an option nor an aspiration. It is the non-negotiable commitment of a preacher who truly desires to do justice to God's Word. This is critical in making a reputable attempt to fulfill one's calling from God to preach the Word.

Here then is our task, if we are to be faithful in fulfilling our calling from God to preach the Word—we are to put the contents of the Bible into the minds and into the hearts of those who hear, with all the saving and sanctifying power inherent in those biblical truths. And because the Scriptures do furnish us "a book of final values for all who would live nobly," we make it the sufficient and enduring basis of our preaching.[2]

As we preach, then, we must codify statements of theological principle from the Bible through carefully chosen words that express the fullest meaning of the passage we are able to achieve. The theological principles must reflect the most precise meaning we are able to articulate in single statements. The statements of theological principle composing the main structure of a sermon must be, in the words of Stephen Olford, "biblical" and "faithful to the text." He writes, "The integrating thoughts (main points) should come out of the text. They should not be imposed on the text. Thus, a good outline should reflect the primary integrating thoughts of the text. The minor modifying phrases, or subordinate movements or thoughts, should be reflected in sub points or in the flow of the message, but not in the main points."[3]

The main points of the sermon, that is, the statements of theological principle must be indicative of the passage we seek to expound in our preaching. If our sermon structure cannot or does not accomplish this then the sermon structure is defective. To the degree that the outline of a sermon establishes relevant theological insight that is congruous to the preaching passage, it is a good outline.

An outline that is congruent to the meaning of the preaching passage provides a brief understanding of the text as well as documenting the main insights of the sermon. The gist of the sermon, the main structure, identifies for the hearers what the preacher intends to say. These statements of theological principle can be analyzed, pondered, accepted, or rejected by the hearers but by virtue of the sermon structure the hearers can identify what the preacher is saying. Without the substance of a good sermon structure that reflects the meaning of the preaching text, it may become apparent to many that the preacher is deserving of the stinging indictment—"He had nothing to say and he said it."[4]

In regards to the textual congruity an outline must have, it should be understood that the exposition of the text, parceled out by the structure of the sermon, must be congruous to the text also. This will mean that the time spent in one point will not be balanced or equal to the time spent on the other points in the sermon. Greater detail supplied in a text for a one sermon point will require more time for the exposition of the text associated with that sermon point. Other points coming from the text that are not accompanied by as much detail will not receive as much time in exposition of its content as the more detailed portion of the text. This is an inevitable result in expository preaching marked by textual congruity.

In essence, fidelity to the text will guarantee an imbalance of time spent on the various points of a sermon. As Blackwood wrote regarding the symmetry or proportion of the main points of a sermon outline, the law of symmetry does not require that "all of the main divisions need to run exactly the same length" but requires that "every part receive as much time and stress as its importance demands, and no more."[5] Expounding the text according to the various depth of detail within the passage being preached will assure that each sermon point receives the needed, yet distinct, time and attention each point should receive. There is a definite point of departure between homiletical theory and expositional practice regarding two matters—allegiance and symmetry. The allegiance of the Bible expositor is to the Bible, not the sermon. The symmetry that the expositor is to be concerned with has to do with an expository sermon that is symmetrical to the text from which he is preaching. Expository preaching cannot excel under the restraints of homiletical artistry and gamesmanship exhibited by proportional time spent between various sermonic points. Expository preaching is not a matter of trying to bow to homiletical contrivances but it is a matter of bowing to the text and being faithful to rightly reflect the meaning of the passage. Expository preaching must result in textual congruity but it has no requirements for sermonic symmetry!

Purposefully Specific in Terminology

The requirement of a preacher in outlining a sermon is to communicate, in each statement of sermon structure, a summarizing principle that will be general enough to convey all that will be said in exposition of the point. This reflects the extent of the passage's meaning as well as this meaning in connection with the hearer's life. Yet, at the same time, the summarizing principle must be specific enough to convey, with some precision, what will be said regarding the essence of the exposition for the passage. Both the specificity and the generality of the preacher's terminology are crucial for his sermon structure. Grady Davis communicated this well as he argued that all the points, the structural assertions, of a well-organized sermon are particulars of the central concept. In like manner, each structural point is a generalization that contains and relates all the particulars used in its development. Or, conversely, every detail in an orderly discussion of a point is a particularizing of the point. The points are particularizations as compared with the central thought, but generalizations as compared with the detail.[6]

The preacher must calculate and weigh the terminology of his sermon points in regards to specificity and generality. An appropriate balance must be sought for each sermon point in regards to the generality versus the specificity of terminology within each statement of theological principle. If an expositor is to be concerned with balance regarding the points of sermon structure, he should make sure that each statement of theological principle is as general as it must be and at the same time as specific as it can be in order to reflect adequately what the meaning of the text is and what the exposition of the text will be. The terminology of sermon points must be weighed according to generality and specificity so that one's principlization of the text is an accurate depiction of what the text teaches in essence and extent.

Before we consider various terminologies, errors, and classifications associated with statements of theological principle, let's use an example of a non-biblical subject-matter, baseball, and see how a variety of erroneous statements can be deduced about the 1985 World Series through the use of terminology that is too general or too specific. Of the many things that could be said of the 1985 World Series, let's codify one principle and then introduce 5 classifications of "final product errors" of this principle.

An accurate statement would be as follows:

"The National League Champion St. Louis Cardinals lost to the Kansas City Royals in the 1985 World Series by turning in an uncharacteristic subpar performance."

A *hyper-principlized statement* would be as follows:

"The St. Louis Cardinals, representing the National League in the 1985 World Series, suffered a humiliating defeat to the Kansas City Royals by playing horrible baseball for most of the series."

A *supra-principlized statement* would be as follows:

"The St. Louis Cardinals, representing the National League, lost the 1985 World Series although they were a much better team than the Kansas City Royals."

Two meta-principlized statements would be as follows:

"The St. Louis Cardinals, the best team in baseball in 1985, played horribly for most of the '85 World Series."

"The St. Louis Cardinals threw the '85 World Series even though they played well throughout the series.

A sub-principlized statement would be as follows:

"The St. Louis Cardinals, representing the National League, lost to the Kansas City Royals in the 1985 World Series even though the Cardinals played well throughout the series."

An under-principlized statement would be as follows:

"The Cardinals were a World Series team in 1985."

For the sake of future reference, the *essence* of the accurate statement of principle is "The National League Champion St. Louis Cardinals lost to the Kansas City Royals in the 1985 World Series" while the *extent* of the statement of principle is "by turning in an uncharacteristic subpar performance."

It is observable that a number of inaccurate things can be said about the outcome of the 1985 World Series because of terminology that is too general or too specific, thus leading to statements that are completely overstated, partially overstated, overstated and understated, understated, and completely understated. All six of the erroneous statements include one or both problems of not stating what should have been stated, or stating what should have never been stated. The same kind of errors can accompany statements of theological principle that misrepresent a portion of Scripture rather than codifying the truth of a biblical text. Certainly this must not happen, but we must understand how to prevent it so it can be curtailed.

Erroneous Principlization Processes and Products

Clarification must be made between erroneous *products* of the principlization process versus erroneous *processes* of the principlization effort. Of course, the erroneous products of principlization are due to an erroneous principlization process. Regarding erroneous principlization processes, there are two: a sub-principlization process or effort and a supra-principlization process or effort. Regarding erroneous principlization products, there are five which are referred to as "final product errors": hyper-principlization, supra-principlization, meta-principlization, sub-principlization, and under-principlization. Note that sub-principlization and supra-principlization are terms that apply to an erroneous principlization process and to two of the five "final product errors" of principlization.

SUB-PRINCIPLIZATION OF SCRIPTURE

If a preacher does not carefully calculate his terminology he will err in sermon structure by articulating statements of theological principle that are less than what the text teaches—less than what the text teaches in essence, less than what the text teaches in extent, or both. This describes a less-than-the-text problem with sermon structure. We can refer to a less-than-the-text problem in outlining as a sub-principlizing effort in outlining or formulating statements of theological principle. Sub-principlization, saying in a statement of theological principle less than what the text actually means, in essence or extent, can take place because the terminology used is either too specific or too general.

Explicit sub-principlization occurs from terminology that is too specific. Implicit sub-principlization occurs from terminology that is too general. When a statement of theological principle is a sub-principlized "final product error," it will be so because the terminology was too specific. In this case, the only error is the use of terminology that is too specific and, therefore, the only resulting product is one of sub-principlization. However, using terminology that is too general can lead to an initial, implicit error of sub-principlization along with the explicit error of supra-principlization. When this is the case, the sub-principlization is an initial, implicit error which is accompanied with and overshadowed by the more dominant, explicit error of supra-principlization. Sub-principlization as the only error in a statement of theological principle results from terminology that is too specific. Sub-principlization as the initial error of a statement of theological principle results from terminology that is too general. When sub-principlization occurs initially and implicitly because of terminology that is too general, the explicit terminology used, being too general, will give rise to a statement of theological principle that is also supra-principlized, thus, the "final product error" will be a statement of theological principle that is meta-principlized. Meta-principlization combines the initial, implicit error of sub-principlization along with the more dominant, explicit error of supra-principlization due to terminology that is too general. In such cases, the terminology is so general that what should have been stated was not stated, which is sub-principlization, and that which was stated was overstated, which is supra-principlization. When the combined errors of sub-principlization and supra-principlization occur in a statement of theological principle, the "final product error" is a statement of theological principle that has been meta-principlized.

We will discuss and illustrate the "final product errors" of supra-principlization and meta-principlization later in this chapter. What must be understood about the sub-principlization process at this point is the difference between explicit and implicit sub-principlization. Explicit sub-principlization is a "final product error" occurring from terminology that is too specific. Implicit sub-principlization is an initial error that will be combined with and overshadowed by the error of supra-principlization, both errors occurring through the use of terminology that is too general.

A preacher cannot afford to codify, as a theological principle of a text, something that is so specific it necessitates exposition of subject-matter that is other than the more general, true subject-matter of the text. The too specific subject-matter then actually replaces the more general subject-matter of the text which should rightfully be expounded. In this case, the preacher will be codifying a principle that is less than what the text means in essence. He is so specific that his sermon point really never suggests the more general, actual essence of the text because the essence of the text has been understated. Therefore, the essence of a statement of theological principle has to do with an accurate articulation of the subject-matter of the statement of theological principle which identifies the exact subject-matter of the portion of the text from which the statement of theological principle is drawn.

On the other hand, however, one cannot afford to codify as a theological principle of a text something that is so specific it fails to project all of what the text teaches about the subject-matter in a given portion of the text. In this case, the preacher will be codifying a principle that is less than what the text means fully, or what the text means in extent. In other words, he is so specific that his sermon point really never describes comprehensively the extent of the text's meaning because the extent of the text has been understated. Therefore, the extent of a statement of theological principle has to do with an accurate articulation of what is being said about the subject-matter so that the statement of theological principle provides an appropriate limitation for what insights may be deduced about the subject-matter of a given portion of text.

When sub-principlization occurs because of terminology that is too general, the initial error is that of saying less than what the text means by muting the text's true meaning. This less-than-the-text problem is an initial error. However, the error of using terminology that is too general does not stop with an initial, implicit error of muting the true meaning of the text. It will ultimately give rise to an explicit statement that is more than what the text means. So, the "final product error" of using terminology that is too general is one of meta-principlization since there is a combination of implicit sub-principlization and explicit supra-principlization.

In contrast, when sub-principlization occurs because of terminology that is too specific, there is no initial, implicit error giving way to an explicit error. There is only an explicit erroneous statement that says less than what the text means.

Supra-principlization of Scripture

Likewise, if a preacher does not carefully calculate his terminology he will err in sermon structure by articulating theological principles that are more than what the text teaches—more than what the text teaches in essence or more than what the text teaches in extent. This describes a more-than-the-text problem with sermon structure. We can refer to a more-than-the-text problem in outlining as a supra-principlizing effort in formulating statements of theological principle. Supra-principlization, saying in the statement of theological principle more than what the text actually means, in essence or extent, can take place because the terminology used is too general. Still, the essence relates to an accurate depiction of the subject-matter and the extent relates to an accurate limitation of the insight about the subject-matter.

Let's consider a more-than-the-text problem arising because of a preacher's unwillingness to carefully weigh the specific and general nature of his terminology. Consider a situation in which the essence of the text is supra-principlized. In this case, the preacher uses terminology that is so general that he ascribes as the meaning of the text more than what the text teaches in essence. He is so general that his sermon point really never accurately describes the essence of the text. The true meaning of the text is never surfaced because the more limited understanding of the text's essential meaning is replaced by a meaning that is overstated and more general than was intended by the biblical writer.

However, a preacher may use terminology that is so general that he provides a meaning for a text that is more than what the text teaches in extent. He is so general that his sermon point never limits accurately the extent of the text's meaning. What the text actually means in extent is never understood because the more limited understanding of what the text means in extent is replaced by a meaning that was never intended by the biblical writer.

Additionally, a preacher can use terminology that is so general that what is stated has no right to be stated because what is stated replaces the more specific statement that should have been made. When this is done, there is a simultaneous problem of sub-principlization and supra-principlization occurring in the same statement of theological principle, which yields a "final product error" of meta-principlization. An erroneous process of sub-principlization has occurred because what should have been stated was not, it was omitted altogether, and an erroneous process of supra-principlization has occurred because what should not have been codified was codified. This inadequate disclosure of the text's meaning combines an implicit sub-principlization process, by muting the true meaning of the text's essence through use of terminology that is too general, and an explicit supra-principlization process since the terminology is too general to accurately depict the more limited, true essence of the text. The simultaneous errors of a sub-principlization process and a supra-principlization process joined together in a statement of theological principle is *a problem of replacement—the exclusion of that which should have been included* and *the inclusion of that which should have been excluded, which mutes what should have been stated and states what never should have been stated.*

The problem of inaccurately depicting the meaning of the text through statements of theological principle may stem from two *causes*—the statements may be too general or they may be too specific. The text may suffer misunderstanding in two *ways*—the essence of the text's meaning is distorted or the extent of the text's meaning is distorted because the statement of theological principle is too general or too specific. The two *resulting processes* from being too specific or too general are that of a sub-principlization or supra-principlization process, both of which lead to a misunderstanding of the text. The use of terminology that is too general or too specific, thus resulting in sub-principlization or supra-principlization, will yield an erroneous statement of theological principle which can be classified by one of five "final product errors." The five "final product errors" for a statement of theological principle are hyper-principlization, supra-principlization, meta-principlization, sub-principlization, and under-principlization.

Before we examine examples of statements of theological principle, we need to understand exactly what constitutes the two components of a statement of theological principle—the essence of the statement and the extent of the statement. What determines the essence of a statement of theological principle? The essence of a statement of theological principle is the portion of the statement that identifies the subject-matter. This is similar to the subject component of the plural noun proposition which, you will recall, answers the question, what is he talking about? The essence of a statement of theological principle identifies what the preacher is talking about. The extent of the statement of theological principle is analogous to the complement of the plural noun propositional statement which answers the question, what is he saying about what he is talking about? In other words, the extent of the statement of theological principle comprises the boundaries or the limitation of how the subject will be modified, or what will be said about the subject-matter.

Sub-principlization and Supra-principlization Exemplified

Some examples of possible sermon points that fail to incorporate carefully weighed terminology might be helpful at this point. Two examples will be given that incorporate differing degrees of difficulty.

Example One—First, let's look at a concise verse of Scripture—John 10:30, which says, "I and the Father are one." For the sake of clarification, let's agree that a carefully weighed statement of theological principle from this verse might be:

"Jesus is God and he affirmed his deity as being, in full essence, the same as his Father's."

The following paragraphs will include some possible statements trying to convey correctly the essence and extent of John 10:30 but will fail to do so because sub-principlization and/or supra-principlization processes have occurred. Also, an evaluation will be provided after each statement which uses the following symbols: +Sp: indicates the problem of terminology that is too specific; +Gn: indicates the problem of terminology that is too general; 0s1 indicates that the first part of the essence of the text was omitted; -s1 indicates that the first part of the essence of the text is not codified fully; s1 indicates that the first part of the essence of the text has been codified fully; 0s2 indicates that the second part of the essence of the text was omitted; -s2 indicates that the second part of the essence of the text is not codified fully; s2 indicates that the second part of the essence of the text has been codified fully; +s2 indicates that the second part of the essence of the text has been more than fully codified; 0x indicates that the extent of the text was omitted; -x indicates that less than the extent of the text has been codified; x indicates that the extent of the text has been codified fully; +x indicates that more than the extent of the text has been codified; B, < T indicates that sub-principlization has occurred and the statement codifies less-than what the text means; P, > T indicates that supra-principlization has occurred and the statement codifies more than what the text means. With the above statement of theological principle from John 10:30 in mind, the essence and extent of passage would be as follows:

"Jesus is God" = s1 "and he affirmed his deity" = s2 "as being, in full essence, the same as his Father's" = x

Two assertions form the essence of the text— s1 and s2. One assertion forms the extent of the text— x. With these symbols identified, they will be used to help explain various statements that are inadequate as statements of theological principle for this text.

Statements of theological principle incorporating terminology that is too specific are:

#1 "Jesus affirmed that he is God." +Sp: 0s1, s2, 0x = B, < T
#2 "Jesus is God and he affirmed his deity." +Sp: s1, s2, 0x = B, < T

Each statement above is true. Furthermore, each of the statements is true in light of the text of John 10:30. But the problem with each of the above statements is that neither one of them adequately summarizes all of the verse. Statements #1 and #2 rightly depict a portion of what the verse teaches. A less-than-the-text problem is indicated in each statement. In other words, sub-principlization "final product error" has occurred due to a sub-principlization process. Each of the statements above demonstrates a less-than-the-text problem since each provides less than what the text means in essence or extent.

Statements #1 and #2 clearly assert the second component of the text's essence—that Jesus clearly made a claim of his deity. Statement #2 includes the fact of Jesus' deity. Statements #1 and #2, though conveying a portion or the complete essence of the text, fail to capture the extent of the text's instruction—that he is God in full essence as his Father, or he is no less God than his Father. So the problem with each of the above statements as potential statements of theological principle for John 10:30 is that each one fails to adequately depict the truth of the text in essence or extent. Each statement depicts less than what needs to be said about the verse in one sentence. If either of these potential statements of theological principle were incorporated in a sermon outline, sub-principlization would be the result—a sub-principlization process yielding a "final product error" of sub-principlization. Neither of the statements is general enough to codify a correct understanding of the passage in extent, and #1 fails to codify a correct understanding of the passage in essence.

Additional statements of theological principle incorporating terminology that is too specific are:

#3 "Jesus became God and he affirmed his deity." +Sp: -s1, s2, 0x = B, < T
#4 "Jesus, though God, never affirmed his deity." +Sp: s, -s2, 0x = B, < T
#5 "Jesus is God and he affirmed his dietty as being, in essence, less than his Father's." +Sp: s1, s2, -x = B, < T
#6 "Jesus is God, in full essence, the same as his Father but he never affirmed his deity." +Sp: s1, -s2, x = B, < T

Statement #3 asserts for the first component of the text's essence less than what must be stated, namely, that he is God. The claim that he "became" God is simply heresy. The second component of the text's essence was stated clearly. The extent of the text was omitted. A less-than-the-text problem is demonstrated in both the essence and the extent of the text's meaning.

Statement #4 asserts the first component of the text's essence though the second component of the text's essence was negated. Therefore, a less-than-the-text problem is indicated since the essence of the text was not fully stated and the extent of the text was not stated.

Statement #5 asserts accurately both components of the text's essence but the text's extent is less than what must be stated, namely, that his deity is in full essence the same as his Father's. Therefore, a less-than-the-text problem is indicated in the extent of the statement.

Statement #6 asserts accurately the first component of the text's essence as well as the text's extent. However, the second component of the text's essence was explicitly negated. Therefore, a less-than-the-text problem is indicated in the essence of the statement.

Now let's exemplify the opposite problem—the use of terminology that is too general to depict accurately the essence or the extent of the text. In other words, let's see some examples of various instances of supra-principlization. Notice that statements #7—#12 suffer from sub-principlization and supra-principlization while statement #13 suffers from supra-principlization only.

As you will discover, using terminology that is too general leads to significant error. However, it is important to clarify a few things about many of the following statements from #7— #27. *It is safe to believe that some of the following statements are so erroneous that they would not be codified by anyone making a serious attempt to formulate an accurate statement of theological principle. I am simply trying to illustrate how errors can occur through imprecision. Admittedly, some of these statements are intentionally exaggerated to illustrate clearly the various degrees of error which arise from imprecise terminology.*

#7 "Jesus affirmed that his Father is God." +Gn: 0s1, 0s2, 0x = B, < T
$$\text{+Gn: +x = P, > T}$$

#8 "Jesus affirmed that there is only one true God."
$$\text{+Gn: 0s1, 0s2, 0x = B, < T}$$
$$\text{+Gn: +x = P, > T}$$

#9 "Jesus affirmed his unity with the Father."
$$\text{+Gn: 0s1, 0s2, 0x = B, < T}$$
$$\text{+Gn: +x = P, > T}$$

#10 "Jesus affirmed his submission to the Father."
$$\text{+Gn: 0s1, 0s2, 0x = B, < T}$$
$$\text{+Gn: +x = P, > T}$$

#11 "Jesus, though God, became man in perfect agreement with his Father."

$$+Sp: s1, 0s2, 0x = B, < T$$
$$+Gn: +x = P, > T$$

#12 "Jesus affirmed his deity and his distinct role from the Father."

$$+Sp: 0s1, s2, 0x = B, < T$$
$$+Gn: +x = P, > T$$

#13 "Jesus is God and he affirmed that he alone is the Promised Lord and Savior and, therefore, his deity is in full essence the same as the Father's.

$$+Gn: s1, + s2, x = P, > T$$

Statements #7, #8, #9, and #10 are so general that they fail to assert either component of the text's essence, the fact that Jesus is God and claimed to be God. Therefore, these statements completely fail to portray the essence of the text. Sub-principlization has occurred regarding Christ's deity and his explicit claim of deity. In other words, statements #7—#10 are examples of initial, implicit sub-principlization. What should have been stated was not stated at all. Statements #11 and #12 fail to incorporate either the fact of, or Christ's affirmation of, deity. Therefore, explicit sub-principlization has occurred in regard to one of the two components of the text's essence in each of these two statements because the terminology is too specific. Neither statement #11 or #12 provide a complete statement of the essence of the verse, both provide only a portion of what should have been stated. However, all six of these statements (#7—#12) fail to incorporate the quality, or the extent, of Jesus' assertion—that he is God in full measure with his Father. Therefore, all six of these statements lack specificity regarding deity in full measure so that each one is sub-principlized in the specific extent of the passage. Sub-principlization has occurred because the extent of the text's meaning has not been codified in any of the statements #7—#12 above, each one being too general to accurately principlize the text.

However, notice the way supra-principlization is demonstrated in each of these six statements (#7—#12). All six statements incorporate a theme that is certainly true about God but these incorporated themes go beyond the teaching of this verse. Therefore, each of the first six statements is too general to reflect the actual extent of the meaning of the verse. Actually, statement #7 simply states a correct inference of this verse, that his Father is God. Statements #8—#12 go well beyond the extent of instruction of the text. The truths of monotheism, incarnation, unity, submission, and distinct roles within the Godhead are taught in Scripture but if these truths are incorporated in a statement designed to clarify John 10:30, they will only shift the emphasis away from what must be said about this text in extent.

Notice that statement #13 exemplifies supra-principlization only, while statements #7—#12 join sub-principlization with supra-principlization. Remember, we refer to statements combining both faults simultaneously in a statement of theological principle as meta-principlization. Meta-principlization will be indicated as M, < > T.

Statements #11 and #12, even though they reflect a component of the essence of the text, and even if they were made to include the true extent of the passage, would still be misleading because of the supra-principlizing component in each of them. In other words, these two statements could accurately reflect a portion of the text's essence as well as the extent of the text, only to go beyond the true extent and still end up reflecting a more-than-the-text problem of supra-principlization. Here's how this could be done.

#11a "Jesus, though God, in full essence with the Father, became man in perfect agreement with his Father." +Sp: s1, 0s2, x, = B, < T
$$+Gn: +x = P, > T$$
$$+Sp, +Gn: s1, 0s2, x, +x = M, < > T$$

#12a "Jesus affirmed his deity as being equal to his Father although possessing a distinct role from his Father."
$$+Sp: 0s1, s2, x, = B, < T$$
$$+Gn: +x = P, > T$$
$$+Sp, +Gn: 0s1, s2, x, +x = M, < > T$$

In both of the statements above, only one of the two components of the text's essence is captured—Jesus is God, or Jesus affirmed his deity. Therefore, explicit sub-principlization occurs in each statement. The extent of the text is captured in each statement—his deity is no less than his Father's. However, both of these statements also include an assertion that is certainly true but it does not come from this text. The extra-textual addition ultimately renders these two statements to be an inexact reflection of the extent of the text's meaning because supra-principlization enters into the statements. Because statements #11a and #12a combine sub-principlization and supra-principlization each statement ultimately represents the "final product error" of meta-principlization.

Statement #13 accurately reflects the fact of Jesus' deity, the first component of the text's essence as well as the text's extent, that his deity is in full measure the same as his Father's deity. However, statement #13 includes far more than just an affirmation of Jesus' claim of deity and includes an affirmation of his identity as Messiah and a fulfillment of Old Testament prophecy. Of course, Jesus is the Messiah and he did fulfill many Old Testament prophecies in his first coming into the world but these realities go beyond the instruction of this verse.

It is helpful to clarify degrees of sub-principlization and supra-principlization. We can refer to instances of sub-principlization in essence *and* extent as under-principlization. This is a case of *total* sub-principlization. *Using terminology that is too specific can lead to sub-principlization or under-principlization.* Therefore, let's clarify our thinking about sub-principlization with the two statements used previously to exemplify terminology that was too specific, statements #1 and #2.

We can refer to statement #2 as sub-principlization since there was a less-than-the-text meaning occurring from an inadequate reflection of the extent of the text's meaning. Statement #1 reflected an understated meaning of the text that lacked in essence *and* extent. This is total sub-principlization, and therefore, under-principlization which we will designate by the symbol U, <<T. Notice that while statement #1 omitted one of the two components of essence of the text, still there is sub-principlization occurring in this portion of the statement. Since the statement is sub-principlized in essence and extent, under-principlization has occurred.

#1 "Jesus affirmed that he is God." +Sp: 0s1, s2, 0x = U, << T
#2 "Jesus is God and he affirmed his deity." +Sp: s1, s2, 0x = B, < T

We refer to instances of supra-principlization as a statement in which there is an overstatement of the meaning of either the essence or the extent of a passage. We will refer to instances of supra-principlization in essence *and* extent as hyper-principlization. This is a case of total supra-principlization. Hyper-principlization will be designated by the symbol H, >> T.

As we have seen, there are times when a combination of sub-principlization and supra-principlization occurs in the same statement. Such an occurrence is reflected by a statement that uses terminology that is too general in part or all of the statement. The terminology may be so general that it causes the essence of the text to never be expressed resulting in implicit sub-principlization, while the extent of the text is replaced by an overstatement, an explicitly supra-principlized assertion. Remember, this combination of sub-principlization and supra-principlization occurring in the same statement is referred to as meta-principlization, designated by the symbol M, < >T. *Using terminology that is too general can lead to implicit sub-principlization, supra-principlization, meta-principlization, and hyper-principlization.*

Let's clarify our thinking about supra-principlization, meta-principlization, and hyper-principlization with the six statements used previously to exemplify terminology that was too general.

#7 "Jesus affirmed that his Father is God."

We represented this statement earlier as +Gn: 0s1, 0s2, 0x = B, < T and also as +Gn: +x = P, > T. The true extent of the text was never reflected in the statement which caused the statement to be sub-principlized, yet an extra-textual addition was supplied so that the statement ended up being supra-principlized in extent. Since both components of the essence of the text were sub-principlized and the extent of the text supra-principlized, we can designate the meta-principlized statement above as follows: +Gn: 0s1, 0s2, 0x, +x = M, < > T.

The explanation given above for statement #7 is also true for statements #8—#10 below. Therefore, each one of them are indicated as +Gn: 0s1, 0s2, 0x, +x = M, < > T.

#8 "Jesus affirmed that there is only one true God."
+Gn: 0s1, 0s2, 0x, +x = M, < > T.

#9 "Jesus affirmed his unity with the Father."
+Gn: 0s1, 0s2, 0x, +x = M, < > T.

#10 "Jesus affirmed his submission to the Father."
+Gn: 0s1, 0s2, 0x, +x = M, < > T.

#11 "Jesus, though God, became man in perfect agreement with his Father."

In reference to statement #11, we represented this statement earlier as +Sp: s1, 0s2, 0x = B, < T and also as +Gn: +x = P, > T. The true extent of the text was never reflected in the statement which caused the statement to be sub-principlized, yet an extra-textual addition was supplied so that the statement ended up being supra-principlized in extent. Since the second component of the text's essence was sub-principlized and the extent of the text supra-principlized, we can designate the meta-principlized statement above as follows: +Gn: s1, 0s2, 0x, +x = M, < > T.

#12 "Jesus affirmed his deity and his distinct role from the Father."

We represented this statement earlier as +Sp: 0s1, s2, 0x = B, < T and also as +Gn: +x = P, > T. The true extent of the text was never reflected in the statement which caused the statement to be sub-principlized, yet an extra-textual addition was supplied so that the statement ended up being supra-principlized in extent. Since the first component of the essence of the text was sub-principlized and the extent of the text supra-principlized, we can designate the meta-principlized statement above as follows: +Gn: 0s1, s2, 0x, +x = M, < > T.

#13 "Jesus is God and he affirmed that he alone is the Promised Lord and Savior and, therefore, his deity is in full essence the same as the Father's."

In reference to statement #13, repeated above, it was supra-principlized because the second component of the text's essence exceeded Jesus' claim of deity. The first component of the text's essence and the extent of the text were expressed as they should have been. This statement was designated as follows: +Gn: s1, + s2, x = P, > T.

By changing the extent of the statement we can arrive at an example of meta-principlization and an example of hyper-principlization. Notice how this takes place.

#13a "Jesus is God and he affirmed that he alone is the Promised Lord and Savior even though his deity is not the same as the Father's."

If we replace the true extent of the text, "his deity is in full essence the same as the Father's," with a statement that asserts much less than the true extent of the text, "even though his deity is not the same as the

Father's" then meta-principlization results. Meta-principlization results because there is a supra-principlized essence combined with a sub-principlized extent. We can designate this statement as follows:

$$+Gn, +Sp: s1, + s2, -x, = M, < > T.$$

#13b "Jesus is God and he affirmed that he alone is the Promised Lord and Savior and, therefore, his deity is in full essence the same as the Father's even though he accepted a less-exalted position while on earth."

If we keep the true extent of the text, "his deity is in full essence the same as the Father's" and supply a statement that asserts much more than the true extent of the text, "even though he accepted a less-exalted position while on earth" then hyper-principlization results. Hyper-principlization results because more is being stated in the essence as well as the extent of the text's meaning. We can designate this statement as follows: $+Gn: s1, + s2, x, +x = H, >> T.$

The problem of using terminology that is too specific leads only to a sub-principlization process, whereas the problem of using terminology that is too general can lead to an initial, implicit sub-principlization process as well as a supra-principlization process. Though the problem of using terminology that is too specific leads only to sub-principlization— a sub-principlization process and a sub-principlization "final product error," the use of terminology that is too specific will lead to a "final product error" of under-principlization if is totally sub-principlized, that is, sub-principlized in essence and extent.

Since the problem of using terminology that is too general can lead to sub-principlization as well as supra-principlization, the use of terminology that is too general will result in meta-principlization if sub-principlization and supra-principlization occurs in the same statement while hyper-principlization will result from supra-principlization in essence and extent. Therefore, supra-principlization certainly is no less of an inaccuracy than sub-principlization. Although both errors must be judiciously withstood, *using terminology that is too general is more egregious than using terminology that is too specific. To say less than what the text means is undesirable since we fail to communicate the fullness of the text. However, to ascribe a meaning that is more than what the text means robs the text of its meaning since it is given a meaning that it does not have. In other words, a partially correct understanding of a text must compare favorably to a complete misunderstanding of the text.*

Example Two—Let's continue with a different statement of theological principle and consider how sub, under, supra, hyper, and meta-principlization may result. The statement is one we considered in an earlier chapter. The statement is,

"God is pleased with parents who are devoted to him in spite of their imperfections."

Unlike example one, this statement of theological principle has only one component for its essence and one component for its extent. The essence of the statement is "God is pleased with parents who are devoted to him" and the extent of the statement is "in spite of their imperfections." Notice that the extent is a negative reality, that is, the parents are not perfect in their daily walk. To assert, in the extent of this negative statement, an assertion of no imperfection or perfection, is to say *less* than what needs to be indicated. However, to assert excessive sinfulness beyond what the text indicates is to say *more* in extent than what the text means. In other words, when dealing with a negative assertion, if a more positive statement is supplied then the statement will err by being a less-than-the-extent meaning, indicated by –x. If a more negative assertion is made than should be made then the statement will err by being a more-than-the-extent meaning, indicated by +x.

In order to economize the explanation for each of the following statements, principlization indicators will be used to help identify that which is accurate or inaccurate in each of the statements. The portions that are neither italicized nor underlined are correctly principlized. The portions that are *italicized* include terminology that is too general and are, therefore, supra-principlized. The portions that are underlined include terminology that is too specific and are, therefore, sub-principlized. Let's see how the above statement of theological principle can suffer deviation through terminology that is too specific or too general so that the statements end up stating less than what should be stated or end up stating more than should be stated. We will discover instances of sub, under, meta, supra, and hyper-principlization. These statements will be presented as #14—#27.

#14 "God is pleased with parents who are devoted to him and possess no imperfections." +Sp: s, -x = B, < T

#15 "God is pleased with parents who are devoted to him <u>and perfectly obey his Word</u>." +Sp: s, -x = B, < T

#16 "God is pleased with parents who are <u>religious zealots</u> in spite of their imperfections." +Sp: -s, x = B, < T

#17 "God is pleased with parents who are <u>religious zealots and possess no imperfections</u>." +Sp: -s, -x = U, << T

#18 "God is pleased with parents who are <u>religious zealots and perfectly obey his Word</u>." +Sp: -s, -x = U, << T

#19 "God is pleased with parents who are devoted to him *even though they intentionally and consistently disobey him*." +Gn: s, +x = P, > T

#20 "God is pleased with parents who are devoted to him *even though they dishonor each other*." +Gn: s, +x = P, > T

#21 "*God prevents hardship from occurring to parents who are devoted to him* in spite of their imperfections." +Gn: +s, x = P, > T

#22 "*God prevents hardship from occurring to parents who are devoted to him even though they intentionally and consistently disobey him*."
 +Gn: +s, +x = H, > > T

#23 "*God prevents hardship from occurring to parents who are devoted to him even though they dishonor each other*." +Gn: +s, +x = H, >> T

#24 "*God prevents hardship from occurring to parents who are devoted to him* <u>and possess no imperfections</u>." +Gn, +Sp: +s, -x = M, < > T

#25 "*God prevents hardship from occurring to parents who are devoted to him* <u>and perfectly obey his Word</u>." +Gn, +Sp: +s, -x = M, < > T

#26 "<u>God is pleased with parents who are religious zealots</u> *even though they intentionally and consistently disobey him*."
 +Sp, +Gn: -s, +x = M, < > T

#27 "<u>God is pleased with parents who are religious zealots</u> *even though they dishonor each other*." +Sp, +Gn: -s, +x = M, < > T

It is clearly demonstrated that the terminology used to codify a statement of theological principle must be carefully weighed. The specificity and/or the generality of our statements can be the cause of codifying statements that lead to error. The statements will be erroneous because they codify more than what should be stated or less than what should be stated in order to be an accurate reflection of the text's meaning. The inaccuracy may be found in the essence of the text, the extent of the text, or both.

Purposefully Limited in Theology

The problem of incorporating terminology that is too general or too specific to accurately depict the teaching of a text in essence or extent, stems from the fault of imprecise thinking about, or synthesis of, the details of the text. Therefore, imprecise thinking will cause a preacher to be too specific or too general in stating his sermon points, or statements of theological principle.

However, being too general with one's terminology in a statement of theological principle may be the result of the preacher wanting to teach the truths of other texts while he is preaching the text at hand. This is not a problem stemming from imprecise terminology but a problem stemming from an imprudent methodology. Let's assume the imprudent methodology, though actual, is unintentional. The imprudent methodology is to use the text at hand so superficially that it becomes, in effect, a pretext to teach the truth found in another text or other texts when the conscripted truth from another text or other texts has, at best, only an apparent but no actual connection with the text at hand and the statement of theological principle drawn from the text. This is simply prescribing a meaning to a text, expressed by the statement of theological principle that is not the meaning of the text. The meaning of the text is never understood because of imprudent methodology just as much as when the preacher uses terminology for a statement of theological principle that is too general so that the meaning of the text is never expressed.

In the case of such imprudent methodology, the problem is *not* that a preacher is informed of how other passages deal with the subject-matter of his passage in more general or more specific ways than the instruction provided on the subject-matter contained in the text being preached. The problem is *not* that the preacher would quote, paraphrase, or cross reference other passages while trying to expound the text at hand. The problem *is* that the preacher incorporates the truths of other texts regarding the subject-matter of the text he is preaching, into statements of theological principle that supposedly come from the text he is preaching, when, in fact, the sermon points are more indicative of the instruction of other texts more than the text he is attempting to expound.

This causes the text to be used as a spring board to teach things that only relate in some way to the teaching of the text, while the truth of the text the preacher should be expounding is minimized or never surfaced at all. When this happens, the result is not exposition of a text but the suffocation of a text via theological avalanche!

Walter Kaiser provides good insight in regards to the "essential substance" of a passage. This deals with the issue of the "biblical theology" of a passage, the theology taught in a specific passage of the Bible, in relation to the "systematic theology" of the rest of Scripture. Kaiser's "emerging theology," in contrast to "informing theology," is helpful in establishing both the more basic theological understanding provided by a specific passage as well as the fuller, more developed theological understanding of the doctrinal content found within a given passage.

The Emerging Theology of the Passage

The basis for Kaiser's emerging theology is indeed strong. When a passage of Scripture is understood only on the basis of what is more widely known from Scripture, so that a passage is not understood on the basis of its content in its context, then the significance of that passage will never be understood. When this is the case, "people and pastor continue to go blithely on their way, unaware that instead of experiencing God's Word from the passage under investigation, they are bringing in material from some unknown location in the Bible and foisting that material onto the present text."[7] Accordingly, Kaiser continues, "it must be stressed, however, that in no way may a theological grid be arbitrarily dropped over the text as a substitute for a diligent search for a unifying theological principle through the process of induction."[8] It is intolerable to usurp the specific instruction of a given passage by imposing an imported theological system onto the text in order to provide the meaning of the passage. Kaiser writes:

> In the past grids that had been devised outside of the text were dropped in place over the text to yield some theological payload from the Bible. But everyone knows this is as wrong as sin itself. At best, it restructures the Bible according to one's favorite schema or pet doctrine; but what authority and guidance are left after the text has been treated so subjectively?[9]

In response to an objection that some are sure to raise, Kaiser contends:

> Should someone complain that no Christian exegete can or should forget that part of the Bible which was completed after the text under investigation, we respond by saying, "Of course, no one expects the exegete to do that." Subsequent developments in the revelation of theology (subsequent to the passage we have under consideration) may (and should, in fact) be brought into our conclusion or summaries after we have firmly established on exegetical grounds precisely what the passage means. We do, in fact, have the whole Bible; and we are speaking (usually) to a Christian audience. Therefore, in our summaries we should point out these later developments for the sake of updating and putting everything in its fullest context. However, in no case must that later teaching be used exegetically (or in any other way) to unpack the meaning or to enhance the usability of the individual text which is the object of our study.[10]

The path is made for Kaiser's "emerging theology" as he asserts, "Biblical theology will remain incomplete and virtually barren in its results, as far as the Church is concerned, without a proper input of 'informing theology.'"[11] Kaiser asserts that emerging theology "must take precedence over the legitimate concerns of a systematic theology." However, Kaiser places a subsequent and secondary allowance for informing theology. He writes, "in our summaries of each main point, in the sermon outline, or in the whole passage, we may jump over the centuries and bring to bear all that God subsequently revealed on the theological issue being examined."[12]

Kaiser's "emerging theology" has tremendous benefits for the accurate handling of the doctrinal content of the text being expounded as well as relating the theology of the passage to the antecedent and subsequent theological instruction of the rest of Scripture. But if we state main points to reflect emerging theology only, then later in the exposition of the point include instruction from other passages, which have been given to us by God through progressive revelation, are our statements of theological principle accurate enough, that is, general enough for the exposition we will be giving? No, not entirely. On the other hand, if we state the statements of theological principle to reflect in insights of progressive revelation of other texts, are we not prescribing a meaning for the passage more than it actually means? Yes, we are.

Since we are not able to express the meaning of the passage at hand in a way that will truly reflect the text and the rest of Scripture's instruction regarding the same subject-matter, we must favor or give preference to the meaning of the text at hand in formulating statements of theological principle. We must concern ourselves with the emerging theology of the text as opposed to the informing theology of the rest of Scripture for our statements of theological principle. Though the informing theology must be dealt with after the text has been investigated in its context, if the text will be allowed to have a specific theological voice at all, the statement of theological principle should reflect the emerging theology that will be brought out in the discussion to be provided for the main point.

A statement of theological principle cannot equate fully the exposition the text will receive which shows how the subject-matter of the statement of theological principle is developed further by other texts because of the progressive revelation of Scripture. Therefore, a statement of theological principle will be limited to providing a timeless truth of the passage, what it meant to the original audience and what it means to us now. The *exposition of the passage* will validate the statement of theological principle so that what the passage meant and means to us will be understood as well as what this passage means to us in light of the completed canon of Scripture. Therefore, the theological understanding of the passage, the emerging theology of the text, is made known by the statement of theological principle. The exposition of the passage will reveal how other texts build upon and relate to the theological understanding of the passage being expounded.

The Informing Theology of Scripture

Obviously, in expounding the text the expositor will have to be clear as to what the text meant to the original recipients and what the biblical writer was saying to them. But the expositor will reflect later biblical insight because he is preaching to people who have the whole canon of Scripture. The emerging theology must be understood as well as the informing theology of subsequent revelation. An expositor's ultimate goal is to provide an accurate understanding of emerging theology of the passage he is expounding in concert with the informing theology of the whole of Scripture.

Again, the systematic understanding cannot be represented as the specific and therefore, more limited, emerging theology of the passage. Yet, the emerging theology of the text must represent only a portion of what God has revealed about the subject-matter of the passage. This is the instruction Stephen Olford provides in his scheme of principlizing Scripture in preaching. Having discovered the original meaning of the text and thus having principlized the meaning of the text, Olford emphasizes the need for the principlization to reflect the broader biblical and Christological perspective, which the text can and should eventually have. Olford is clear in asserting that the insights of such broader study are not to be read into the text in such a way that the text loses its meaning, theology, and dynamic. Olford's counsel is to "seek that fair understanding of the theology and principles of the text, and then consider the broader biblical and Christological perspective."

Specifically, Olford writes regarding the main structure, "the preacher ought to express the abiding truths, the principlized truths that arise from the original meaning of the text. These essential principles or truths, expressing the doctrine and theology of the text, are given perspective by viewing them biblically/canonically and specifically christologically." Additionally Olford writes, "Essentially our concern is to discern the truth of God in the text." We want to hear his "voice," and understand the truth and its implications. "What God is saying through what He has said" is our concern and our goal.[13] What God is saying through what he has said is both a matter of the text under study as well as other texts in which God has provided additional insight and instruction about the same subject-matter one is dealing with from the passage being preached. We do not want to provide a partial understanding about a subject-matter when God has provided a fuller disclosure. What God is saying through what he has said is not limited to one passage alone. Certainly, we must provide clear understanding of what God has said in the passage being preached, a textual understanding, but we also must provide understanding about what God has revealed in the rest of Scripture, a scriptural understanding.

If we are to establish in our preaching a theological understanding, then we must begin at the correct starting point, the text at hand which we intend to expound. How can Scripture as a whole have any comprehensive meaning if its numerous individual passages do not possess a specific meaning? Our preaching must result in a theological understanding—a theological understanding of the passage being expounded and how this textual theological understanding contributes to a broader theological understanding provided by the whole of Scripture. A. J. F.

Behrends speaks persuasively about the matter of processing theological statements in our preaching as he writes:

> The point of urgency is this, that your theology must be the outcome of your preaching, not its antecedent, superimposed condition and limitation. It must be forged anew, link by link
> ... The Word of God is a hammer, a coal of fire, a two-edged sword. A hammer breaks; fire burns; the sword pierces; and you must have a theology which does all that.[14]

The theology of the text being preached must be explained. It must not become a recipient of the meaning of other texts which are ascribed to it. Each text has theological meaning and this must be discovered and explained. However, each text's theology makes a contribution to a wider system of theological understanding and the connection of the text's theology to this wider understanding must be explained as well. If we cannot relate the theology of the text to other texts, how can we accrue a theological understanding? Therefore, Behrends's next assertion is no less significant,

> So I say again, and would repeat it a thousand times: Be theologians. Let your theology be practical, never swinging in the air, but let there be theology. You must have something to say, and the thing which you say must be an expression of the thought of God, and of the mind of Christ; which again amounts to this, that the Christian preacher must be a Christian theologian.[15]

So again, in the attempt to articulate statements of theological principle for the main points of an expository sermon the question is raised—do we discover what the text meant to the original audience or do we seek the meaning of the passage for the present time? And again, the answer is both. For a text to have meaning at all, it must have had meaning for the original audience and this is the starting point for the meaning of the passage—what it meant to the original audience. However, that is just the starting point. Having discovered what the text meant originally we must establish the meaning that the text should have for our present time, culture, and circumstances. What we must do in preaching is to codify the timeless truths of Scripture.

All will agree that the preacher must explain what the text meant to the original readers and what it means to us today—people who live in a different culture and people who are in possession of the whole canon of

Scripture. Under the direction of a capable expositor, the process of exposition will accomplish both, what the text under consideration meant and what it means to us. However, our present concern is with the statements of the main points of the sermon—the statements of theological principle. Are they to reflect the more limited, initial meaning that will be explained early in the process of exposition for each of the points or are they to reflect timeless truths that can summarize meaning for the original recipients as well as meaning for us? *Remember, the main points must summarize what is to be said in explanation of the meaning of the passage, what it meant and means.* The main point must summarize more than just the meaning the text had for the original readers, that is, the explanation that will be provided in the beginning of the explanation process. If the main point provides a summary only of the original meaning, then explanation should not go beyond the summary statement for the original meaning and this is certainly unacceptable. But since the process of exposition will start with the meaning of the passage originally then move to the meaning it has for us, then the statement of the point should reflect this by codifying statements of theological principle that are timeless truths.

Once the meaning of the passage has been discovered and a timeless statement of theological principle has been formulated for the passage, the preacher now has a statement of truth that is not only indicative of what the passage meant to the original readers of the passage but also a meaning for the present hearers of the sermon. Care must be taken to not overload the actual exposition of the passage with too many cross references which show how the subject-matter of the preaching passage has been subsequently refined through the progressive revelation of Scripture. More basic insights of Scripture must be understood in the light of later biblical texts but discretion must be incorporated so that the progressive revelation of Scripture is understood. What is to be avoided is providing more material than is necessary to chart clearly the path of theological enhancement the subject-matter has undergone. A clear treatment is what is sought. Overloading the exposition with too many cross references may obfuscate rather than clarify the matter.

Spurgeon remarked upon the "almost universally needed" corrective of not overloading a sermon with "too much matter." He offered the following comments in the attempt to curtail this negative trend in the preaching of his time:

> All truth is not to be comprised in one discourse. Sermons are not to be bodies of divinity. There is such a thing as having too much to say, and saying it till hearers are sent home loathing rather than longing. An old minister walking with a young preacher, pointed to a cornfield, and observed, "Your last sermon had too much in it, and it was not clear enough, or sufficiently well-arranged; it was like that field of wheat, it contained much crude food, but none fit for use. You should make your sermons like a loaf of bread, fit for eating, and in convenient form." It is to be feared that human heads (speaking phrenologically) are not so capacious for theology as they once were, for our forefathers rejoiced in sixteen ounces of divinity, undiluted and unadorned, and could continue receiving it for three or four hours at a stretch, but our more degenerate, or perhaps more busy, generation requires about an ounce of doctrine at a time, and that must be the concentrated extract or essential oil, rather than the entire substance of divinity. We must in these times say a great deal in a few words, but not too much, nor with too much amplification.[16]

Spurgeon makes a crucial point. It is scary to think that if such statements were true in his day, how much more so in this present day. But in his day or ours, there is a delicate balance that must be struck regarding cross references used in connection with the preaching text, namely—it is important not to overload the sermon with supporting references just as it is necessary not to be presumptuous toward our hearers and fail to provide them with the needed validation of other passages to show them that what we say the passage means is accurate.

Gordon Wilson provides argumentation for giving our hearers sufficient data so that preachers do not deal with Scripture and their hearers unfairly. He writes:

> A blind acceptance of facts, without even knowing that they are facts, can best be called by the term "prejudice." We insist that those who reject Christianity without examining its claims and evidences are prejudiced, and we criticize them for denying the truth of something about which they know little or nothing. If our criticism of unbelievers is a fair one, then why do not they have the right to criticize Christians who accept Christianity without examining its claims and evidences? If it is prejudice to deny without knowing, then it is surely prejudice to accept without knowing.[17]

A preacher must, in order to expound the text but not drown the text, limit his thinking theologically to codify theologically only what his preaching passage teaches and how the instruction of the preaching passage is understood in terms of its meaning then and now.

In codifying a sermon point, which is a statement of theological principle of a text, the preacher is saying—"This is what *this* passage means." He must be as specific as the text is specific. He must be as general as the text is general. He cannot afford to ascribe as the meaning of the passage more than what the text teaches or less than what the text teaches. He should only be content to bring out the essence and extent of the text in his statements of theological principle. Yet, the exposition of the text must not be limited to a meaning that is true only for the original readers as though God's revelation is not progressive in nature, so that a principial teaching of a given text is taught on that level *only* without receiving any additional insight from subsequent revelation of Scripture. Therefore, through statements of theological principle a preacher, in effect, is not only saying—"This is what *this* passage means" but he is saying with equal force "This is what this passage *means*." What he is not saying is, "This is what this passage *meant*" as though he were about to conduct a lecture on a biblical text.

The effort to explain the theology of the text being expounded as well as the effort to show the connection that the text being expounded has to other passages that support the same theological understanding is an acceptable practice of preaching throughout the history of the Church. Since the Reformation, the theology of the expounded text was argued and defended with great diligence. Don Wardlaw says regarding the preaching of the medieval schoolmen or the post-reformation dogmatists, "the sermon became an exercise in reasonableness, a discourse in theological refinement." With Luther and Calvin, preaching assumed a commonsense air, beginning with a simple explanation of Scripture, followed by appropriate application to daily life. But "the appeal almost invariably rested on the framework of argument" and "preaching mostly assumed a debater's stance."[18]

Before going further, it may be helpful to pose a question regarding the legitimacy of using references to other texts when expounding a passage rather than expounding the preaching text with no consideration to outside references. Is the consideration to outside reference legitimate and/or necessary when expounding a passage? The incorporation of extra-textual references is both legitimate and necessary. Extra-textual references must be used to support what is being taught from the preaching passage. Obviously, they should not be used in so great a number or treated in such detail that they cause the text to be lost from sight. After all, the purpose for their incorporation into the sermon is to clarify the sermon and the preaching text, not to deflect attention away from the text. As we have already seen, in expository preaching the primary exposition is of the text.[19] If the text is not expounded then the text, in effect, becomes a pretext for the preacher to say anything he wants to say. Unfortunately, this is all too common. But on the other hand, once the text is expounded then implications of this truth and subsequent instruction from the rest of Scripture can be understood and appreciated as an extended connection to the text.

Expository Preaching and Theology

Expository preaching must be understood, primarily, as an attempt to explain the meaning of the text being preached and, in a secondary sense, to relate the meaning of the passage to the wider scope of Scripture. In prioritizing the primary sense, Nathaniel Van Cleave defines an expository sermon by four criteria—it is usually involving a longer text than a topical or textual sermon would deal with; it draws its main divisions and sub-divisions only from the text being preached; it treats the passage not just the subject suggested by the passage; and it is usually preached in a series of sermons drawn from a biblical book.[20] Van Cleave's last three assertions are essential for understanding the nature of expository preaching.

Much preaching is not and cannot be expository preaching for one of two completely opposite reasons. If a preacher does not expound the text that he is supposedly preaching from, then expository preaching will not be the result of his preaching. If, however, the text is expounded yet the implications of the text not drawn out and supported by progressive revelation of the subject-matter of the passage, then the result will be an irrelevant, partial explanation of what the text means for us who possess the complete canon of Scripture, and this too is not expository preaching.

A preacher must understand that outlining a passage is not expounding a passage. The outline of the passage, point by point, establishes what must be attended to in the exposition of the text at hand

and, thus, identifies what will be attended to in exposition of that passage. However, no outline, no matter how precise it is, and how carefully expressed it may be in its terminology, no matter how many points of main structure and substructure there may be in the outline, no outline is capable of equating the exposition of the text. The outline is only suggestive of what must and will be said in the exposition of its text. The exposition of the text is the comprehensive detailing of what the outline, and therefore, what the text actually means.

The ultimate, full expression of meaning for a passage comes from the exposition of the text not the outline of the text. An outline always will be too concise to ever denote all of what must be conveyed about a passage of Scripture. The outline is the skeleton, the appropriate framework, for the expository sermon. The actual exposition is the muscle affixed to the skeleton of an expository sermon. One of the most enlightening distinctions of an expository sermon is made by Van Cleave when he writes:

> Furthermore, the expository sermon is a treatment of the passage of Scripture, while the topical and textual sermons are treatment of the subject. Though the textual sermon gets its main headings from the text, it is really a treatment of a subject as suggested by a text and the subject is the principal thing. An expository sermon will have a subject, but the subject is subordinate to the text; the text is the principal thing.[21]

Both the skeleton and the muscles of a sermon are significant to preaching just as both, the skeleton and the muscles of one's anatomy, are significant to an individual. Both muscle and bone have a function to perform and are therefore valuable, though distinct. And though they are distinct, they are interrelated.

Perhaps an analogy reflecting the course expository preaching should take will clarify the matter. The exposition of a passage is like a train-ride experienced by passengers on a train. A train-ride is experienced only as the train (the exposition of a text) runs on the rails of the train track (the outline of the text) according to the actual ticket purchase necessitating precise stops and an exact termination the passengers have a right to anticipate (the limitation of theological excursions). Once purchasing train-fare for travel from Tampa to San Diego, the expectant passengers will be cheated and disappointed if the train never shows up at the Tampa depot. If the train shows up at the Tampa depot for travel to San Diego, the passengers should not have to endure an excursion to Seattle. And if the train ever jumps the tracks resulting in a train wreck, the passengers have every right to be less than impressed about the whole journey and probably will rethink any future travel on that train. So it must be in our preaching. We don't want to cheat the people who hear us preach, so we must begin with the intent to expound the passage from which we will preach. As we proceed, we must not jump the track and wreck because of rails that have been negligently laid. Certainly, we must stay the intended course and not encounter stops we should not be making on this trip. Finally, we must not become unnecessarily detained so that we end up arriving at our destination in much more time than it should have taken to get there!

Scripture Interprets Scripture as Homiletical Procedure

As stated previously, the use of cross references is not illegitimate and unwarranted in expounding a passage of Scripture. In outlining a text, the teaching of the text or the statement of theological principle from the text must be exactly that and nothing more than that—the teaching of this passage, what it meant and what it means for us. Once the meaning of the text has been crystallized, based upon the substance of the text, then cross references may be used in expounding, supporting, and validating the detailed understanding of the passage being preached. "Scripture interprets Scripture" is a sound hermeneutical principle and it is a sound homiletical procedure for an expositor seeking to bring clarity and persuasion to those who hear him in effect saying, "This is what the passage meant, here is why it meant that, and this is what that means for us."

Whenever we deal with a passage of Scripture, we understand that other passages deal with the same subject-matter found in our preaching text. This is so because Scripture has come to us in a progressive revelation from God to man. Themes are addressed over and over with variously more general or more specific levels of instruction and insight upon the theme. The crucial reality is that we must be like God, in that, we are content to provide limited instruction upon the subject-matter of the passage from which we are preaching as God was content to limit his revelation of the subject-matter at the time of its Holy Spirit guided inscripturation. This must be our initial resolve and commitment. But, since God has given additional revelation regarding the subject-matter elsewhere in Scripture, we can and should feel welcome to understand and incorporate various other passages to help us promote a clear and accurate understanding of the text we are expounding. But we, like God, will not declare everything that could be said about the subject-matter at any one time.

In the process of exposition, we can refer to passages which also treat the subject-matter of the text we are expounding but we must be careful to clarify the more developed or less developed level of insight compared to our preaching text. This will help to bring understanding of the preaching text if we are careful to say, in effect, the meaning of this text is more than this incipient meaning found there, and yet, less than this developed meaning found here. Various levels of theological development can be important for establishing a correct understanding of a text in the process of exposition as one compares and contrasts the insights of other texts. But, in outlining every main point of sermon structure, what must be done is to represent in one sentence what this specific passage of Scripture means in the context of this biblical book and what that meaning now means to us. In the exposition of the text, the text will be interpreted and explained in regards to its immediate and wider context as well as the much broader context of the totality of God's Word. Lloyd-Jones reflects his view regarding the treatment of a passage in connection with the whole of Scripture.

> To me there is nothing more important in a preacher than that he should have a systematic theology, that he should know it and be well grounded in it. This systematic theology, this body of truth which is derived from the Scripture, should always be present as a background and as a controlling influence in his preaching. Each message, which arises out of a particular text or statement of the Scripture, must always be a part or an aspect of this total body of truth. It is never something in isolation, never something separate or apart. The doctrine in a particular text, we must always remember, is a part of this greater whole—the Truth or the Faith. That is the meaning of the phrase "comparing Scripture with Scripture." We must not deal with any text in isolation; all our preparation of a sermon should be controlled by this background of systematic theology.[22]

I would interject what I believe to be an important revision regarding the "control" that systematic theology should have upon the text being expounded. Systematic theology can clarify the text but I think "control" is too strong of a term. I am more comfortable with the understanding that systematic theology makes a "contribution" to the text being expounded, just as the text being expounded makes a contribution to systematic theology. Systematic theology certainly can, and should, "weigh in" on the exposition of a text but it must not be allowed to "outweigh" the text!

The general criteria of clear arrangement, statements of theological principle, and textual congruity allow sermon structure to be effective. In general terms, good sermon structure affects clear, timeless truths, derived very obviously out of the passage being expounded and harmonized with the completed revelation of Scripture.

CONSIDER THE FOLLOWING QUESTIONS

1. What is the basis for good sermon structure, initially and ultimately?
2. What is the task of one who desires to faithfully fulfill one's calling to preach the Word?
3. What is it that a sermon outline that is congruent to the text provides for the hearers?
4. What is the inevitable result of expository preaching that reflects textual congruity?
5. What is the correct understanding for the law of symmetry for the main divisions of a sermon?
6. How does expository preaching depart from homiletical theory in regards to allegiance and symmetry?
7. What is the preacher required to communicate in each of the points of his sermon outline in regards to the generality and the specificity of each statement?
8. Rather than concern for the balance of time spent expounding each sermon point, what is the concern the expository preacher must have regarding his sermon structure?
9. How is a less-than-the-text problem of sermon structure described, and by what term is reference made to this kind of effort to deduce a statement of theological principle?
10. Sub-principlization can take place because of what kind of terminology used in a statement of theological principle?

11. What kind of sub-principlization occurs through the use of terminology that is too general? Is this a "final product error"?

12. What kind of sub-principlization occurs through the use of terminology that is too specific? Is this a "final product error"?

13. Initial, implicit sub-principlization will be accompanied with and overstated by what kind of principlization error? What "final product error" will result from this combination?

14. In an instance of meta-principlization what is erroneous about the statement that has been sub-principlized and what is erroneous about the statement that has been supra-principlized?

15. What must happen in order for a preacher to codify a statement of theological principle that, in reference to essence, is a less-than-the-text problem?

16. The essence of a statement of theological principle relates to what?

17. What must happen in order for a preacher to codify a statement of theological principle that, in reference to extent, is a less-than-the-text problem?

18. The extent of a statement of theological principle relates to what?

19. Supra-principlization can take place because of what kind of terminology used in the statement of theological principle?

20. What is the meaning of supra-principlization as being a more-than-the-text problem of sermon structure?

21. Why is it that the simultaneous faults of sub-principlization and supra-principlization, when joined together, become a problem of replacement?

22. In reference to stating a sermon point inaccurately, what are the two causes for stating a sermon point that will lead to a misunderstanding of the text, what are the two ways the sermon point will suffer a misunderstanding of the text, and what are the two resulting processes of the text's misunderstanding because of inaccurate expression?

23. What are the five "final product errors" that result from sub-principlization and/or supra-principlization?

Sermon Structure and Textual Congruity

24. How do the five "final product errors" of principlization compare and contrast with each other?
25. How does the problem of using terminology that is too general compare with the problem of using terminology that is too specific in reference to the error that can be caused by each?
26. What fault is behind the problem of a preacher incorporating terminology in statements of theological principle that are too general or too specific?
27. What imprudent methodology contributes to a preacher codifying a statement of theological principle that is too general to be a correct meaning of the passage and what is the result of this methodology?
28. Why must we favor or give preference to the emerging theology of the text over the informing theology of the rest of Scripture as we attempt to establish theological understanding in our preaching?
29. What does it mean to discover "what God is saying through what he said?"
30. What is the correct starting point for establishing theology in our preaching and what is the rationale for insisting upon this starting point as being the correct one?
31. What will the process of exposition accomplish under the direction of a capable expositor?
32. What is the rationale for statements of theological principle, as timeless truths, to incorporate more than the meaning the text had for the original audience?
33. What is the delicate balance that must be struck regarding the supporting references used in connection with the preaching text?
34. How does the use of supporting references limit Christians from the criticism of prejudice?
35. What two things is a preacher saying "with equal force" through the use of statements of theological principle and what is he not saying through the use of them?
36. What are the two completely opposite reasons that keep much preaching from being expository preaching?

37. What is the rationale for an outline, regardless of the excellence of its composition, being inadequate to equate the exposition of a passage?

38. What sound hermeneutical principle also forms a sound homiletical procedure?

39. What is it that must be done in every point of sermon structure in an outline?

40. What role should systematic theology have in preaching so that it can clarify but not control the text that is being preached?

ENDNOTES

1. Chapell, *Christ-centered*, 147.
2. Brown, *Art*, 61.
3. Olford and Olford, *Anointed*, 145.
4. Brown, *Art*, 70.
5. Blackwood, *Preparation*, 132.
6. Davis, *Design*, 243.
7. Kaiser Jr., *Exegetical*, 133.
8. Ibid., 134.
9. Ibid., 138.
10. Ibid., 140.
11. Ibid., 139.
12. Ibid., 161.
13. Olford and Olford, *Anointed*, 138.
14. Behrends, *Philosophy*, 199–200.
15. Ibid., 212.
16. Spurgeon, *Lectures*, 77.
17. Wilson, *Set*, 8.
18. Wardlaw, *Preaching Biblically*, 12.
19. Van Cleave, *Handbook*, 41.
20. Ibid., 39–40.
21. Ibid., 39.
22. Lloyd-Jones, *Preaching*, 66.

Words to Live and Preach By

The Effectiveness of Well Chosen Words

Anxiety in the heart of man weighs it down,
but a good word makes it glad.
PROVERBS 12:25

A gentle answer turns away wrath, but a harsh word stirs up anger.
The tongue of the wise makes knowledge acceptable,
but the mouth of fools spouts folly.
PROVERBS 15:1–2

A soothing tongue is a tree of life,
but perversion in it crushes the spirit.
Proverbs 15:4

A man has joy in an apt answer,
and how delightful is a timely word!
PROVERBS 15:23

Righteous lips are the delight of kings,
and he who speaks right is loved.
PROVERBS 16:13

The heart of the wise teaches his mouth, and adds persuasiveness
to his lips. Pleasant words are a honeycomb,
sweet to the soul and healing to the bones.
PROVERBS 16:23–24

He who loves purity of heart and whose speech
is gracious, the king is his friend.
PROVERBS 22:11

Like apples of gold in settings of silver is a word spoken in right circumstances. Like an earring of gold and an ornament of fine gold is a wise reprover to a listening ear.
PROVERBS 25:11–12

By forbearance a ruler may be persuaded, and a soft tongue breaks the bone.
PROVERBS 25:15

Oil and perfume make the heart glad, so a man's counsel is sweet to his friend.
PROVERBS 27:9

7

Sermon Structure's Stylistic Components

SPECIFIC CRITERIA FOR QUALITATIVE DEDUCTIVE PREACHING SERMON STRUCTURE

MUCH HAS BEEN STATED regarding clarity, clarity of the sermon proposition, and clarity of the sermon structure. Lack of clarity in preaching is detrimental to qualitative preaching. Obviously then, clarity in preaching is a matter of priority not preference. Likewise, but even more so, accuracy or the truthfulness of that which is made clear must be viewed as obligatory, not optional. John Wood, in his book *The Preacher's Workshop: Preparation for Expository Preaching* suggests that true preaching is defined by the essential elements of truth, clarity, passion, persuasiveness, and color.[1] Obviously then, clarity and accuracy alone are not adequate for ultimate qualitative sermon structure. Clarity and accuracy are bedrock issues in sermon structure. Nothing can be more important than these, and anything else can, at best, bring a measure of enhancement to clear, accurate statements of theological principle. If a measure of enhancement can be attained, then it certainly should be attained. But the question is, how can sermon structure be enhanced beyond clarity and accuracy?

With the general criteria of clear arrangement, statements of theological principle, and textual congruity for sermon structure in mind, we will give attention to nine specific criteria for sermon structure that will bring enhancement to the outlines we use in our preaching. These specific criteria for qualitative deductive sermon structure are; relevance, penetration, parallelism, repetition, alliteration, assonance, sermonic progression, advancement of thought, and substructure. Although these nine will be discussed as specific criteria, it must be noted that all nine may be mutually exclusive of each of the others but substructure is a chief means by which advancement of thought is accomplished most productively.

It is helpful to understand the nine specific criteria in terms of three considerations for sermon structure style. The three considerations are force, form, and flow. The stylistic consideration of force includes two specific criteria— relevance and penetration. The stylistic consideration of form includes four specific criteria—parallelism, repetition, alliteration, and assonance. The stylistic consideration of flow includes three specific criteria—sermonic progression, advancement of thought, and substructure.

THE STYLISTIC CONSIDERATION OF FORCE

Force through Relevance

It has been stated that "the cure for dullness in the pulpit is not brilliance, but reality."[2] The insistence of relevance in preaching in general, and in our sermon structure specifically, is not heavy-handed, or asking too much. Simply put, relevance is not an option! Therefore, it is tragic if preaching is not relevant in sermon substance and sermon structure. Halford Luccock was accurate when he wrote, "It is a tragedy that in an age which cries out wistfully for great preaching, not great in eloquence or brilliance, but great in the deeper sense being the experience and utterance of realities, that there are so many quack substitutes in the pulpit of one kind or another."[3] Luccock was right. At the time he wrote the previous statement in the late 1920s, the leading proponent of life-situation preaching, Harry Emerson Fosdick, was advocating what he believed was the corrective for irrelevant preaching. The problem with his attempt to provide correction was that his preaching emphasized relevance but radically deemphasized revelation—the Word of God. Coach Fosdick put the Word of God "on the bench" and gave the "starting role" to man, placing ultimate worth, confidence and value to man, his problems, his solutions, his interests, and his wisdom in the enterprise of preaching! Unfortunately, in the preaching of many today the Word of God is still "on the bench," is still a "bench-warmer," relegated to peripheral duty in a backup or supporting role! Almost as unfortunate, are those who make the Word of God very central in their preaching but it is preaching that is fairly perceived as irrelevant, irrelevant in the substance and the structure of their sermons!

Having correctly diagnosed a common problem of poor preaching in any era, Harry Emerson Fosdick remarked that, "The sermon is uninteresting because it has no connection with the real interests of the people."[4] This assessment was correct. However, his solution was wrong, just as the problem of irrelevant preaching is wrong! Life-situation preaching is not the solution for irrelevant preaching! Preaching that is relevant is the solution to irrelevant preaching! Relevant preaching must begin with the sermon introduction but in reference to the body of the sermon, relevant preaching must begin with sermon structure composed of statements of theological principle reflecting the timeless truths of the text as well as the relevance of these textual truths.

The beginning point for qualitative enhancement for sermon structure must be the insistence upon the relevance of the sermon points, or statements of theological principle. According to Stephen Olford, "Preaching involves the 'contemporization' of the textual message." In order to do this he says, "Make sure that the points are principles or statements put in the present tense. You are stating your point in such a way that it is true and applicable for the contemporary listener, even as it was for the original listener."[5] If principlization has actually occurred, it will be demonstrated by theological statements that are not latent with dated, past tense terminology. Walter Kaiser's assertions regarding the preacher's care in constructing the main points of a sermon reflect the criticality of authentic principlization. According to Kaiser, the major concern for the preacher in formulating the main points of the sermon is that they "will not only preserve the precise meaning of the original text, but will also provide an invitation, challenge, and instruction to moderns." But this will only be the case if "each proposition is worded as to preserve the abiding, permanent, and fixed teaching of the text."[6]

The use of dated, historically proper terminology suggests to all who hear that the preacher will be lecturing more than preaching, and that his material is not intended to be "for you" as much as it is intended to be "about something." What is necessary is that the hearers easily discern that the conveyance of the truth of the text, through the terminology of the main point, is "relevant to all."[7]

It is not adequate for a preacher to be content that his sermon substance is relevant even if the structure of the sermon seems to belie that fact. The point being, his sermon structure must be just as relevant as his sermon substance. Spurgeon wrote:

> I know a minister whose shoe latchet I am unworthy to unloose, whose preaching is often little better than sacred miniature painting—I might almost say holy trifling. He is great upon the ten toes of the beast, the four faces of the cherubim, the mystical meaning of badgers' skins, and the typical bearings of the staves of the ark, and the windows of Solomon's temple: but the sins of business men, the temptations of the times, and the needs of the age, he scarcely ever touches upon. Such preaching reminds me of a lion engaged in mouse-hunting.[8]

This certainly is a lamentable depiction of one's preaching in regards to the substance of the sermon. But it is no less inexcusable for the structure of one's preaching to be marked by the same appalling trait—an attempt to codify something that is next to nothing in regards to its pertinence to the hearer's lives. It is a giant leap forward regarding the relevance of a sermon if the main structure of the sermon outline is cast in statements of timeless truth which reflect the personal relevance of the truth for the hearers.

Clear, accurate, relevant statements of truth are helpful to understand what is being said about a passage of Scripture—this is what the text meant, as well as, what it means for us. The relevance of our sermons and the individual statements of our sermon structure are significant but they are a matter of secondary importance—trumped only by the accurate recovery of the text's meaning. Only two things are worse than irrelevant preaching! The first is preaching that is marked by error—false doctrine, misinterpreting the text, codifying inaccurate meaning. The second is preaching that is not only marked by error but error that is made very relevant—relevant falsehood, prescribing how to walk in error, how to live according to wrong doctrine. Therefore, relevance, though essential, is not the controlling essential. George Zemek provides valuable insight as he suggests the two general essentials that characterize textual exposition. The controlling essential is the sermon's objectivity and the dynamic essential is the sermon's applicability.[9] Regarding the controlling essential Zemek states, "Most importantly, objective data from a biblical text must determine the body of a sermon. Based on its grammatical and syntactical phenomena, the text must be allowed to surface and evidence itself in the sermon outline . . . The outline should progressively communicate the development of a unit of Scripture."[10] Regarding the dynamic essential Zemek asserts, "Without violating the original intention(s) of the author of a text, it should be handled in a fashion conducive to application in contemporary life. Make the text live!" Provide "timeless abiding truths with special focus on the application of those truths to the current needs of the Church."[11] Expository preaching should be characterized by sermon structure that exposes the meaning of the text and the application of that meaning.

Examine the following outlines[12] from James 1:5–8. These outlines will be examined for other purposes later in this chapter, but for now, give attention to the varying degrees of relevance apparent in the sermon points of these three outlines.

Outline #1

I. In order to mature as a believer in the midst of trials we need to pray wisely.

II. In order to mature as a believer in the midst of trials we need to pray sincerely.

III. In order to mature as a believer in the midst of trials we need to pray expectantly.

Outline #2

I. Practical wisdom for the ordering of life is a common requirement of Christian Disciples.

II. Practical wisdom for the ordering of every-day life and relations is a Divine gift.

III. Practical wisdom for the ordering of life is obtained only on conditions.

Outline #3

I. A universal want.

II. An abundant source of supply.

III. An easy method of obtaining.

IV. An indispensable requisite to success.

Obviously, outline #3 does not contain complete sentences. Therefore, statements of theological principle are not advanced. The result is that there is no clear, accurate description of the main truths of this passage. Moreover, this outline indicates no relevance and is the kind of outline that is to be strenuously avoided. Outlines #1 and #2 not only contain statements of theological principle but they reveal relevance, with the more specific relevance depicted in outline #1 since it describes how the believer is to pray in times of trial.

As we think about the relevance of our preaching generally and the relevance of our sermon structure specifically, we must agree that our Lord's sermons were very clear, accurate, and practical so far as doctrine was concerned. The Sermon on the Mount is a very model of practicality and plainness. There is nothing in it from beginning to end that puzzles the mind. Various portions of the Law that had been misunderstood in doctrine and practice were surfaced and corrected—corrected meaning and corrected application were provided. As a result, his sermon was contrasted favorably to the teaching of the scribes. Those who heard the sermon said that he "spoke with authority." This authority was perceived, due in part, because he spoke in such a way that they knew what he meant. "There were no puzzling questions concerning knotty points of the Law, which had been discussed and controverted over and over again by opposing schools, but *principles laid down, and precepts founded upon them, in a way which could not but commend itself to every honest heart."* (Italics added)[13]

Before leaving the subject of Christ's preaching it should be noticed that Jesus did not have sermon points in his preaching of what is known as the "Sermon on the Mount." Matthew is recounting the teaching he provided for the large crowds that were following him at that time. Matthew says Jesus began "*'to teach'* them saying . . ." After Matthew recounts the pointed and insightful instruction Jesus provided he writes, "When Jesus had finished these *words*, the crowds were amazed at his *teaching*: for he was *teaching* them as one having authority, and not as their scribes." Matthew was obviously emphasizing the content of what Jesus taught and the authority with which he taught it. This authoritative content, both the content and the authority, was drastically different than the teaching of their scribes. Was Jesus preaching a sermon? Yes. Did he use sermon structure? No. In fact, Jesus was providing instruction in keeping with the pedagogy of the culture which, in this case, did not use structure. Sermon structure would have been very strange in their culture. Structured sermons are not strange in our culture and structured pedagogy is very much at home in western culture. If one must use the Sermon on the Mount to argue for or against structure in preaching then one should conclude that a preacher should, as did Jesus, provide in his preaching what the culture views as normative and what they can profit from rather than offering that which would be strange to that culture. However, to "argue from silence" from this passage for the sake of insight for preaching would not be wise since that would not be consistent with what Matthew was providing. Furthermore, if one finds it mandatory to use this sermon as an argument for not having sermon structure because, "You don't see Jesus doing that in this sermon," fair enough, if you don't stop with sermon structure! Continue this tactic and see what else you would need to rule out to be consistent. Such procedure would produce the following:

- Don't have points in your sermons, Jesus didn't have any
- Don't pray before you preach, Jesus didn't pray before he preached
- Don't use a pulpit when you preach, Jesus didn't use one
- Don't stand when you preach, Jesus sat down
- Don't use any notes when you preach, Jesus had no notes at all
- Don't use a biblical passage when you preach, Jesus didn't have a biblical text for his sermon
- Don't study before you preach, Jesus didn't study, he simply saw a crowd and began to teach them
- Don't preach in a building, Jesus preached outside on a hill
- Don't offer any form of public response or personal counsel for hearers when the sermon is completed, Jesus didn't do that
- Don't follow up the sermon with anything—no prayer, no singing, no benediction, just simply finish the sermon and walk away like Jesus did

Now, the Sermon on the Mount is an excellent source for homiletical insight and instruction! Much of my thinking about preaching is derived from this sermon. My concern is that it not be used as a basis to rule out things pertaining to preaching simply because they are not seen here.

To refocus upon what Matthew desired others to know about our Lord's teaching—his amazing content and his amazing authority—let's not miss an obvious insight about Christ's preaching contrasted with so much of the preaching of today. It is easy to contrast the preaching of Jesus with the scribes, to agree that their instruction was woefully deficient in comparison! It is not so comforting to agree that the preaching of many, who are followers of Jesus Christ, more resembles the preaching of Christ's enemies than it resembles the preaching of the One they follow! This is a grievous error in a true discipleship of Jesus Christ as well as a grievous error in a responsible proclamation of truth! The following is an accurate, and unfortunately, a well justified criticism, "It is the great defect of us theologians—we do not think out vigorously and clearly, and the consequence is a vagueness and haziness and a cultivating of platitudes, which takes all the interest and grip out of our sermons."[14] Statements of theological principle are not vague or hazy. They replicate the essential substance of our Lord's preaching—accurate, plain doctrine with unmistakable relevance!

In order to get back on track, to make a break from "scribal instruction" and preach with a semblance of affinity to the Lord's preaching will not be convenient but it can be done. For this to be done, T. Harwood Pattison suggests that three hurdles will have to be overcome. As a starting point, what must be overcome is any "temptation to resent a distinct and clearly arranged division of the text chosen for the sermon."[15]

> Clarity in form and structure is a major factor in making what the preacher says intelligible. It is not the Holy Spirit's responsibility to take sermon globs and make them intelligible, it is the pastor's responsibility. Furthermore, it is a major factor in making what he says aesthetically pleasing. He is not laboring for oratorical floridity, but rather he is aiming at doing everything in his power to make the sermon pleasing to the senses. No amount of passion can cover chaos.[16]

Additionally, one must overcome "the temptation to indolence and insufficient preparation for a sermon."[17] And finally, one must overcome the temptation to prepare and deliver anything that would fall short of an expository sermon, that is, a sermon which "should be a careful and intelligent exposition and enforcement of the passage."[18]

The exposition of Scripture and expository preaching, when rightly pursued, leads to practical application. The truth or idea which has been obtained from the text "is not left to expatiate and wander in the mind; out of all the conduits into which it flows, it is gathered and confined in one conduit into which all the others issue, that of the will; and thus it receives a course towards action, more or less rapid."[19] As Alexander Vinet phrased it many years ago, "There is no truth which has no practical bearings direct or indirect; nothing is level, all is inclined; nothing still water, all is a river or a torrent . . . On the whole, I conclude that to have unity in a sermon, it must be reducible to a doctrinal proposition, which is readily transformed, and is in fact transformed into a practical proposition."[20] Accurate doctrine and the practical bearing of doctrine must be reflected in the individual points of the sermon. This will be the case when the sermon structure is composed of statements of theological principle because they reflect the timelessness and the timeliness of the passage.

It is also worthy to note that the relevance of our sermon structure is not only appropriate, in that, it has an essential place in preaching, but it is also valuable, in that, it produces interest in our preaching. Vinet reminds us that, "Christian doctrine and Christian morality form the proper and peculiar matter of pulpit discourse—doctrine, so far as it has a practical bearing; and morality, in its immediate and natural relation to doctrine."[21] Additionally, Vinet writes, "Purely oratorical interest reveals itself in a sense of the manifest importance of our taking such or such a proposed determination. When no determination is to be taken, oratorical interest has no place."[22]

Remember, the cure for dullness in the pulpit is not brilliance, but reality. Much preaching today needs this cure, now more than ever before. Former President of the United States of America, Woodrow Wilson, made this personal observation concerning the preaching of his day. "I have heard a great deal of preaching and I have heard most of it with respect; but I have heard a great deal of it with disappointment, because I felt that it had nothing to do with me."[23]

If former President Wilson were hearing sermons today he may be forced to a greater level of disappointment—preaching that had little to do with the Bible as well as preaching that had nothing to do with him personally. The incorporation of statements of theological principle is the starting place to resolve both deficiencies. Observe the following outline, noting the relevance of the statements of theological principle.

I. You will find that obeying the Lord, at times, will be extremely difficult.

II. You will find that obeying the Lord, at times, may be extremely frightening.

III. You will find that obeying the Lord, ALWAYS, will be extremely beneficial.

Force through Penetration

In describing three types of preachers, according to the affect of their preaching, J. Patterson Smyth wrote: "There are some preachers whom you *cannot* listen to; there are some preachers who you *can* listen to; there are some preachers whom you *must* listen to. I think there is a considerable number of the first, a very great number of the second, and extremely few of the third—extremely few—and I do not believe this need be so."[24] Smyth was right in his general declamation of preaching as well as his appraisal that better preaching is certainly an obtainable prospect. Sermon structure cannot be the singular corrective measure for better preaching but it can make a certain contribution to preaching effectiveness.

The stylistic consideration of force is the first of three considerations that must be scrutinized and, when necessary, strengthened in order for sermon structure to make a certain contribution to preaching effectiveness. In reference to sermon structure, the stylistic consideration of force is not only a matter of relevance but also a matter of penetration. If sermon structure is truly forceful, it must be attended by the qualities of relevance and penetration. What is involved in sermon structure that bears the quality of penetration? In a phrase, penetration allows the hearers to not only understand but to feel the significance of a statement of theological principle.

The effectiveness of penetration in sermon structure should be apparent by what was said of Scottish pastor Robert Murray McCheyne. "The heads of his sermons," said a friend, "were not the milestones that tell you how near you are to your journey's end, but they were nails that fixed and fastened all he said. Divisions are often dry; but not so *his* divisions—they were so textual and so feeling, and they brought out the spirit of a passage so surprisingly."[25] Sermon outlines consisting of statements of theological principle stand the best chance to affect hearers by penetrating their understanding, feeling, and volition to the truth brought out in the sermon.

Penetration as Plain Proofs

I believe it is revealing that the points of main structure in a sermon commonly were referred to as "proofs" in older homiletical texts. This described the function for a sermon's main points in reference to the sermon's proposition. The purpose of each main point or "proof" was to provide a convincing argument in regards to the proposition. The understanding of a sermon point as a proof which provides a convincing argument necessitates that each point possess the qualities of force and distinctiveness. Force and distinctiveness were viewed as "fundamental properties ... indispensable to good sermonizing."[26] The quality of distinctiveness is associated with the criterion of sermonic progress, which will be discussed later. The present concern is to show the fundamental requirement that sermon structure must be accompanied by force, in general, and penetration, more specifically.

What is true of a preacher's sermonic style, or the style of his sermon as a whole, is equally true for his sermon structure style specifically. Accordingly,

> The principal quality in a forcible style, and that which first strikes our attention, is penetration. While listening to a speaker of whom this property is a characteristic, our minds seem to be pricked as with needles, and pierced as with javelins. His thoughts cut through the more dull and apathetic parts, into the quick, and produce a keen sensation. Force is electrical; it permeates and thrills. A speaker destitute of energy never produces such a peculiar sensation as this ... Our feeling is merely that of complacency. He has not cut sharply into the heart of his subject, and consequently he has not cut sharply into the heart of his hearer.[27]

The stylistic consideration of force in sermon structure, due to the stylistic criterion of penetration, sets in motion a domino effect that is indispensable to all preaching that is truly effective—conviction. Where there is a heart that has been convicted by truth there is a heart that has been penetrated by the force of the truth. This is true for those who preach sermons as well as those who hear them.

In understanding force as a matter of penetration, it must be obvious that the statements of theological principle must be clear and accurate statements for the meaning of the passage. We have considered this already, but the mentioning of it at this juncture is to underscore the fact that *an obscure statement will have no force and cannot penetrate.* A penetrating statement must be a plain statement. Plainness and penetration will always be interlinked. "He who has secured plainness may secure force, while a failure to attain the former carries with it the failure to attain the latter."[28]

Because of the clarity of a sermon, made clear through the means of sermon structure, Henry Ward Beecher wrote, "When you have finished your sermon, not a man of your congregation should be unable to tell you, distinctly, what you have done."[29] A true sermon is a well arranged progression of thought in the elucidation of the theme, "so clear that the wayfarer though a fool may follow it directly to its destination."[30] The points of sermon structure must be clear, they must be forceful, and they must penetrate the hearts of the hearers so that the volition, or the will, of the hearers may be impacted. Points of sermon structure that are forceful, because of their relevance and penetration, become serviceable means to affect the only true end for all preaching, that is, the persuasion of the hearers. Sermon structure must assure that the sermon is clear and instructive but, beyond these, that the main points of the sermon may wield "an overpowering impression and influence upon the will."[31] However, if it is that the will of the hearer is not influenced by the sermon and its structure or even if they reject the message preached, it must be that "they reject it because they too clearly understood and not because it seemed like a mass of unrelated tidbits of truth."[32]

Penetration by Persuasion

I am afraid that too many men in the pulpit seldom give themselves completely to the accomplishment of the true end for preaching—persuasion. John Broadus recognized this in his day, and though it has been many years since he wrote of this common fault, the intervening years have only corroborated his assertion that, "Preachers, especially the educated, have too often regarded instruction and conviction as the aim of their labors, when they are but means of leading men to the corresponding feeling, determination, and action."[33] Furthermore, the present climate in preaching almost forbids a man to even consider the thought of impacting the emotions of his hearers. Because of excess appeal to the emotions by some, others have conceded this area altogether, as though it is an illegitimate thing for people to be impacted emotionally by the truth. Even when seeking to persuade the will, some would prefer to bypass the emotions so that the affect of their preaching moves from cognition to persuasion, without even registering upon the emotions. They fail to understand that the invigorating of the emotions is a natural and unavoidable part of persuasive preaching because the emotions are an integral corollary of volition. In order to affect a response, the emotions need to be reached. They are a pivotal, not a peripheral, part of the response sought after in the preaching of God's Word—an intelligent, heartfelt, commitment to live one's life according to the truth of Scripture.

It is possible to convince a person on the cognitive level of the truth of a certain proposition or idea, but for one to act upon that idea in a meaningful way, that person must be touched and motivated, not exclusively but inclusively, in the area of the emotions.[34] *Penetrating statements of sermon structure will not be produced by a preacher who intends that his preaching must not inundate the emotions.*

What is equally problematic is for a preacher to desire to impact his hearers, emotionally and volitionally, with truth that has failed to captivate his own emotions and volition. When a preacher can construct his sermon structure and the statements of theological principle yet these fail to penetrate his own heart and fail to captivate his own mind forcefully, is it any wonder that his hearers will not be gripped by the same truths that have failed to impact him? The weight and worth of the statements of theological principle in a preacher's sermon structure must inundate his soul or else he will dispense valuable truth glibly through a heart and mind that can only devalue the significance of what his mouth utters.

> Archbishop Sancroft once asked Betterton the tragedian, "How is it that when you speak everybody listens to you although you speak fiction, but when we speak the people do not listen though we speak the words of Divine truth?" "I think, your Grace," replied the actor, "the reason is this, you speak truth as though you believed it to be fiction, whilst we speak fiction as though we believed it to be truth." We have to acknowledge that there are grounds for this criticism. What is the cause? Not insincerity or doubt about the facts which we teach but chiefly failure to realize them, to grip them as realities, often deep, fascinating, exciting realities. Many a preacher is a mere juggler with phrases, floating

on a sea of *words*, not getting down to *things*. So the preacher loses power in preaching. So the people lose interest in listening.[35]

Persuasion and Grip

Grip is an appropriate term to express *that manner of preaching which impresses a hearer with a strong belief that the preacher feels that he has something to say which is worth saying, and which ought to be said.* Grip is the preacher's personal conviction regarding the content of the specific passage he will be preaching. Grip is prerequisite for every preacher who would fulfill the counsel that a preacher should "Stand up in your pulpit not because you have to say something but because you have something to say. Make sure of that first. Then say it."[36] This impression carries the mind away from the speaker to the thing spoken. It is obvious that the effect of a sermon ought to be, not an admiration of the preacher, but a sense of having heard something which one will never forget, or of having formed a good resolution for the future, or of having had light thrown upon some point previously obscure, or of having in some way or another received a benefit to the soul.[37] In other words, those who hear the preacher's message are left with the same affect that the preacher himself received as he was studying the passage he was preparing to preach.

Grip results when the preacher has grasped the truth mentally, in a meaningful way so that the implications of the truth is known and can be articulated. Grip is apparent when the preacher dispenses truth that has brought conviction to his own heart and the force of the truth is discernable so that it penetrates the hearts of the hearers. The value of grip must not be underestimated because "The common mind loathes a counterfeited enthusiasm but it is ever ready to listen to a really earnest and forcible man."[38] However, really earnest and forcible men seem to be the exception, not the rule. Walter Kaiser is on target with his statement that, "Regardless of what new directives and emphases are periodically offered, that which is needed above everything else to make the Church more viable, authentic, and effective, is a new declaration of the Scriptures with a new purpose, passion, and power."[39] However, a new declaration of the Scriptures with a new purpose, passion and power will have to be declared by a man who has been penetrated by the truth of Scripture and can articulate the truths he will proclaim forcefully through the force of relevance and the force of penetration. Examine the following outline and try to appraise the penetration of the points of sermon structure, that is, the ability of the statements to convey the spirit/feeling of the passage as well as the ability of the statements to prick the hearts and minds of the hearer.

I. The Dilemma of a rich fool is "What can I do to enhance my cause?"

II. The Determination of a rich fool is to expend great effort to enrich himself.

III. The Delusion of a rich fool is to believe he will find true fulfillment in wealth.

IV. The Dismay of a rich fool will be that much of his life will have been wasted!

To persuade a hearer that he or she may be a rich fool and must terminate such a lifestyle is a tall order. However, the task can be accomplished if they can relate to the dilemma, determination, delusion, and dismay of the rich fool as presented in the biblical passage. The task can be accomplished even more effectively if the hearers are forced to feel the selfishness, greed, folly, and futility of living such a life. Grip is not automatic. There are requirements that must be met in order for grip to be a reality in sermon structure.

Four Requirements for Grip

The first requirement for grip, or for preaching with force and wielding truth that truly penetrates the hearts of the hearers is fervent prayer—the headwaters of spiritual power. I believe that prayer is THE vital component for powerful preaching.[40] James Rosscup asserts, "If the preacher is to deliver God's message with power, prayer must permeate his life and furnish a lifelong environment for the fruit of the Spirit."[41]

The second requirement for preaching with force and wielding truth that truly penetrates the hearts of the hearers is sufficient time to allow the truths which God has revealed to permeate the soul. "You must think, and muse, and meditate, and be alone with God, and let your mind and your soul and your heart play over the teaching till it glows and becomes alive and grips hold of you."[42]

The third requirement for preaching with force and wielding truth that truly penetrates the hearts of the hearers is fruitful revision. There must be a willingness to revise the statements of theological principle time and time again until they possess a razor sharp edge. The following counsel is applicable to written or spoken communication, including preaching. This counsel is especially appropriate in the formulation of statements of theological principle:

> It is not always enough that a thought be expressed clearly and correctly. For even then it may be dull and tedious, lacking in vigor and interest. It must hold people's attention, stimulate them to think and realize what is said; it must also be adapted to slow and heavy minds as well as to minds bright and attentive. *This fact makes it generally necessary to impart more distinction than its merely intelligible expression would demand.* (Italics added)[43]

Adequate expression of thought is rarely derived from the earliest attempts. "We must put ourselves in the place of those who are to hear us, and try on our own heart the train of thought which we give to our discourse, to ascertain if one be suited to the other, and whether we may confidently expect that the heart of the hearer will be penetrated by what is stated."[44] Interest, a word which expresses both the subjective and the objective, denotes, in the objective sense, the property of an object to draw our thought and soul to itself, so that our happiness, in some measure, depends on it. In a subjective sense, interest consists in identifying ourselves more or less profoundly and permanently with an object which is out of us.[45]

The fourth requirement for preaching with force and wielding truth that truly penetrates the hearts of the hearers is *more courage* in proclaiming these truths when we have found them. The courage required to declare God's Word is important for the deepening of your own grip as well as for its value in the instruction of your hearers. The lack of this courage in speaking for God by declaring his Word is responsible for a good deal of uninteresting preaching.[46] Back of any real power must lie, after all, strength of thought and conviction.[47] Can one speak courageously if it is known that what is spoken is not so much God's Word as it is one's sermon? I don't think one can. Courage comes through speaking God's Word, not your sermon! More courage means more of God's Word must be the substance of the sermon. Statements of theological principle spearhead the timeless meaning of Scripture and incorporate more of God's Word than any other type of sermon structure.

Persuasion and Order

The purposes of preaching are to instruct, to interest, and to persuade. In considering only the first of these, we see that order is all important. We are instructed commensurate with our ability to comprehend and retain; but we comprehend and retain easily, surely, only in the proportion in which the matters on which our understanding is exercised are consecutive and connected. It is futile to think that it should be different in persuasion or influence on the will. A discourse badly ordered is obscure, and that which is obscure is weak. "Decision cannot be conveyed to the soul of another by one who bears the tremulous impress of indecision."[48]

A sermon's ultimate purpose is to persuade; and a connected argument or train of thought is necessary to that end. A collection of soldiers is no more an army as is a heap of stones an arch or is a plurality of ideas a persuasive sermon. Other things being equal, a discourse is powerful in proportion to the order reigning in it. Where something is placed makes a difference in the effectiveness of use. As one man graphically put it, "Suppose a man had an arm where one of his legs ought to be, and the leg was socketed at his shoulder-blade—what kind of a man would he be for doing things?"[49] The statements of theological principle must be so arranged, by the expression of each one of them and in the order of their presentation, that they shall be best fitted to do things like instruct and persuade. This means that the order in which we present the statements of theological principle may not at all times follow the consecutive order of the text from which we preach. This will be an uncommon event and it will only occur as an effort to make emphatic what is emphatic in the text or to make our final appeal what the text ultimately requires of us even though it was found earlier in the passage. The order of the following outline, taken from Ecclesiastes 5:1-7, does not follow the sequential order of the text. The last point in the outline comes from the first verse in the English Bible.

I. You may fail to keep your vows to God which is the encumbrance of true worship.

II. You may fail to guard your heart before God which is the exercise of true worship.

III. You may fail to draw near to God which is the essence of true worship.

IV. You may fail to fear God which is the epitome of true worship.

V. You may fail to hear God which is the excellence of true worship.

A sermon must never be a lake, it should be a river; it should have movement from a point of origin to a point of termination. If a preacher in preparing his sermon has a definite objective in view, all his thinking should be concentrated upon the accomplishment of that objective, and the sermon should move with increasing power toward the ultimate result. This quality of movement is more than mere logical continuity. In a chain, each link depends upon and is connected to the preceding link, but the last link does not differ in size, strength, or significance from those which preceded it; but each contributing stream adds to the volume and force of the river. The sermon should be a river, not a chain! It should be so constructed that every new thought should not only advance to the ultimate conclusion, but should reinforce the principles previously discussed: for the object of the sermon is not merely to convince the understanding, it is to transform life; and its value depends, therefore, not merely upon its logical completeness, but upon its reinforcing power.[50] Examine the cumulative progression of the outline below. Notice how the order of the structure moves from that which is most basic to that which is most important for abundant living.

I. Living the abundant life means that you are concerned for the interests of others more than your own interests.

II. Living the abundant life means that you are content with your station of life as it is right now.

III. Living the abundant life means that you are confident you will overcome all things in Christ.

Penetration by Focalizing

Contrary to a belief which has become too common, I believe that divisions can excite interest in the minds of our hearers. They can foster expectation. Certainly they assist the mind to understand and carry away the particular line of thought which the preacher is enforcing. "Assist them to follow your message, and you have gone a long way toward assisting them to accept it." Besides, the clear and natural partition of your subject is likely to produce the precise effect aimed at in your sermon. Every sermon which deserves the name must have an aim, and the divisions assist the preacher in taking his sight as a skillful marksman should do.[51] *An outline is necessary to the pursuance of a coherent, progressive and convincing argument.* The outline secures unity. Branching and scattering are fatal homiletic vices. Sermonizing is focalizing.[52]

Sermonic focalizing means focusing upon the text so that one's sermon clarifies the text in its major and minor assertions. Therefore, as important as lexical studies are in understanding and rightly expounding a biblical text, even more so "the syntax and structure of a passage lie at the very heart of true expository preaching." Additionally, "Failure to reflect the author's theme, outline, and central idea is a departure from true exposition."[53] Sermon structure is not an afterthought for expository preaching but the DNA of it. Without statements of theological principle reflecting the major assertions of the biblical text, the penetrating forcefulness of the sermon is limited since the essence of the passage cannot be grasped by the hearers.

FOCALIZING FOR BREVITY

The outline is necessary for conciseness. Brevity is demanded of preaching these days. "Say what you have to say and be done with it" is pretty much a universal sentiment of sermon hearers. But that is impossible unless a preacher has a clear understanding of what he proposes to say before he undertakes to say it. "Time was when preachers could go round about by the way of the wilderness, double on their tracks and camp in parentheses at pleasure; but that time has gone by. Thirty minutes to the end of your journey! Across the desert to the Land of Promise! If your sermon has a point, make it."[54] Divisions assist a preacher in meeting the popular demand for brevity with minimal loss of power.

The demand for briefer preaching time is a threatening evil and exponentially increases the difficulty for a preacher to provide an understanding of the passage and the relevance of the passage for the hearers. Audiences today will not tolerate the old measurement for the length of a sermon. A preacher cannot control the public taste but he must accept it and make the best of it. Therefore, the task of the preacher is to compress into the smallest amount of time in the delivery of the sermon the greatest amount of solid yet interesting matter. To achieve this, well-framed divisions are indispensable. Short, crisp statements of the salient thoughts of a biblical passage cut down on the time needed to provide the text's meaning and application. Statements which carry in themselves the force of argument is the style of divisions now needed in the pulpit.[55] Each statement of theological principle must serve as an arrowhead that penetrates the heart and mind of the hearer so that the shaft of the biblical text may be carried away as well.

Focalizing for Recollection

Divisions help the preacher in his delivery of the sermon. They impress upon his mind the map of what he must say and thus help him to master the contents of the sermon. "They insure method, and 'without method memory is useless.'"[56] Not only does sermon structure aid the preacher, but the divisions of a sermon promote permanence of impression for those who hear preaching. We may safely say that, other things being equal, the best sermon is that which furnishes the most effective means of holding it in the memory of the hearers.[57] Spurgeon's strong admonition is enjoyably edifying as he writes,

> Let the good matter which you give them be very clearly arranged. There is a great deal in that. It is possible to heap up a vast mass of good things in a muddle. Ever since I was sent to shop with a basket, and purchased a pound of tea, a quarter of a pound of mustard, and three pounds of rice, and on my way home saw a pack of hounds and felt it necessary to follow them over hedge and ditch (as I always did as a boy) and found when I reached home that all the goods were amalgamated—tea, mustard, and rice—into one awful mess, I have understood the necessity of packing up my subjects in good stout parcels, bound round with the thread of my discourse; and this makes me keep to firstly, secondly, and thirdly, however unfashionable that method may now be. People will not drink your mustardy tea, nor will they enjoy muddled up sermons, in which you cannot tell head from tail, because they have neither ... Put the truth before men in a logical, orderly manner, so that they can easily remember it, and they will the more readily receive it.[58]

Three Inviolable Imperatives for Producing Penetrating, Relevant Structure

Earlier in this section we discovered four requirements for a preacher's possession of grip, or his ability to preach with force and wielding truth that truly penetrates the hearts of the hearers. These were prayer, time, revision, and courage. But is that all that is needed? These requirements for grip are valuable in order to preach with force. However, there are more to consider in order for one to preach with maximum relevance and penetration. The question is—what is imperative, methodologically, in order to make our sermon structure, composed of statements of theological principle, forceful so that they are relevant and penetrate? There are three inviolable imperatives, containing contrasting couplets, which must control one's methodology in structuring a sermon so that the sermon will be a product derived from the text and thus bearing its force in penetrating relevance. The three inviolable imperatives in constructing sermon structure are: Let the passage dictate to you; don't dictate to it. Find the Outline; don't create it. Communicate the message; don't just outline it.[59]

Three Cardinal Commitments for Producing Penetrating, Relevant Structure

But, when the four requirements for a preacher's possession of grip are adhered to and the three inviolable imperatives for sermon structure methodology are honored, is there anything else that is essential in order for one to preach with maximum relevance and penetration? Additionally, three cardinal commitments will help immeasurably in the effort to construct outlines that will be effectively forceful to penetrate the hearts of the hearers. Cardinal commitment number one has to do with the preacher's resolves regarding *the preaching process*: the preacher must resolve to preach from the passage, preach from the heart, and preach for changed lives.[60] Cardinal commitment number two has to do with the preacher's understanding of *the preaching context*: the preacher must remember that he will be preaching to hurting people.[61] Cardinal commitment number three has to do with the preacher's intentions for *the preaching opportunity*: the preacher must intend that his sermon will be an offering to the Lord, and as such, that his sermon can be an acceptable sacrifice to the divine author of Scripture.[62]

These requirements, imperatives, and commitments are not mutually exclusive but are interrelated in processing a text to be preached, preparing the message to be preached, and preparing the heart of the preacher to preach the passage. But each of them has a role in the formulation of statements of theological principle that possess force of relevance and penetration. In order for a statement of theological principle to possess the force of relevance and penetration: each one must be the subject of prayer, must be given sufficient time to formulate an accurate statement of theological principle, must be revised to state it more precisely, and must be proclaimed courageously; each one must be dictated by the passage, must be discovered in the text, and must be communicated as one part of the broader message of the passage; each one must be preached from the passage, must be preached from the heart, must be preached for changed lives, must be preached for the encouragement of hurting people, and must be preached as an act of worship of a great God. Obviously, preaching with the force of penetrating and relevant structure is not just a matter of preparing the statements of theological principle that make up the sermon structure, but it also includes preparing the heart and mind of the preacher himself.

We have been trying to understand the stylistic consideration of force for sermon structure through the specific criteria of relevance and penetration. Let's look at the contrasting outlines depicted in the introduction of this book and test the force, or the lack thereof, discernable through the relevance and penetration of each outline.

I want you to see five things from our passage this morning.

I. The man

II. The motive

III. The ministry

IV. The mission

V. The means

As we examine our text this morning I want you to see 5 characteristics of the servant whom God uses greatly in his Kingdom work.

I. God greatly uses servants who have been tested severely and approved thoroughly.

II. God greatly uses servants who seek only to glorify him in their lives.

III. God greatly uses servants who fervently love fellow believers.

IV. God greatly uses servants who are burdened for the lost and committed to win them to Christ.

V. God greatly uses servants who sacrifice much in their opportunity to serve him.

Obviously, the first outline affects no force due to its absence of penetrating, relevant truth in the absence of statements of theological principle.

THE STYLISTIC CONSIDERATION OF FORM

The main points of the message will take on greater meaning and greater ability to be remembered if they are structured in such a way that they possess an enhanced auditory quality as they are stated from the pulpit. An enhanced auditory quality for relevant statements of theological principle is achieved by using parallelism, repetition, alliteration, and assonance. Eugene Hall and James Heflin insist that "how language sounds matters" in regards to the expressive basis of preaching. How the language of the statements of theological principle is impacted by parallelism, repetition, alliteration, and assonance is an important matter in expository preaching.[63] Hall and Heflin suggest expressing the statements of theological principle aloud as they are being refined in the construction stage. Speaking these statements aloud provides an aural assessment of the main structure, thus allowing the language of the sermon points "to fall upon the ear—how it sounds to you is an important clue to its effect upon others."[64] Greater aural impact is achieved by the use of parallelism, repetition, alliteration, and assonance.

Parallelism

Parallelism, or parallel structure, is the arrangement of the terminology of one's sermon points so that each of the points is similar to the others with the exception of a key word, several key words, or a phrase. In stressing the importance of parallelism in sermon structure, Kaiser describes what constitutes parallel structure:

> If one is a phrase, then all should be phrases instead of a single word or a sentence. If one is in the imperative form or an interrogative, then it is best that the others also follow suit. Likewise, nouns should correspond with nouns, verbs with verbs, and prepositions with prepositions. Thus, if the first point begins with a preposition, so should each of the other main points.[65]

Parallelism must be incorporated into the statements of the sermon's main points if they will be found to be memorable by the majority of the hearers of the sermon.

Through parallelism the main points of the sermon outline become memorable. Olford writes, "By memorable we mean both 'worth remembering' and also that it can be remembered, it is memorizable. This helps both the preacher and the listener. If something is worth remembering, we should try to express it in such a way that it can be remembered."[66] It is certainly advisable that the substructure reflects parallelism as well. As one succinctly stated, "Parallelism is essential at all levels of an outline so as to avoid mixing apples and oranges."[67]

Parallelism of the main points of a sermon helps the hearers to grasp both the unity and the diversity of each point of the sermon. Through the parallel portion shared by each sermon point the hearer is caused to reflect again upon the sermon proposition. Through the non-parallel portion of the sermon points, the listener is caused to understand the unique and diverse contribution that each sermon point makes in relation to the sermon proposition.

Parallelism clarifies to the hearers the unity among the diversity of the structure as well as clarifying the diversity among the unity of the sermon structure. Parallelism works both ways. "Parallelism acts as an audio flag" waving before the hearers to say, in effect, "Hey, here is another main point in this message!" And yet, "Parallelism draws the attention of the ear, and focuses the mind on what differs among the points."[68] Parallelism helps to clarify what must be made clear to the hearers—the unity and the diversity of the sermon.

Parallelism is significant for good sermon structure because it helps the hearers recognize the fact that each sermon point is just that—one of a series of major clarifying statements that this sermon will have. The role of parallelism for good sermon structure is supported by Stephen Olford's statements:

> Beginning each point with the same words or phrases or the same first letter in words, etc., draws "audio" attention to a pattern, a sequence. You are drawing attention to parallel thoughts by placing them in parallel form with distinctive characteristics. There is nothing wrong with creativity to enhance clarity. A little work to shape an outline in this regard may be very helpful for the communication of the message ... With all the possible distractions, as well as the regular details of a good message, drawing attention to the primary truths of a message is needed. The outline can sound forth with more clarity and distinctiveness if attention is

given to the way the points sound ... Helping people hear your outline is all we are encouraging you to do.[69]

A few examples of parallelism in sermon structure might help to clarify the matter. A sermon proposition and outline for a sermon from Matthew 7:7–12 is:

"In this passage we find 3 minimum daily requirements for living as a child of God."

To Live As A Child of God You Must ...

I. Pray persistently for the unique necessities of your life

II. Trust unquestionably in the perfect faithfulness of your God

III. Strive exclusively for the equitable treatment of your neighbor

The parallelism of the main structure is demonstrated in several ways. Each of the three main points begins with the phrase "To live as a child of God you must." Then each main point incorporates a verb—*pray, trust, strive*. In each main point the verb is modified—pray *persistently*, trust *unquestionably*, strive *exclusively*. Following the modified verb, there is a preposition, followed by the definite article, which begins a prepositional phrase—pray persistently *for the*, trust unquestionably *in the*, strive exclusively *for the*. In each point, two words follow the definite article, an object of the preposition being preceded by a word modifying the object of the preposition—pray persistently for the *unique necessities*, trust unquestionable in the *perfect faithfulness*, strive exclusively for the *equitable treatment*. In each of the points, there is a three word phrase that ends each statement. The last word, which describes a possession, is preceded by the words "of your." Pray persistently for the unique necessities *of your life*, Trust unquestionably in the perfect faithfulness *of your God*, Strive exclusively for the equitable treatment *of your neighbor*.

Without going into the same depth of analysis for parallelism as in the sermon outline above, notice how the 3 main points of a different outline[70] are parallel.

I. You must identify sin as an internal disposition

II. You must equate sin against man as sin against God

III. You must act to minimize the consequences of your sin

Though the parallelism of this outline is not as prominent as in the former outline, it is still observable. The extent of consistent parallelism for all three points is limited to "You Must," although the first two points share further parallelism not achieved in the third point.

Lest one think that parallelism is simply a means by which the form of the statements of theological principle are cast, one should understand that parallelism is vital to produce outlines that stay on track with the passage and help in codifying statements that convey what the text meant and what it means to us. Two very valuable suggestions to help construct sermon outlines that incorporate the objectivity and applicability of the text are: "be descriptive, and maintain parallelism in phraseology."[71]

Parallelism will not be achieved initially, that is, when an accurate statement of theological principle has been synthesized. The accurate statement of theological principle, once formulated, must be rephrased to produce as much parallelism as possible without losing any accuracy in the transfer to a more parallel statement. Notice how the following outlines move from accurate statements to more parallel statements without losing any accuracy in the transfer. The underlined words in the initial form of the first outline designate the words that need to be changed to enhance greater parallelism achieved in the final form of the first outline which deals with unfruitful people. The bold words reflect the degree of parallelism found in both the initial form and the final form. Notice in the final form of outline one how the "r" alliteration of the key words "reconcile," "repent," and "radiate" provide the hearer with a greater ability to recall the structure after the sermon is completed.

Outline One: Initial Form

I. **Unfruitful people** are ignorant of their need to reconcile with their opponents.

II. **Unfruitful people** <u>suppose they have no</u> need <u>of repentance</u>.

III. **Unfruitful people** are <u>unaware of the consequences of living fruitless</u> lives.

Outline One: Final Form

I. **Unfruitful people are ignorant of their need to** reconcile with **their** opponents.

II. **Unfruitful people are ignorant of their need to** repent of **their** sins.

III. **Unfruitful people are ignorant of their need to** radiate fruitfulness in **their** lives.

In the second outline, which deals with the humble servant of God, the underlined words of the final form indicate the changes necessary to provide greater parallelism beyond the initial form. Again, the bold words reflect the degree of parallelism found in both the initial form and the final form.

Outline Two: Initial Form

I. **The humble servant of God** fulfills one's God ordained ministry.

II. **The humble servant of God** is used as God sees fit.

III. **The humble servant of God** experiences joy in the process of completing one's ministry.

IV. **The humble servant of God** desires to exalt Christ Alone In Ministry.

Outline Two: Final Form

I. The **humble servant of God possesses** <u>the faithfulness necessary to fulfill</u> one's God ordained ministry.

II. The **humble servant of God possesses** <u>a willingness to be</u> used as God sees fit.

III. The **humble servant of God possesses** <u>an increasing</u> joy in the process of completing one's ministry.

IV. The **humble servant of God possesses** <u>the motive that</u> Christ Alone <u>Must Be Exalted</u> In Ministry.

In the final form of outline two, parallelism was enhanced by only one word, "possesses." However, this one word found in each of the four statements of theological principle is the unifying concept that ties together the individual attributes of the humble servant of God. The one word addition to each of the four statements only marginally enhanced parallelism but the continuity, or the cognitive glue, provided by this one word will increase dramatically the hearer's ability to understand and remember what distinguishes the humble servant of God from all others.

Sometimes parallelism will not be able to be achieved except in a limited way. It must always be sufficient in the mind of the preacher for clarity and accuracy to dominate regardless of the degree of parallelism! Look at the following outline observing that parallelism is limited to the initial eight words of each statement of theological principle while the remainder of each of the statements reflects significant diversity.

I. **Satan tempts you to sin against God by** seeking physical needs more than spiritual necessities.

II. **Satan tempts you to sin against God by** challenging his oversight of and concern for you.

III. **Satan tempts you to sin against God by** diverting worship from God to other things.

Repetition

Repetition of a key word, or key words, in the statements of theological principle adds to the increased aurality of the sermon structure. In the outline below the key word "SIN" is found in all three points. This absolutely had to be the case since the proposition intended to demonstrate 3 correctives for common misunderstandings regarding sin.

I. You Must Identify Sin as an Internal Disposition

II. You Must Equate Sin against Man as Sin against God

III. You Must Act to Minimize the Consequences of Your Sin

The repetition of a key word, or key words, is "an audio cue" that another main point is being presented. Hundreds of sentences and sentence fragments whistle past listeners' ears during a sermon. When the hearers hear the key word of the sermon points stated they perceive that the preacher has moved on to the next point of the sermon.[72]

Repetition of the key words of a point of sermon structure serves as a cue that a transition is being made from one point to the succeeding point of sermon structure. Transitions provide a sense of march to the sermon, help to supply the connective tissue which holds the whole address together, and furnish an opportunity to underscore the genuine concerns of the message. When the main points are given a parallel structure, the structure itself serves not only to build a transitional bridge from one point to another but to summarize what has gone before thus adding impact to the clarity of the exposition.[73] Notice the high degree of "component repetition" in the following outline. You will observe that the amount of "component repetition" is as complete as possible in the effort to make related, but distinct statements. Only the underlined words are not repeated in all six of the statements, yet the two underlined words of each statement are grammatically parallel in each statement.

I. The grace of Christ is demonstrated by <u>assisting</u> the <u>needy</u>.

II. The grace of Christ is demonstrated by <u>accepting</u> the <u>humble</u>.

III. The grace of Christ is demonstrated by <u>instructing</u> the <u>ignorant</u>.

IV. The grace of Christ is demonstrated by <u>forgiving</u> the <u>repentant</u>.

V. The grace of Christ is demonstrated by <u>rebuking</u> the <u>errant</u>.

VI. The grace of Christ is demonstrated by <u>encouraging</u> the <u>faithful</u>.

Repetition, however, is not limited to a word or phrase used consistently in each sermon point. This kind of repetition is component repetition. A component is repeated from point to point because it was intentionally included as a part of each point of the sermon. This kind of repetition, component repetition, is achieved by the preacher in his study as a he pores over the structure word-smithing the statements to affect as much aural enhancement as he can achieve. Remember that the greatest care must be taken with the phraseology of a statement of theological principle. Each one ought to be expressed in the most exact, and concise language.[74]

However, there is also a "cumulative repetition" that elevates the aurality of the statements of theological principle. This is repetition that is achieved in the pulpit as the preacher reiterates his points, saying them over and over, in the process of expounding the text and progressing through the outline. It is not enough to clearly state a proof. It should be fully unfolded. It should be resolved in the preacher's mind, and before the hearer's mind, until all that is latent in it has been elicited. The maxim, then, in respect to the number of main points or divisions is, "Amplify, rather than multiply."[75] However, the maxim in respect to the treatment of the main points of the sermon is "amplification through repetition." A. W. Blackwood acknowledged, "As a lover of sermons, all sorts of sermons, I always find it difficult to name any present-day master of the preacher's art who has not learned the value of meaningful repetition."[76] Repetition of the statements of theological principle will help the hearers to remember the structure throughout and perhaps beyond the preaching event.

Component repetition within the structure of the sermon points will work to impress the hearers regarding the style of the statements of theological principle. Cumulative repetition of the structure of the sermon points will work to impress the statements of theological principle upon the hearers. Component repetition affects the appreciation of the sermon points whereas cumulative repetition affects the recollection of the sermon points.

The combination of component and cumulative repetition enhances the unity of the discourse so that the continuance of textual exposition within a given sermon does not become a competing force but a complimentary force. Through the ongoing discussion of the text, the unity of the passage becomes more evident. As the expositor continues to preach, the sermon gains greater unity which enhances the cognitive understanding of the sermon and text in the minds of the hearers as well as a greater unity which facilitates a volitional response to the sermon and text in the hearts of the hearers. Repetition is crucial for the kind of unity that brings both strength and beauty to a sermon, apart from which a sermon can only be good incidentally, not intentionally. Dabney writes,

> The nail is only driven home by successive blows upon the same spot. The engineer who would batter a breach in the enemy's wall does not scatter his cannon-shot. He makes all his guns converge upon a single spot. Thus an irresistible force is applied, before which no masonry can stand, while be the opposite method he would only have scratched the whole surface of the fortress, without breaking down any part.[77]

The Apostles believed intensely a few things and they reiterated them, restated them, repeated them; and it is this reiteration, this studied repetition that makes preaching somewhat difficult, for the preaching of the Gospel moves in a narrow channel. Preaching must speak always and everywhere the old, old story. The New Testament kerygma, which is our standard and our authority, asserts and reasserts, repeats and reiterates a simple and concise message. There is almost a studied monotony about it.

The pastor who has preached to the same people for a generation cannot but wonder why people continue to come for he is saying over again what he has so often said before. Yet, this is the art of preaching. "Mastery," said Lord Acton, "is acquired through resolved limitation." The artist is limited to the colors of the spectrum and must work within his limitation. The musician is limited to the notes of the octave and must work out his melodies within the confines of his art. So too the preacher works within definite restrictions. Make no mistake about this aspect of preaching, it takes time and talent and spade work and imagination, and above all the illuminating work of the Holy Spirit, to tell over and over again in an interesting way the old, old story, precept upon precept, line upon line.[78]

Alliteration

Alliteration is defined as the repetition of the same sound, usually of a consonant, at the beginning of two or more words immediately succeeding each other, or at short intervals. In its application in preaching, alliteration is the arrangement of the terminology of one's sermon points so that key words of each of the statements will begin with the same letter. Most commonly there are four types of alliteration. There is *single word, single letter, repeated* alliteration; *multiple words, single letter, repeated* alliteration; *multiple words, multiple letters, repeated* alliteration; and *multiple words, single letter, varied* alliteration. Three components are used to describe the exact kind of alliteration that may be used in sermon structure. The first component ("single" or "multiple") is in reference to the word/words alliterated. The second component ("single" or "multiple") is in reference to the letter/letters alliterated. The third term ("repeated" or "varied") is in reference to the alliteration of the sermon points from one point to the next point, that is, is the alliteration repeated from point to point or is there varied alliteration from point to point?

An example of *single word, single letter, repeated* alliteration is seen in the following outline. Notice that a single word bearing a single letter "f" alliteration is repeated in each point of the outline.

I. Those who rejoice in the Lord are <u>forbearing</u> toward others.

II. Those who rejoice in the Lord are <u>focused</u> on the Lord's presence.

III. Those who rejoice in the Lord are <u>freed</u> from all anxiety.

IV. Those who rejoice in the Lord are <u>fervent</u> in thankful praying.

V. Those who rejoice in the Lord are <u>furnished</u> with God's peace.

An example of *multiple words, single letter, repeated* alliteration is seen in the following outline. You find multiple words alliterated by the single letter "p" being repeated in each of the points.

I. Those who are being led by the Spirit <u>pursue</u> <u>peace</u> with others at all times.

II. Those who are being led by the Spirit <u>practice</u> <u>purity</u> before others at all times.

III. Those who are being led by the Spirit <u>possess</u> <u>patience</u> toward others at all times.

An example of *multiple words, multiple letters, repeated* alliteration is seen in the following outline. Observe that there are multiple words bearing alliteration of multiple letters in each point "e" and "s" which are repeated from point to point.

I. As Believers Mature in Christ the <u>extent</u> of one's <u>sinfulness</u> seems to increase

II. As Believers Mature in Christ the <u>eradication</u> of one's <u>sinfulness</u> is desired intensely

III. As Believers Mature in Christ the <u>example</u> of one's <u>selflessness</u> is clearly observed

IV. As Believers Mature in Christ the <u>effects</u> of one's <u>selflessness</u> is used to serve others

An example of *multiple words, single letter, varied* alliteration is seen in the following outline. Notice how multiple words in each point bear alliteration of a single letter, but the single letter alliteration of multiple words varies from one point to another. There is a single letter "r" alliteration of multiple words in point one, single letter "h" alliteration of multiple words in point two, single letter "t" alliteration of multiple words in point three, single letter "s" alliteration of multiple words in point four, and single letter "g" alliteration of multiple words in point five.

I. God requires every believer to <u>re</u>flect the <u>ri</u>ghteousness of Christ

II. God requires every believer to <u>h</u>arbor the <u>h</u>ope of salvation

III. God requires every believer to <u>t</u>rust the <u>t</u>ruthfulness of Scripture

IV. God requires every believer to <u>s</u>eek the <u>s</u>alvation of the lost

V. God requires every believer to <u>g</u>uard the <u>g</u>ospel of God

Notice how the following outline contains the same letter alliteration of two key words underlined in each statement, but the alliteration of the two key words is different from point to point, and as such is another example of *multiple words, single letter, varied* alliteration.

I. The perfecting of faith requires submission to the <u>w</u>ill and <u>W</u>ord of God.

II. The perfecting of faith thrives in the <u>p</u>resence and <u>p</u>ower of God.

III. The perfecting of faith results in the <u>a</u>ffirmation and <u>a</u>doration of God.

Some people will quickly attack the validity of alliteration, poke fun at it, set it aside as being something that is insignificant or injurious to preaching. There can be no doubt that some preachers have gone overboard with alliteration to the degree that their sermon points are nothing other than a display of their own cleverness. In hearing such highly alliterated statements one cannot help to wonder *if the preacher is trying to communicate truth to people or trying to communicate his cleverness before people.* The sinfulness, or excesses, of some should not rule out alliteration from being used as a means of earnestly trying to communicate God's truth to his people.

There is nothing that compares to the device of alliteration that allows people to recall what were the main points, or the statements of theological principle. At the time of this writing, I can recall a sermon I heard preached almost thirty years ago, and will probably never forget, because of the alliteration that was used in the main points. The sermon had to do with the will of God. Selected New Testament references were compiled that stated something as being God's will. The expositor structured the statements so that the key word of each sermon point began with an "s." The will of God was described in a most unforgettable way.

I. God's will is that you be **S**aved.

II. God's will is that you be **S**pirit-filled.

III. God's will is that you be **S**anctified.

IV. God's will is that you be **S**ubmissive.

V. God's will is that you be **S**uffering.

VI. God's will is that you be **S**aying "Thanks."[79]

If alliteration helps people who hear sermons remember main points of the sermons, then shouldn't preachers consider employing something to help their hearers recall the truth they proclaimed to them? I believe they should! I also believe if a preacher really doesn't care whether the truth he preaches is remembered or not remembered, then he should quit preaching! The crucial issue to be decided then is this—does alliteration help me or hinder me in my attempt to accurately communicate truth in such a way so that those who hear the truth might remember the truth? In reality, it works and it can work well!

One of the characteristics of Puritan preaching was their great desire to bring edification to the hearers. Alliteration was a choice means by which the Puritans would seek to bring understanding and recollection of the messages they preached since they typically had very extensive sermon structure. For example, Richard Baxter preached a sermon on the "Chiefest Helps of Your Salvation" which included: Powerful Preaching, Prayer, Prudence, Piety, Painfulness, Patience, Perseverance.[80] For those who heard this sermon preached, or for one who reads this sermon, desiring to recall what are the "chiefest helps of one's salvation" one may do so simply because of the alliteration used in identifying the seven helps of salvation. Of course, we have in mind alliteration found in sermon points consisting of statements of theological principle rather than sermon points consisting of a word or a phrase.

Assonance

"Assonance is the repetition of a dominant or concluding vowel or, perhaps, vowel and consonant combination."[81] The "ate" ending of the words: articulate, terminate, validate, hesitate, and indicate reflect simple assonance. A higher level of assonance is achieved if the consonant preceding the "ate" ending is the same for a series of words such as: indicate, complicate, and explicate. In this case, the "icate" ending provides a stronger sound since the same vowel precedes the common "c" consonant of each word. Finally, assonance is affected even more fully if the words: indication, complication, and explication are used since they share a three vowel ending—"i/ca/tion".

Earlier in this chapter three outlines were depicted from James 1:5-8. Examine the first of the three and notice the simple assonance of the three modifiers of prayer.

I.   In Order to mature as a believer in the midst of trials we need to pray wisely.

II. In Order to mature as a believer in the midst of trials we need to pray sincerely.

III. In Order to mature as a believer in the midst of trials we need to pray expectantly.

The simple "ly" ending for each of the three prayer modifiers helps hearers to recall how they are to pray in the midst of trials so that they may mature as a believer.

The assonance of the following outline is more pronounced since it bears a stronger aural quality.

I.   Salvation as God's declaration of one's righteousness is Justification

II. Salvation as a process of becoming more like Christ is Sanctification

III. Salvation as an immortal, imperishable, bodily resurrection is Glorification

The endings of all three significant, theological terms end with the same four syllables, i/fi/ca/tion.

Assonance can be applied to the points of substructure as well. Notice how assonance in the "less" ending of all 5 points of substructure provide easy recall for Christ's disconnected branch simile in John 15:6.[82]

A. A Disconnected Branch Becomes Worthless

B. A Disconnected Branch Becomes Lifeless

C. A Disconnected Branch Becomes Defenseless

D. A Disconnected Branch Becomes Helpless

E. A Disconnected Branch Becomes Hopeless

The stylistic consideration of form bears the potential to achieve greater aural impact through the means of parallelism, repetition, alliteration, and assonance when applied to sermon structure.

THE STYLISTIC CONSIDERATION OF FLOW

Faris Whitesell, in the effort to establish an accurate understanding of expository preaching described what is NOT expository preaching. Of the ten components listed which prevent expository preaching from occurring, half of them directly related to the absence of sermon structure. These include the following:

> It is not running commentary from word to word and verse to verse without <u>unity, outline and persuasive drive</u>.
>
> It is not rambling comment and offhand remarks about the passage apart from thorough exegesis and <u>logical order</u>.
>
> It is not pure exegesis, no matter how scholarly, if it lacks <u>theme, thesis, outline and development</u>.
>
> It is not a chopped-up collection of grammatical findings and quotations from commentaries without being fused together into a <u>smooth, flowing, interesting and compelling message</u>.
>
> It is not a discussion of a Bible passage ... lacking <u>sermon structure and rhetorical factors</u>.[83]

Sermon structure is pivotal in preaching, and as Whitesell points out, sermon structure is paramount in expository preaching. Sermon structure is invaluable in aiding the flow of a sermon. In the case of expository preaching the sermon flows in a horizontal fashion—moving from point to point, which is sermonic progression, and in a vertical fashion—providing depth of treatment for each point, commonly by means of substructure, which is referred to as advancement of thought. We must understand the flow of a sermon in both the horizontal and vertical sense.

The flow of a sermon is perceptible for the hearers when distinct segments of the theme of a biblical passage are identified, when the first segment is given sufficient explanation so that a portion of the passage is understood and its relevance to the hearers is discernable, and when there is a transition to the next identifiable segment which is given sufficient treatment. This pattern of identification, explanation, transition, identification, explanation, transition, etc. continues until the entirety of the biblical passage and its theme has been covered. But the question is, covered to what extent? The extent of coverage afforded any passage will determine the unique quality of flow for a given sermon.

The extent of vertical flow, or advancement of thought, somewhat retards the horizontal flow, or sermonic progression. Sermonic progression and advancement of thought are both essential for expository preaching but they do, in a sense, work against each other, in that, it is hard to make progress on the horizontal axis of a sermon if there is too much advancement of thought occurring on the vertical axis. In the same way, it is hard to make advancement of thought on the vertical axis if there is a great need to make progress on the horizontal axis. In other words, it is difficult to accomplish exposition of a text which provides both depth and breadth of treatment in one sermon. This requires the expositor to make crucial decisions regarding how thoroughly each point will be covered. Obviously, a sermon with seven points will be covered rather superficially since much sermonic progress, or horizontal movement from point to point, is required. However, a sermon with two points does not require much horizontal movement from point to point. The requirement of this sermon is to deal thoroughly with the points, allowing much detail and insight to be brought to the points which accomplishes advancement of thought.

The non-negotiable is this—regardless of the number of points in the sermon, whether a twofold structure highly modified with abundant substructure or many points with little or no substructure, the hearers must sense that the biblical passage is being covered well. What matters is that the text is treated in such a way that the meaning of the passage is understood. Therefore, the structure exists only for the purpose of clarifying the meaning, whether by the means of a sermon structure that achieves great sermonic progression or a sermon structure that affords much advancement of thought upon a few points, or a sermon structure that achieves a good balance of both advancement of thought and sermonic progression in the same message.

Sermonic progression, advancement of thought, and substructure will be given a more thorough treatment in the following chapters but a brief discussion will be offered here in connection with the stylistic consideration of flow.

Flow through Sermonic Progression

It has been suggested that all "other things being equal a good outline is the guaranty [sic] of a good sermon; and, *per contra*, an imperfect outline (or, still worse, none at all) is the occasion of much flat, stale and unprofitable discourse."[84] Why is this so? Without an outline, flow through the sermon is indiscernible, it cannot be tracked. Therefore, what could have been perceived as advancement of thought on a sermon point ends up being just additional clutter to an unorganized, chaotic, and rambling mass of material. As Vinet wisely remarked,

> The human mind inherently demands unity . . . The strongest thoughts, which are not interconnected, injure one another, and the more in proportion to their strength. Only very powerful minds can obtain profit from that which is without unity, or from that which is inconsistent with itself. Attacked by a crowd of mutually self-neutralizing impressions, we are made captive by none, and are fixed by nothing.[85]

It is the interconnecting of points, as all the points are related to but are making a distinct contribution toward the understanding of a theme being explained in a point by point fashion, which allows for sermonic progression.

We may affirm that, other things being equal, the power of a sermon is proportional to the order which is apparent in it, and that a sermon without ordered structure is comparably feeble. A sermon "has all the power of which it is susceptible, only when the parts proceeding from the same design, are intimately united, exactly adjusted, when they mutually aid and sustain one another like the stones of an arch."[86]

If it is true, as Bridges suggests, that "Some of the best pulpit talents—such as fluency of utterance, richness and variety of illustration—without an orderly distribution, fail in arresting the attention, or fixing permanent impression" then sermon structure is even more imperative for those who do not possess "the best pulpit talents" to begin with.[87] No preacher is above the need for his sermon to make marked progression by dealing with the truths of his text in a clearly discernible point by point fashion. But the expository preacher in particular has a greater need for the sermonic progression secured by sermon structure. The eloquence of a sermon "should be a discourse that exhibits singleness of aim, and a converging progress towards an outward practical end," which in the case of expository preaching the expositor "must in this instance be less successful" since expository sermons typically "are more defective in respect to unity of structure, and a constant progress towards a single end, than in any other respect."[88] Therefore,

> The expositor will need to employ his strongest logical talent, and his best rhetorical ability, to impart sufficient of the oratorical form and spirit, to the expository sermon. He will need to watch his mind, and his plan, with great care, lest the discourse overflow its banks, and spread out in all directions, losing the current and the deep strong volume of eloquence. This species of sermonizing is very liable to be a dilution of divine truth, instead of an exposition.[89]

Unfortunately, this is the tendency of many who are especially adept at showcasing rich insight and interesting detail from a biblical passage.

How Sermonic Progress Benefits Hearers

In reference to the need of the expository preacher to make sermonic progression, four benefits may be offered. The first benefit is the concentration of attention. "Divisions call attention to one thing at a time: therefore they concentrate attention."[90]

The second benefit is the consciousness of achievement. In reference to sermon divisions assisting the preacher to make progress in his sermon, Phelps remarked, "Organization achieves in discourse that which it achieves in everything else, —rapidity of execution ... The same expedient assists a hearer, also, in perceiving progress of discussion. Few things are so essential to impressive discourse as the sense of progress. Hearers crave the consciousness of achievement."[91]

The third benefit is the coherent apprehension of truth. Coherence is concerned with the logical connection between one point and another. Some sermons do not lead logically from one point to another. There are no transitions to make a logical bridge from one point to the next.

Coherence is most obviously needed when the sermon is structured so that each point depends upon the previous one.[92] Good divisions are nothing more than the clear analysis of any given theme of a sermon. They assist the hearer to follow the discussion of a passage which prevents the sermon from becoming a mass of incoherent and confused matter.[93]

The fourth benefit is the consolation it affords the hearers. Sermon divisions "refresh the mind and memory both of the speaker and the hearer. They introduce breaks; they enable the mind to repose a moment, and take a view of the field, to recall what has gone before, to note the progress which has been made, and to look forward to what is to come. The mind rests in the trench in which it is working its way up to the stronghold, looking both backward and forward."[94] The benefits of sermonic progression as concentrated attention, consciousness of achievement, coherent apprehension of truth, and consolation afforded to the hearers are an impressive rationale for sermon structure. Observe the outline below and notice how the fourfold structure allows sermonic progression to occur as the subject of fervent prayer is developed by four statements of theological principle.

I. The reason for fervent prayer is the onslaught of crisis

    A. People pray fervently when normality gives way to crisis

    B. People pray fervently when the crisis escalates

    C. People pray fervently when disaster seems eminent

II. The reliance upon fervent prayer is the means of God's power

    A. God's power is available in the worst circumstances

    B. God's power may not be recognized initially

    C. God's power can change life completely

III. The response to fervent prayer is the demonstration of God's will

    A. Christians are to covet God's will for their lives as they pray

    B. Christians are to be content with God's will having prayed

III. The result of fervent prayer is the declaration of God's glory

    A. Christians must aspire to see God's glory through answered prayer

B. Christians must acknowledge God's glory in answered prayer

C. Christians must announce God's glory for answered prayer

Sermonic progression results from sermon structure. However, the mere presence of sermon structure does not achieve sermonic progression. Qualitative sermon structure achieves sermonic progression. You may be certain that any confusion in divisions in a sermon, any difficulty in keeping the thoughts expressed in them in their right places, must be traced to a lack of clearness in the preacher's understanding of what he wants to communicate. As one man so eloquently expressed it, "You have not attended to your fences, and the sheep are straying from one pasture to another. The remedy for this is not to run after each sheep that wanders, but to repair and strengthen your fences."[95] The fences of a good sermon structure are certainly worth the effort to build and maintain. People easily give up on a sermon and its preacher once they determine that the sermon and the preacher are equally unorganized and confusing. There may be difficult textual matters that are hard to resolve in a clear, concise, convincing manner but what the subject of the text and sermon is, and how the subject is being clarified in a point by point manner must never be uncertain.

If you tell a man about a great sermon you've recently heard, his first question is; "What was its subject-matter?" that is, "What was it about?" He never asks you, "What were its subjects?" because a sermon must be a discussion of one subject. Unity of subject, in order to be real and to be felt, involves, unquestionably, a convergence or a gravitation of all the parts, even the minutest, towards the center.[96] Therefore, the actual unifying theme of the passage must be discovered so that the outline is not forced upon the text. How does one know if this is ever being done? If staying in the text, examining all of the details in the passage does not validate a statement of theological principle and the statement of theological principle is not comprehended more fully through the examination of the passage, then the statement of theological principle has been forced upon the text, it did not rise out of the text.

Therefore, if a statement of theological principle, in support of a proposition, is not *genuinely* demonstrative, and *distinctively* demonstrative, it should not constitute a part of the sermon structure. "All arguments that do not, so far as they reach and relate, really evince, and afford new elements of conviction, ought to be energetically rejected."[97] Even more importantly, every statement of theological principle that cannot be validated from the text, not just part of the statement of theological principle but the whole of it, has no right to see the light of day in a sermon from that passage. Not only would this hinder sermonic progression, but it would be ruinous to expository preaching.

For sermonic progression to occur as it should, every statement of theological principle must establish the proposition. It is not enough, that they bear some affinity to the theme of the discourse; that they are not heterogeneous. They must be of the nature of demonstration, and carry conviction to the hearer's mind. At the conclusion of each point of the sermon structure, the hearer should feel that the proposition has received an additional, authentic support. *This requires that each statement of theological principle exhibit a distinct contribution to the understanding of the theme as validated by the details of the biblical text.* This means that each point should not contain elements of proof that are found in other points. For sermonic progression to flow in an unhindered way, no one point can be a mere modification of some other point, but a distinct, and additional, item in the mass of argument.[98] The outline below suggests three distinct insights regarding purity in the Church of Jesus Christ. Notice how each statement of theological principle provides fresh insights to the subject of church purity.

I. The purity of the church necessitates yielded rights from each member

    A. Resulting in untroubled relationships with others

    B. Resulting in unhampered ownership of possessions

    C. Resulting in unhindered fellowship with God

II. The purity of the church is demonstrated by meeting each other's needs

    A. By extensive personal sacrifice

    B. By wise distribution of resources

III. The purity of the church is jealously guarded by God

    A. Against the deception of sin

    B. Against the promotion of self

    C. Against the intervention of Satan

D. Against the testing of the Spirit

Flow through Advancement of Thought

In the desire to make a sermon seem free and spontaneous there is a prevalent dislike to giving it formal structure. The statement of the subject, the division into points, the recapitulation at the end, all such attempts to bring structure to a sermon are out of favor, and there is a great deal of derision about them, today more than ever. Structured preaching has always had antagonists. The response of Phillips Brooks, made years ago, is still vital for today. Brooks's testimony in the face of such antagonism was,

> I can only say that I have come to fear it less and less. The escape from it must not be negative but positive. The true way to get rid of the boniness of your sermon is not by leaving out the skeleton, but by clothing it with flesh... and the more thoroughly the outlines of your work are laid out the more freely your sermon will flow, like an unwasted stream between its well-built banks. I think that most congregations welcome, and are not offended by clear, precise statements of the course which a sermon is going to pursue, carefully marked division of its thoughts.[99]

The antagonism against structure in and for preaching is not completely unfounded, yet it stems from abuse, obvious abuse, which needs to be corrected rather than dismissing structure as unproductive for preaching.

But the truth is some sermons exhibit a body of proof which, owing to the multitude of the divisions and subdivisions, is wholly unsuited to the purposes of persuasive preaching. They are good illustrations of the infinite divisibility of matter, but produce no conviction in the popular mind, because they are antithetical to preaching. This fault will be avoided, if the preacher asks, in respect to each and every statement of theological principle: "Does this proposed statement of theological principle really prove the proposition?" And, "Does it afford a distinctively new principle that is not contained in any other point?" These two questions, rigorously applied, will prevent minor assertions in the sermon from becoming the major assertions of the sermon and every statement of theological principle will exhibit a unique contribution, so *distinct* and *diverse* from that of all preceding or following points, as to impart a marked, and distinguishing logical character to it.[100] If a prospective statement of theological principle does not meet these criteria then the point is not a main point but rather a point of substructure, providing modification and amplification of a statement of theological principle, but not another statement of theological principle. Amplifying and modifying substructure makes a major contribution in advancing the thought of a given statement of theological principle. In other words, a major contribution is made by a minor point, a point of substructure in a sermon. Again, in the case of expository preaching is this especially true. So much of the insight of expository preaching takes place through advancement of thought, provided through the substructure of the sermon. In the outline below, notice how the substructure provides an array of amplification to make the two statements of theological principle understood well beyond what could be known simply from the articulation of the two points in the delivery of the sermon.

I. Every Believer Needs to Be Encouraged in Their Walk with the Lord
   A. The need for encouragement
   B. The focus of encouragement
      1. faith in the Lord
      2. love for the saints
   C. The means of encouragement
      1. gratitude from others
      2. prayer by others

II. Every Believer Needs to Be Enlightened in Their Knowledge of the Lord
   A. The need for enlightenment
   B. The focus of enlightenment
   C. The areas of enlightenment
      1. His calling
      2. His inheritance
      3. His power

Eugene Hall and James Heflin correctly assert that an expository sermon, since the end of the third century, was distinguished from a homily, or running commentary, due to orderly structure for the sermon and that "all sermons should first be expositions of Scripture."[101] The exposition of Scripture, the fiduciary responsibility of the preacher, must not be inhibited by sermon structure but rather aided by it. This means that the substance of the text must be dealt with. Such dealing with the substance of a passage means that the textual matter will furnish detailed modification and amplification of a statement of theological principle. Advancement of thought is the leading tenant of good expository preaching. The text stays under scrutiny and statements of theological principle are understood as the details of the passage validate the points of the sermon's main structure.

Structure, main structure and substructure, promotes interest for the hearer. Austin Phelps hinted at this in his statement that, "The interest of the hearer is dependent upon good divisions. The unity which they create prevents the tedium of confused thought; and nothing is more tedious than confused thinking. The divisions invite interest in their expansion."[102] Main structure, with its contribution of sermonic progression which allows a theme to be clearly identified through point by point treatment along the horizontal axis of the sermon, allows interest to be a potential reality, or as Phelps indicated, it prevents the disinterest that confusion brings. But substructure explores and develops the points of main structure. It is in the advancement of thought, secured by the insights obtained through the detailed examination of the text, where interest is achieved in an expository sermon. In fact, this is the real genius of expository preaching which is preaching that is dependent upon the biblical text for its framework and its content.

Unlike preaching that is not expository, there may be points for the sermon but the points are not developed by the text. In expository preaching, the points and the development of the points rise out of the passage. The relation between the statement of theological principle and the exposition of the text which generated the principle is depicted by the closed palm of logic and the open palm of rhetoric. Now, a statement of theological principle is logical in nature; it is like a hard, closed fist. The explanation, development, modification, amplification of a statement of theological principle is rhetorical in nature; it is like an open hand. The hand can be opened or closed but it cannot be both at the same time. There is the closed hand and the open hand like there is the statement of a theological principle and the explanation of the principle. To attempt to unite the two in one sentence is like attempting to open and shut the hand by a single volition, and by one set of muscles. The hand cannot be shut by the muscles that were made to open it. The statement of a theological principle cannot be the development and amplification of it.[103] Therefore, a statement of theological principle must be examined and validated through a thorough explanation of the passage which provides advancement of thought regarding the statement of theological principle.

The necessity of divisions and the amplification of the divisions is what Blaise Pascal called the "geometrical spirit." He contended that the most profound thinking involves the "tendency to geometrize." That is, "it involves that bent of mind which defines, which proves, which demonstrates, which therefore affirms positively in the end. Divisions and the amplification of the divisions represent this type of thinking in the pulpit and "the disuse of the one is destructive to the other."[104] The need to "geometrize" is crucial for advancement of thought so that a given statement of theological principle stays in focus long enough to receive depth of treatment by seeing how the details of the text bring valuable insight to the statement of theological principle. In other words, the sermon structure as a whole and each statement of theological principle must fully comprehend the portion of the passage from which it is drawn.

> A simple illustration may serve to clarify what this means. The text, or theme, could be likened to an orange from which the juice is to be extracted. Each division represents a squeeze which the preacher should give that orange until all the juice, or truth, has been extracted. These divisions should therefore be successive squeezes, until no more truth can be obtained from the text. Naturally, the *fewer* these divisions are, the *more* truth must be extracted with each squeeze. The more these divisions are, the *less* truth will be obtained with each squeeze.[105]

Structure and substructure, specifically, assist a hearer in perceiving and appreciating the comprehensiveness of discussion and provide what is so necessary for preaching—interest. As Phelps commented, "St. Peter's at Rome makes no such impression of magnitude from an outside view as from the interior. *So it is with a complete discussion. To be appreciated, it must be explored; the parts of it, in their order, must be seen.*" (italics added)[106] Advancement of thought is a crucial stylistic consideration of flow which is extremely significant in expository preaching.

Interest, the interest that accompanies the advancement of thought produced from the exposition of a biblical text, is the stylistic hallmark of sermon structure for the expository preacher. Interest and understanding Scripture is forfeited when advancement of thought is not achieved. Substantial advancement of thought necessitates preaching the text, not preaching about the text, nor preaching from the text, but preaching the text which entails a thorough examination of the passage. Therefore, advancement of thought with its byproduct of interest and understanding occur when the text is thoroughly examined. A thorough examination will require substructure so that advancement of thought can be apprehended clearly. Notice in the outline below how the main points are understood more fully through the means of the substructure. The limitations of established believers are not evident unless specified through the substructure. The past which new believers must overcome requires amplification, otherwise the statement of theological principle is too general to be helpful. Overall, church renewal cannot be understood biblically until the text is considered fully by means of the substructure.

I. The Church Is Renewed as Established Believers Overcome Their Limitations

   A. By being forced to abandon prejudices
   B. By being focused on eternal priorities
   C. By being faithful to God's purposes

II. The Church Is Renewed as New Believers Overcome Their Past

   A. By procuring the virtues of other believers
   B. By proclaiming Christ to unbelievers
   C. By presenting a changed life before all
   D. By persisting in the faith of the Apostles
   E. By portraying the fruit of the Spirit
   F. By practicing the teachings of Scripture

Vinet sounded a warning long ago that is being flagrantly set aside by many preachers in our day. The warning had to do with the pulpit pandering to the things of the world for the sake of interest in preaching. He wrote,

> Never should the Christian pulpit be sold to the interests of this passing life. There was a time when the pulpit had to do with subjects of worldly interest almost exclusively. When the church, undermined by infidelity, undermined especially by the corruption of her ministers, had to ask compassion for what remained to her of existence, she gave herself, as if she had been a mercenary, to the circulation of whatever ideas she was furnished with, in order to gain a miserable subsistence.[107]

A miserable subsistence would be an accurate, yet deplorable, assessment of preaching that is observable in many pulpits. Why? For the sake of interest, so much is attempted other than that which God has provided, that which can only be of true interest, an insightful discovery of his Word, a rich and thorough understanding of Scripture achieved through a careful examination of the biblical text. A careful detailing of a passage of Scripture in which advancement of thought occurs is not inconsistent with the concern for interest in preaching, but it is actually the chief means of achieving it. The chief means of facilitating advancement of thought is through the use of substructure.

Flow through Substructure

Substructure is the means by which advancement of thought takes place commonly and productively. Marked advancement of thought is dependent upon substructure. Why is this so? Because clear mental action works instinctively by plan, and each assists the other. You understand a subject the better for having reduced it to a plan of discourse. Divisions also assist the hearer to clearness in understanding a discussion. Why should not a hearer, in this respect, profit by a statement of a plan, as well as a preacher by the existence of a plan?[108] This has been the foundational conviction of this book. The plan of a sermon entails not only the major assertions of the passage but the minor assertions which provide understanding of the major assertions.

In the case of expository preaching, sermon structure commonly incorporates more than the points of main structure. In the process of stating a main point of sermon structure, a statement of theological principle, and validating the accuracy of such a statement by the examination of the biblical text, substructure is invaluable in helping the hearers to understand the wealth of insights that allow the statement of theological principle to be validated as true.

Divisions assist the memory of both preacher and hearer in understanding a sermon in its details. Cicero taught that it is chiefly order that gives distinctness to memory. There is scarcely any one of so strong a memory as to retain the order of his language and thoughts without arrangement and the "observation of heads."[109] If Cicero was right, and I believe he was, that order is needed to understand a sermon then the same principle is valid for the understanding of a point within a sermon. Order will be required. In fact, substructure is especially valuable when dealing with the many insights brought out in thorough exposition of a passage. A few points of substructure are valuable to provide hooks to hang the insight discovered in the text in order to validate a statement of theological principle.

The contents of Scripture and their discussion in the pulpit "are such as to render divisions necessary to clearness, to bring the themes within the reach of the common mind, and to secure for them an intelligent and interested hearing."[110] The connection between structure and clarity is operational for main structure and substructure as well.

"As it is necessary to divide the theme, so also is it sometimes necessary to divide the divisions. The fewer the number of the main divisions the more need is there for subdivisions, in order to analyze and unfold the leading thought. Usually, divisions should not extend beyond the second degree."[111] In the outline below, the third level of substructure is included but this is limited and necessary.

I. Trials Are A Blessing Since They Are Produced by God and Secure Eternal Benefits

    A. The fact of blessing

    B. The condition of blessing

    C. The explanation of blessing

        1. Its sequence

        2. Its substance

            a. The approval of God

            b. The crown of life

II. Temptations Are A Detriment Since They Are Produced by the Flesh and Secure Lifelong Devastation

   A. The fact of devastation

      1. Temptation may result in blaming God

      2. Temptation is a reality for believers

      3. Temptation CANNOT be of God

   B. The condition of devastation

      1. Temptation is personal in scope

      2. Temptation is personally damaging

   C. The explanation of devastation

      1. Lust continues to plague the believer

      2. Sin begins with the satisfaction of lust

      3. Death results from the presence of sin

Substructure in a sermon is much like seasoning in food—its presence is definitely a good thing but too much of it definitely is not good. Profitable subdivision requires restraint. The objective to divide a statement of theological principle until it is impossible to divide it further is not division but pulverization. A "pulverizing of the subject is not true division."[112] However, the need is to subdivide the statements of theological principle into "as many parts as we can do so profitably, that is, without approaching the point at which attention is wearied and interest destroyed."[113] John Broadus is helpful in his statement that,

> Where the subject specially requires explanation and argument, it will commonly be advantageous to have clearly stated divisions, and frequently subdivisions also; but these must not be so multiplied, nor so stated, as to prevent the discourse from standing out as a living whole, or to interrupt its progressive movement towards the practical end in view.[114]

In expository preaching, however, the subject always requires explanation because the subject comes from the passage. Therefore, the passage must be explained so that the subject of the passage can be understood by the only reasonable means—explanation of the passage. This establishes the need for substructure in expository preaching.

As with the main structure, the several divisions of substructure should be stated in similar forms of expression, when this can be done without artificiality. Such similarity of statement brings out the symmetry of the divisions, rendering them clearer and also more pleasing.[115]

Whenever we instruct and persuade, we must employ economy of discourse, have a plan and follow it, because we must impart to the mind, not a general impression, but a distinct interpretation of a biblical text, based upon the data of the passage being preached.[116] In other words, the substructure is the means by which the statements of theological principle, that which has been synthesized, can be analyzed so that the hearers may accept them having been provided comprehension, validation, and persuasion.

Henry Ward Beecher suggested that the practice of separating analysis and synthesis in preaching as "one of the great mistakes into which preachers fall."[117] That which is analyzed, the biblical text to be preached, must be synthesized, thus yielding statements of theological principle. But ultimately, that which is synthesized, the statements of theological principle, must be analyzed through the means of substructure to produce a clear and more accurate sense of truth. Beecher used Generals Grant and Sherman to illustrate the resulting shortfall of analysis and synthesis not working in tandem—being left with a partial rather than more complete understanding of truth.

> I will describe to you two men who are as different as they possibly can be,—General Grant and General Sherman; and I will say that both of them have very great fortitude; that both of them have very great patience, running even to obstinacy; that both of them have very sharp and clear intellects; that both of them have foresight; that both of them have very great sympathy with their fellow-men; that both of them are very skillful; and that both of them are apt to be victorious. Those terms describe them both generically, and yet they are as different as it is possible for them to be in other respects. General grant is square, short, and thick; and General Sherman is long, lean, and lathy. General Grant is very taciturn; and General Sherman is never silent,—I suppose he talks in his sleep! General Grant thinks everything out, and General Sherman sees things by intuition. General Grant is secretive, and General Sherman is open as a child. You must go further than the *genus*, or you do not describe men.[118]

Thus, the analysis provided by the substructure results in definitive description of the more general synthesized statements of theological principle.

The outline helps to provide comprehension of the truth of a passage, and thereby, the possibility of a permanent impression. It serves as a mnemonic help. There are many hearers of a sermon who carry away little or nothing except the points; and this they cannot do unless the preacher is a party to it.[119] But when a preacher discovers how the passage divides into major and minor assertions, which become the main structure and substructure of the sermon, the preacher can provide for his hearers sermonic progression and advancement of thought in a message that helps them to understand God's Word. The outline below demonstrates both sermonic progression and advancement of thought through substructure. A substantial amount of substructure develops the thought of each statement of theological principle, providing much movement on the vertical axis, while the four statements of theological principle keep the sermon moving on the horizontal axis.

I. A Believer's Soul Is Strengthened by Resolving to Be a Peace-Maker

    A. The need for a peace-maker

    B. The objective for a peace-maker

    C. The responsibilities of a peace-maker

II. A Believer's Soul Is Strengthened by Rejoicing in the Lord

    A. The specifics of rejoicing

    B. The significance of rejoicing

III. A Believer's Soul Is Strengthened by Revealing a Forbearing Spirit

    A. The requirement of forbearance

    B. The recipients of forbearance

    C. The reason for forbearance

IV. A Believer's Soul Is Strengthened by Reversing Anxiety through Prayer

    A. Man's perpetual problem of anxiety

        1. The meaning of anxiety

2. The restriction of anxiety

 B. God's supernatural solution for anxiety

   1. The privilege of prayer

      a. its appropriateness

      b. its accompaniments

   2. The promise of peace

      a. its description

      b. its protection

Force, form, and flow—three significant considerations for sermon structure style. When these three considerations are apparent in sermon structure composed of statements of theological principle, the sermon is more able to accomplish the purposes of a sermon—to instruct, to interest, and to persuade. If these three considerations of sermon structure style are not apparent then the sermon structure, though present, will only be a shadow of what should have been.

CONSIDER THE FOLLOWING QUESTIONS

1. If clarity is to be viewed as a matter of priority, not preference in preaching, what is to be viewed as obligatory, not optional?
2. Of the nine specific criteria for qualitative deductive sermon structure, which ones relate to the stylistic consideration of force, which ones relate to form, and which ones relate to flow?
3. What was Harry Emerson Fosdick's correct assessment of the problem of preaching and what was his attempt to correct the problem?
4. What was the problem with Fosdick's solution?
5. What is the solution to the problem and where is the starting point for the solution of the problem for the sermon as a whole, and where is the beginning point of the solution in the body of the sermon, specifically?
6. What is the beginning point for qualitative sermon structure?
7. What is necessary for the points of a sermon in order for them, in the words of Olford, to involve contemporization of the message?

8. What is the major concern of the main points, in addition to preserving the precise meaning of the original text, according to Kaiser?

9. What does the use of dated, historically proper terminology in the statements of the sermon structure suggest to the hearers?

10. What is even more important than the relevance of our sermons and sermon structure?

11. What are the two things that are worse than irrelevant preaching?

12. What are the two general essentials that characterize textual exposition and what are the implications of each essential for the sermon structure?

13. What three hurdles must be overcome to prevent preaching from being more like "scribal instruction" rather than the preaching of Jesus?

14. How is the timelessness and timeliness of a biblical text reflected when the sermon structure is composed of statements of theological principle?

15. What was Patterson Smyth's description and conclusion for "three types of preachers?"

16. What is it that force through penetration allows for the hearers?

17. What must be provided by a main point as a "proof" and what qualities are required for this effect?

18. What cause precedes the effect of a "heart that has been convicted by the truth" which is true for those who preach and hear sermons?

19. How can one argue for penetration on the basis of plainness of speech and argue against penetration on the basis of obscure speech?

20. What is the true end for preaching and what two means toward this end are too often regarded as the aims for preaching?

21. If a hearer fails to be influenced by, or even rejects a preached message, it must be because of what reason?

22. What is it that preachers who seek to persuade hearers without affecting their emotions fail to understand?

Sermon Structure's Stylistic Components 245

23. What intention of a preacher will prevent him from producing penetrating statements of sermon structure?
24. What must happen for a preacher who desires to impact his hearers emotionally and volitionally in order for this to become a reality for his hearers?
25. What is the cause for people listening more attentively to the fiction spoken by actors more than divine truth as spoken by preachers?
26. What is the impression upon the hearers that a preacher's "grip" achieves?
27. Grip is prerequisite to fulfill what counsel germane to preaching?
28. What benefit is received by hearers who have heard a preacher who preaches with grip?
29. How is grip apparent in a preacher and why must it not be underestimated?
30. What, according to Walter Kaiser, is needed to make the Church more viable, authentic, and effective?
31. What are the four requirements for grip and which of these is most vital?
32. According to James Rosscup, what is required in order to preach with power?
33. How is interest understood in its objective sense and in its subjective sense?
34. What lies behind real power in preaching and what allows one to speak courageously in preaching?
35. What is the implication of arranging one's sermon structure to instruct and persuade?
36. What is the rationale for the analogy that a sermon is more like a river than a chain?
37. What is the requirement and rationale that likens a preacher to a marksman?
38. What is meant by sermonic focalizing?
39. Why is sermon structure the DNA of expository preaching?

40. How does sermon structure help a preacher in his task regarding brevity?
41. How does a statement of theological principle serve as an arrow's arrowhead in preaching?
42. What are the three inviolable imperatives for constructing sermon structure?
43. What are the three cardinal commitments for constructing sermon structure?
44. What must be prepared beyond statements of theological principles in order to preach with the force of penetrating and relevant structure?
45. How does Kaiser describe what constitutes parallel structure?
46. In what two ways does parallelism, as an audio flag, clarify the hearer's understanding of the sermon's structure?
47. How does component repetition contrast with cumulative repetition?
48. What is the impression that component repetition makes upon the hearer as compared to the impression that cumulative repetition makes upon the hearer?
49. What are the four types of alliteration in sermon structure?
50. What is assonance in reference to sermon structure?
51. How does a sermon's flow in a horizontal fashion contrast to a sermon's flow in a vertical fashion in reference to sermon structure?
52. How do hearers perceive that a sermon is progressing?
53. How is it that the vertical flow of advancement of thought works against the horizontal flow of sermonic progression?
54. What are the four benefits that sermonic progression affords an expository preacher?
55. How can it be determined if a theme, or a statement of theological principle, has been forced upon a text?
56. What must each statement of theological principle do in order for sermonic progression to occur and what does this require?

57. How does substructure make a major contribution to expository preaching?

58. Why is advancement of thought the leading tenant of expository preaching?

59. What factors combine to establish the genius of expository preaching?

60. How does the analogy of a closed and open palm depict the relationship between a statement of theological principle and the text which generated it?

61. What is the stylistic hallmark of sermon structure for the expository preacher?

62. What is forfeited when advancement of thought is not achieved?

63. What does substantial advancement of thought necessitate, entail, and require?

64. Why is a careful detailing of a biblical text not inconsistent with interest in preaching?

65. How can substructure be analogous to seasoning for food?

66. How does pulverization contrast with division of a statement of theological principle?

67. In expository preaching what is the only reasonable means by which the subject of the sermon may be discussed?

ENDNOTES

1. Wood, *Workshop*, 20.
2. Luccock, "Reality in Preaching," 17.
3. Ibid., 18.
4. Mayhue, "Rediscovering," 6.
5. Olford and Olford, *Anointed*, 148.
6. Kaiser Jr., *Exegetical*, 157–58.
7. Ibid., 158.
8. Spurgeon, *Lectures*, 76.
9. Zemek, "Grammatical Analysis," 158.
10. Ibid., 160.
11. Ibid.
12. Outline #1— Awbrey, "Taking Initiative." Outline #2— Tuck, "Wisdom," 499–502. Outline #3— Jerdan, "Ask," 9–10.
13. Goodwin, "Plain Sermon?" 126.
14. Smyth, *Preacher*, 75.
15. Pattison, *Making*, 174.
16. Borgman, *Thy Cause*, 155.
17. Pattison, *Making*, 174.
18. Ibid., 174.
19. Vinet, *Homiletics*, 57.
20. Ibid., 58–59.
21. Ibid., 74.
22. Ibid., 69.
23. Blackwood, *Fine*, 123.
24. Smyth, *Preacher*, 60.
25. Kidder, *Treatise*, 220–21.
26. Shedd, *Homiletics*, 188.
27. Ibid., 83.
28. Ibid., 87–88.
29. Beecher, *Yale Lectures*, 222.
30. Burrell, *Construction*, 55–56.
31. Shedd, *Homiletics*, 148–49.
32. Borgman, *Thy Cause*, 160.
33. Broadus, *Treatise*, 263.
34. Sleeth, *Persuasive*, 60.

35. Smyth, *Preacher*, 71–72.
36. Ibid., 64–65.
37. Goodwin, "Plain Sermon?" 129.
38. Shedd, *Homiletics*, 84.
39. Kaiser Jr., *Exegetical*, 242.
40. I realize that prayer is THE vital component for powerful preaching. My intention is simply to state the connection of prayer with preaching that grips the preacher and penetrates the hearts of the hearers. The subject of prayer in preaching is a matter worthy of lengthy detailing. This has been done by others in various books on preaching throughout many years of writing on the subject, and thankfully so. Though it is not my purpose to enter into a detailed discussion of the necessity of prayer in preaching in this book, the brief treatment of this subject does not suggest that I place little value for prayer in the preaching endeavor.
41. Rosscup, "Priority," 63.
42. Smyth, *Preacher*, 79.
43. Genung, *Outlines*, 116–17.
44. Vinet, *Homiletics*, 23.
45. Ibid., 69.
46. Smyth, *Preacher*, 90–91.
47. Genugn, *Outlines*, 117.
48. Vinet, *Homiletics*, 265–66.
49. Burrell, *Construction*, 55.
50. Abbott, *Christian Ministry*, 212.
51. Pattison, *Making*, 160.
52. Burrell, *Construction*, 54.
53. Mc Dougall, "Central Ideas," 226, 227.
54. Burrell, *Construction*, 56.
55. Phelps, *Theory*, 372–73.
56. Pattison, *Making*, 159.
57. Phelps, *Theory*, 375.
58. Borgman, *Thy Cause*, 156.
59. Mc Dougall, 233.
60. Ibid., 228.
61. Ibid., 228–29.
62. MacArthur Jr., "Delivering the Exposition," 322–23.
63. Hall and Heflin, *Proclaim*, 204–7.

64. Ibid., 204.
65. Kaiser Jr., *Exegetical*, 158.
66. Olford and Olford, *Anointed*, 149.
67. Zemek, "Grammatical Analysis," 163.
68. Chapell, *Christ-centered*, 134.
69. Olford and Olford, *Anointed*, 150–51.
70. Awbrey, "Seeing Sin," Part 1.
71. Zemek, "Grammatical Analysis," 163.
72. Chapell, *Christ-centered*, 134.
73. Demaray, *Proclaiming*, 62.
74. Shedd, *Homiletics*, 191.
75. Ibid., 190.
76. Blackwood, *Today*, 94.
77. Dabney, *Sacred*, 113–14.
78. Kerr, *Early Church*, 43–45.
79. MacArthur Jr., sermon preached at the Grace Community Church entitled "God's will is not secret" aired on the radio broadcast ministry of "Grace To You" GCC tape 1276.
80. Bickel, *Light and Heat*, 28–29.
81. Hall and Heflin, *Proclaim*, 206.
82. Don Scurlock, sermon preached in MN 5111-02 Expository Preaching lab at Midwestern Baptist Theological Seminary, Kansas City, MO, February 21, 2008.
83. Whitesell, *Power*, vii–viii.
84. Burrell, *Construction*, 53.
85. Vinet, *Homiletics*, 56.
86. Ibid., 264.
87. Bridges, *Christian Ministry*, 201.
88. Shedd, *Homiletics*, 146–47.
89. Ibid., 155.
90. Phelps, *Theory*, 371.
91. Ibid., 370.
92. Sleeth, *Persuasive*, 52.
93. Hoppin, *Homiletics*, 384.
94. Ibid., 384.
95. Pattison, *Making*, 169.
96. Vinet, *Homiletics*, 56.

97. Shedd, *Homiletics*, 188.
98. Ibid., 188.
99. Brooks, *Joy*, 133–34.
100. Shedd, *Homiletics*, 188–89.
101. Hall and Heflin, *Proclaim*, 150.
102. Phelps, *Theory*, 373.
103. Shedd, *Homiletics*, 193.
104. Phelps, *Theory*, 376–77.
105. Gibbs, *Preacher*, 208.
106. Phelps, *Theory*, 368.
107. Vinet, *Homiletics*, 73.
108. Phelps, *Theory*, 366.
109. Etter, *Preacher*, 187–88.
110. Phelps, *Theory*, 366.
111. Etter, *Preacher*, 198.
112. Vinet. *Homiletics*, 275.
113. Ibid., 286.
114. Broadus, *Treatise*, 265.
115. Ibid., 272.
116. Vinet, *Homiletics*, 273.
117. Beecher, *Yale Lectures*, 77.
118. Ibid., 77–78.
119. Burrell, *Construction*, 58.

Words to Live and Preach By

The Benefits of Reproof

*My son do not reject the discipline of the Lord, or loathe His reproof,
for whom the Lord loves He reproves, even as a father,
the son in whom he delights.*
PROVERBS 3:11–12

*He is on the path of life who heeds instruction,
but he who forsakes reproof goes astray.*
PROVERBS 10:17

*Whoever loves discipline loves knowledge,
but he who hates reproof is stupid.*
PROVERBS 12:1

*Stern discipline is for him who forsakes the way;
he who hates reproof will die.*
PROVERBS 15:10

*He whose ear listens to the life-giving reproof will dwell
among the wise. He who neglects discipline despises himself,
but he who listens to reproof acquires understanding.*
PROVERBS 15:31–32

*Strike a scoffer and the naïve may become shrewd,
but reprove one who has understanding and he will gain knowledge.*
PROVERBS 19:25

*Stripes that wound scour away evil,
and strokes reach the innermost parts.*
PROVERBS 20:30

Better is open rebuke than love that is concealed. Faithful are the wounds of a friend, but deceitful are the kisses of an enemy. A sated man loathes honey, but to a famished man any bitter thing is sweet.
Proverbs 27:5–7

8

Sermon Structure's Functional Results

PROGRESSION OF THE SERMON

One factor of a good sermon is an outline that will allow the sermon to make progress during the preaching of the sermon. There is nothing interesting about a sermon that seems to be going nowhere. *The Twilight Zone* may have been an interesting television program many years ago but hearers of a sermon do not appreciate being cast into a dimension where linear reasoning disappears for an indeterminate time as a sermon with no structure is preached.

> The story of the bird which got into the sanctuary and flew around during the sermon is to the point. One of the elders was upset by the distraction, but another elder was consoling: "Thank God, something was moving!" The widespread perception that much preaching is uninteresting and dead raises the whole issue of flow and movement within content and how we can get our delivery off dead center.[1]

David L. Larsen is correct in his assessment that the lack of sermon progression is a real problem in preaching.

Progression of a sermon is sensed in two distinct ways—horizontal progression and vertical progression. Horizontal progression is the kind of progression that is typically in reference when the progress of a sermon is being considered. In reference to sermon structure, horizontal progression has to do with the sermon moving from point to point to the conclusion in a clear fashion without any diversions or unnecessary digressions while vertical progression has to do with the progress made within each sermon point.

Vertical progression has to do with the preacher's ability to develop a sermon point by providing insight about the point so that he is explaining the text and providing meticulous attention to the details of a passage that has been summarized by statements of theological principle. Vertical progression will be considered later in this chapter under the heading of *advancement of thought*. For the purpose of clarity, we need to distinguish horizontal and vertical progression. Horizontal progression is the advancement of the sermon while vertical progression is the advancement of the sermon points.

Perceived Progression of a Sermon

A sermon is perceived by the congregation to be progressing when the main points of the message are clearly surfaced and successfully treated. Successful treatment of the main structure means that the hearers can easily discern the unity and distinction of each point as they are stated with emphasis and clarity. Listeners need to know how thought and understanding are advancing throughout the message. If any one point sounds too much like an idea that has already been covered, or if various points seem not to build to a higher purpose, ire develops and interest diminishes. No one wants to waste time listening to a sermon leading nowhere.[2]

As the preacher states the first point and proceeds to validate the integrity of the statement of theological principle through the examination of the verse or verses pertaining to the first point, then moving to the second point etc., he establishes the progression of the sermon. Spurgeon addressed the importance of orderliness and progression as he wrote: "In preaching, have a place for everything, and everything in its place. Never suffer truths to fall from you pell-mell. Do not let your thoughts rush as a mob, but make them march as a troop of soldiery. Order, which is heaven's first law, must not be neglected by heaven's ambassadors."[3] Each main point of structure represents a mile-stone for each and every sermon. The statements of theological principle express the meaning of the text.[4]

Since the hearers know how many sermon points will be coming their way (through the use of a plural noun proposition) they can track certain progress since, at any time in the sermon, they can and should know where they have been, where they are, and where they have yet to go in this sermon. The result being, progression of the sermon can be charted by the hearers. The hearers can sense that steady progress toward the completion of the sermon is happening.

Lack of progression inevitably will cause the listeners to become frustrated, fail to follow the sermon, which will result in a less than complete comprehension and compliance to the truth of the passage being preached. They are likely to be bewildered by tedious expansion, and being unable to maintain a steady attention to what is said, they forget part of what they have heard, before the whole is completed. Furthermore, the feebleness produced by additional expansion will cause the attention to languish even more. And what is imperfectly attended to, regardless of the clarity with which it is presented, will usually be but imperfectly understood.[5]

Progression of the sermon, though helped by structure that is discernable to the hearers and descriptive of the text, can be hindered if the preacher gets bogged down in any portion of his treatment of the passage. Bogging down in a sermon does not mean that a preacher spends significantly more time on one sermon point than others. Remember, there should be no commitment made to providing an equal amount of time for the explanation of each sermon point. The bogging down of horizontal progression has to do primarily with the preacher taking up matters that, in effect, cause him to get side-tracked. His progress has been arrested as he roams and meanders for a while by treating material that should never be dealt with in this particular sermon.

The relationship of the time spent on a sermon point and the bogging down of the progression of the sermon will occur only if the time spent on a sermon point is truly excessive, that is, the same material could have and should have been covered in much less time. When the amount of time used is time spent unproductively, this causes the bogging down of horizontal progression. A lengthy sermon point will not cause the sermon to suffer a bogging down of horizontal progression as long as there is an economical treatment of material that should have been covered in the exposition of the text.

Progress is discernable as long as there is a sustained sense of moving forward—a moving forward from point to point in the sermon outline and, in the instance of expository preaching, a moving forward from verse to verse in the text. Discernable progress in expository preaching, therefore, is sensed by moving forward through the sermon outline as well as moving forward in the biblical text that is being preached.

Expository preaching provides a doubled sense in which sermonic progress may be discerned. One of the benefits of expository preaching is that a biblical text is explained and a subject of a sermon is developed by the use of sermon structure. But this requires that the sermon structure used is actually serviceable so that the biblical text and sermon proposition are progressed as the sermon points are treated.

Progression of the Sermon and Logical Development of Thought

Progression of the sermon takes place as the sermon structure represents a logical development of thought from one main point to the next main point of the sermon outline. The logical characteristic of an outline which allows the sermon to progress is explained by Stephen Olford.

> The outline of integrating thoughts should be understandable and a good representation of the flow of thought or movements in the text. The "logic" of the text should be captured in the outline, and there should be clarity of thought and movement in the outline itself. How do you develop such an outline? First of all, keep each point distinct and mutually exclusive. Make sure that each point is indeed capturing a specific distinct emphasis, thought, or movement in the text.[6]

Olford suggests two simple tests be applied to an outline to help ensure that it will provide progression for the sermon. These two tests are the "key word" test and the "clear thinking" test.[7]

The "key word" test ensures that there is a plural noun that is easily identified with all the points of the outline and the plural noun ties all of the points together. An outline is tested for its "clear thinking" by putting each of the main points into a sentence related to the plural noun proposition. A complete sentence helps to clarify the full thought being expressed in the main points of the outline.

An outline that passes the key word test and clear thinking test spares the sermon from being a communication event in which there is a torrent of words providing a puddle of insight—a sad and too often observed result in preaching. David L. Larsen commented upon the common weakness of the lack of progression in preaching as he wrote, "And we often find what I call the 'ferris-wheel sermon' which goes around and around but never gets anywhere. If there is minimal flow or momentum, the sermon will tend to become circular and repetitive. Few preachers never need help with the factors of flow."[8]

Sermon progression is a valuable commodity in one's preaching. It not only prevents a too-often weakness found in preaching but provides a number of benefits to a sermon that progresses well.

Benefits of Sermon Progression

Interest

A well-organized outline helps to hold the interest and attention of the listeners. The structure of the sermon helps the hearer understand the sermon while it is preached and will help them to remember the sermon after it is preached.

Recall

Good sermon structure also helps the preacher to remember the content of his sermon as he expounds the text. Charles Reynolds Brown's assessment of sermon structure in his preaching is compelling.

> The well-built sermon is always easier to deliver because the points, following each other naturally and therefore inevitably, can be more readily remembered by the preacher himself. When I forget and leave out certain vital points in one of my sermons I always know that the sermon was not well built. If that particular idea had been needed just there in the construction of that sermon, I should not have forgotten it.[9]

Timely Completion of a Sermon Point

It is the *postponed completion* of a sermon point that the preacher has to steer clear of while preaching to his congregation. It is not the length of a sermon point (or, a sermon) as much as it is the uncertain progress of a sermon point (or, a sermon) that frustrates a hearer.

> An auditory will listen with increasing interest to a sermon of an hour's length, provided their attention is kept upon the stretch, by a sermonizer who says just enough, and no more, upon each point, and who passes from topic to topic with rapidity, and yet with a due treatment and exhaustion of each, while they will go to sleep under a sermon of a half-hour's length, in which there is none of the excitement that comes from a skilful management of the heads, and none of the exhilaration of a forward motion. There is less fatigue and weariness, in shooting through two hun-

dred miles of space, in a rail-car, than in lumbering over ten miles of space, in a slow coach.¹⁰

The conception of the preacher and the perception of the hearers regarding the preaching of a sermon point, though not a hundred-meter sprint, should be more in line with a one mile run rather than a marathon, that is, there is quite a bit of ground covered in a brisk pace.

Obvious Sequence and Relatedness of the Sermon Points

Progress of a sermon is made through the main structure as the hearers can understand readily how each point of the sermon is making a contribution to the sermon. Certainly progress is tangible as sermon points are stated clearly and treated successfully with subsequent treatment of the next point. This is a necessity for effective preaching. Again, David L. Larsen insists that progression of the sermon through effective structure is necessary in expounding biblical texts, even narrative passages. He wrote,

> In some marked sense the sermon needs to be sequential. The typical narrative passage catches us up in linear progression, and this becomes one of the interest-sustaining advantages of narrative preaching. If the trajectory of the sermon has a sense of unity, direction, and purpose, we shall sense movement. The crafting of the main points should help us avoid "plot clot," or the clogging of the arterials. Like good shots to the green and the waves of the sea to the shore, so the structure should ease us toward the climacteric.¹¹

Progression of the sermon is not due solely because of a quantitative reality—the dispensing of sermon points and verses of Scripture, be they many or few—but also a qualitative reality—the relation of sermon points to the sermon proposition.

The hearers must be able, with each sermon point, to establish an actual connection to, not just some affinity to, the sermon proposition. With the treatment of each sermon point the hearer should feel that the proposition has received an additional and real support.¹² Each sermon point, if it facilitates the progression of the sermon, must make a "genuine contribution," an actual connection to the sermon proposition. In order for this to happen, each point of the main structure must be one of whatever the plural noun of the proposition is. If the plural noun of a sermon proposition is "benefits" and there are four main points in the sermon, then each of the four main points must be a "benefit." The word "benefit" does not have to appear in the statement of the main points but there can be no doubt about the fact that each of the main point statements is indeed a benefit.

If a sermon point isn't related to the sermon proposition then it is a homiletical rabbit chase, or a sermonette that was preached concurrently with the actual sermon at hand. Progression of the sermon is made, then, as each sermon point bears a genuine connection with the sermon proposition so that the sermon point is not a tangent, a detour, a roadblock in the hearer's understanding of the sermon and the text from which the sermon is preached. Each sermon point must demonstrate unity to the sermon proposition or it cannot positively affect the progression of the sermon.

Adequate Depth of Treatment of Sermon Points

Progression of the sermon requires horizontal movement from the first point to the last point of the message. Yet, vertical movement must be made as well. Sufficient time must be spent on each sermon point to promote understanding, through advancement of thought, of each point in the sermon. A caution here must be given regarding the next two specific criteria for good sermon structure—advancement of thought, and substructure—as they relate and impact progression of the sermon. An elaborate investment of time spent on a sermon point in which a prodigious amount of content is covered "will tire and confuse rather than stimulate and clarify."[13] The expenditure of more time than should have been spent on content that never should have been covered in any given sermon will check sermon progression. Also, an extensive amount of substructure within a sermon point, so that the preacher gets stuck on any given point of sermon structure as he sinks lower and lower into many levels of substructure, will hamper sermon progression. The net effect of too much time spent on a sermon point explored with many levels of substructure may be only this—"no one will remember the sub points, and the sermon itself will get lost."[14] More importantly, they not only will be unable to process so much definitive treatment but they will not even care to do so. This means that sermon progression has suffered another devastating blow.

ADVANCEMENT OF THOUGHT

Just as unity of the sermon points is important for sermon progression, so is distinction of sermon points. Each sermon point must demonstrate that it is a distinct point, yet related to all the other points in this sermon. If a sermon point is not demonstrating its distinct contribution to the sermon proposition, then it is repeating, rehashing, insights of another or other points. Rehashing previously established instruction will not provide progression of a discussion. Therefore, every sermon point, though related to all other sermon points, must make a distinct contribution to the understanding of the passage, proposition, and sermon being preached. In other words, progression of the sermon (horizontal progression) and advancement of thought (vertical progression) operate simultaneously in an effective expository sermon. Yet, the progression of the sermon and the advancement of thought may be obtained independently from the other.

A superficial sermon may demonstrate good horizontal progress, moving clearly from one point to another throughout the sermon. However, because of the terse treatment of each point advancement of thought will be minimal. On the other hand, there may be a sermon that demonstrates tremendous advancement of thought in a point, or even points, of a sermon. However, because of a lack of relating the extensive material to the point to which the material is supposed to clarify and a lack of repeating the structure clearly from point to point throughout the exposition, the hearers may appreciate the detailed insights they have gleaned at various junctures but there will be a negligible impression that what they have heard was sermon.

Advancement of thought is established as each sermon point makes a distinct contribution to the understanding of the text and sermon being preached. Through advancement of thought a biblical text is understood, that is, a thorough understanding of a passage has been attained because what has been expounded was far more than that which was already known by most of the hearers or that which is rather obvious through a brief perusal of the text. Advancement of thought primarily has to do with interpreting and explaining the meaning of the text which, consequently, will clarify and corroborate the insight of the main points or the statements of theological principle. In a secondary sense, advancement of thought also provides an understanding of the truth of the text to the lives of those who hear the sermon, that is, what the text means to the hearers.

> We aren't just giving a lecture about a portion of Scripture; we're seeking to meet the needs of a church family collectively and of family members individually. Any preacher can make a tolerable outline of almost any passage and preach from it, but that would be "sermonizing" and not real exposition of the Word of God.[15]

Wiersbe's comments are extremely insightful. Having a good outline not only does not guarantee that expository preaching will occur, but the outline may guarantee that biblical exposition will not occur if the outline does not advance the thought of the text. Many times a sermon is evidence of the fact that the preacher was caught on the horns of a dilemma—should I preach the text or should I preach my outline? Most often the sermon evidences the fact that the preacher preaches his outline rather than expounding the text through the means of an outline.

Advancement of thought necessitates that each sermon point receives enough time and attention so that insight and understanding become a reality. This means that the preacher has as his purpose to explain the biblical text. The outline is a helpful means to dwell on the text in a way to bring understanding of the text to the hearers.

On the other end of the spectrum, for advancement of thought to occur the text must rise above a host of supporting material, biblical and non-biblical, so that the text is not crowded out by material designed to help the text be understood. The critical issue here is that the expositor must be careful not bury the sermon point through the means of a massive amount of material wielded for the purpose to clarify the point.

Examine the following outlines from James 1:5-8 again, this time giving attention to the various degrees of advancement of thought apparent for the sermon points as provided through the substructure which focuses the exposition on specific portions of the biblical text. Substructure will be considered later in this chapter, but presently notice how progression of the sermon and advancement of thought is possible through the substructure as opposed to instances where substructure is minimal or omitted.

Outline #1

I. In Order to mature as a believer in the midst of trials we need to pray wisely.

    A. The Greatest Deficiency Of Perfection (5a)

    B. The Greatest Source Of Enablement (5b)

    C. The Greatest Assurance Of Reception (5c)

II. In Order to mature as a believer in the midst of trials we need to pray sincerely.

    A. The Requirements For Sincerity In Prayer (6a)

    B. The Reason For Insincerity In Prayer (6b)

III. In Order to mature as a believer in the midst of trials we need to pray expectantly.

    A. The Sentence Of Unanswered Prayer (7)

    B. The Subject Of Unanswered Prayer (8)

Outline #2

I. Practical wisdom for the ordering of life is a common requirement of Christian Disciples.

    A. The Christian discovers that he has a new standard for the management of himself.

    B. But practical wisdom is needed for ordering the commonplace and every-day associations of life.

    C. And as the unexpected is "the thing that happens" even in the Christian life, practical wisdom is needed for rightly meeting the anxieties, trials, temptations, and calamities that come as surprises in every life.

II. Practical wisdom for the ordering of every-day life and relations is a Divine gift.

III. Practical wisdom for the ordering of life is obtained only on conditions.

Outline #3

I. A universal want. (5)

II. An abundant source of supply. (5)

III. An easy method of obtaining. (5)

IV. An indispensable requisite to success. (6–8)

Only in outline #1 is there an apparent blueprint for the progression of the sermon through the advancement of thought. Without verse citations or verse-portion citations enjoined with points of substructure, progression of the sermon and advancement of thought may occur during the preaching of the sermon but without directing the hearers to specific portions of the text and without the divisions of treatment for the main points clarified by the substructure, sermon progression and advancement of thought will not be as apparent as it could be.

Obstacles for Advancement of Thought

INFORMATION OVERLOAD

Information overload is a sure way to prevent a point from being understood well. If a sermon point suffers from information overload it will be like the ore-carrier, the Edmund Fitzgerald, which was filled with twenty-six thousand tons of iron ore and, when accosted by a strong storm over Lake Superior in November of 1975, sank of its own weight. An expository sermon which suffers from information overload will not only fail to advance thought productively but because of its tonnage is destined to sink.

For a sermon point not to sink but to stay afloat and actually advance the thought of the sermon point and, therefore, the text from which the sermon point was derived, the preacher must make the difficult decisions of allowing or preventing some material discovered in thorough study to be incorporated into the sermon. "Content dump is a chief mischiefmaker for the young preacher. Too much is dropped on the congregation. One of the great skills in preaching is the art of resisting the temptation to put it all in the sermon."[16]

No sermon point is capable of receiving both exhaustive treatment and marked advancement of thought at the same time. Thorough treatment is necessary for a sermon point to be advanced, but thorough treatment is not exhaustive treatment. Skinner warns of this excessive treatment as he writes:

> Expository preaching needs care that its sermonic thrust is not lost amid a welter of commentary. It is seldom possible to share the *entire* exegesis or exposition of a given passage in any one sermon, and at the same time, preach effectively. Essential selection will retain only what is of most value in achieving the aim intended, in the time allotted.[17]

Selection of material to be incorporated into the expository sermon will be based upon its ability to explain the passage so that it can be understood by the hearers. There is nothing more exasperating for the man in the pew than to be addressed in words and ideas he does not understand. It all goes over his head. As Spurgeon put it, "the Lord said 'Feed my sheep' not 'Feed my giraffes!'"[18]

Inclusion of Information with No Apparent Purpose or Pattern

David L. Larsen's comments are warranted as well as penetrating. "We need to be part of the diamond-cutting school of preaching. Some preachers are masters of incoherence, and their sermons flow like glue."[19] I believe he is correct in his assessment that "The human brain is programmed to seek patterns."[20] The patterning of a sermon, supplied by the main points and the sub points of sermon structure, must control the content or the subject-matter discussed within each point and/or sub point. If the content does not reflect the point or the sub point, the message is not only hard to follow but it gives the impression that the point or sub point is not critical. When the content amplifies the point or sub point, the point or sub point is not only understood but there is a sense of apparent purpose and significance for it in this sermon.[21]

A sermon point, just like a sermon, can suffer from a lack of progression and advancement of thought if there is no discernable pattern of treating smaller thought blocks in the attempt to understand a larger thought block. Just as it is beneficial for a sermon to have structure, it is equally beneficial for a sermon point to have substructure. Though not advocating main points or sub points in preaching, David Buttrick is correct in his assertion that, "Congregations are remarkably logical, and what they cannot associate, they may well dismiss."[22]

Advancement of thought is enhanced as each main point is developed by carefully articulated substructure. Preaching has languished in our culture's reaction against structure. Expository preaching, especially, thrives in the context of carefully weighed thought—main assertions of truth and smaller considerations that make a vital distinction to the main assertions of a text and sermon.

Good sermon structure will have discernable substructure. The substructure is an enabling element that helps the main structure to be understood and allows the text to be treated thoroughly.

CONSIDER THE FOLLOWING QUESTIONS

1. What kind of progression is made by horizontal progression in contrast with vertical progression?
2. What kind of advancement is made by horizontal progression in contrast with vertical progression?
3. How does a plural noun proposition help the hearers to track the progression of a sermon?
4. What are the inevitable results for the hearers of a sermon that lacks progression?
5. What causes horizontal progression to bog down?
6. How does the time spent on a sermon point become a factor in bogging down of sermon progression?
7. In what way does expository preaching present the possibility of a doubled discernment of progression?
8. What must characterize a sermon outline in order for it to accomplish sermonic progression?
9. What is meant by Stephen Olford's "key word" test and "clear thinking" test for a sermon outline?
10. What five benefits result from effective sermon progression?
11. What must the preacher steer clear of while preaching so not to frustrate his hearers?
12. By what analogy should the preaching of a sermon point be compared and what two analogies provide an inadequate perception?

13. Progression of a sermon is due to what two realities and how are these two realities to be understood?
14. What two cautions regarding advancement of thought and substructure must be heeded for the sake of sermonic progression?
15. How does horizontal and vertical progression operate simultaneously in an effective sermon?
16. How may sermon progression and advancement of thought be obtained independently from one another?
17. How is advancement of thought understood primarily, consequently, and secondarily?
18. How might a sermon outline guarantee that biblical exposition will not occur when it is used in preaching a sermon?
19. What is "the critical issue" that the expository preacher must be certain to do, and not do, regarding the outline and content he will employ in his exposition if advancement of thought is to occur?
20. What are two obstacles for advancement of thought in a sermon?
21. What is the destiny of a sermon marked by information overload and how is this avoided?
22. What is it that a sermon is incapable of receiving simultaneously?
23. What kind of treatment must not be confused with the thorough treatment which a text needs to receive in order for advancement of thought to occur?
24. What is David Buttrick's correct assertion regarding the value for a logical presentation?
25. Why will good sermon structure have discernable substructure?

ENDNOTES

1. Larsen, *Anatomy*, 72–73.
2. Chapell, *Christ-centered*, 136.
3. Spurgeon, *Lectures*, 77.
4. Olford and Olford, *Anointed*, 142.
5. Bridges, *Christian Ministry*, 204.
6. Olford and Olford, *Anointed*, 146.
7. Ibid., 147.
8. Larsen, *Anatomy*, 74.
9. Brown, *Art*, 108.
10. Shedd, *Homiletics*, 142.
11. Larsen, *Telling*, 67–68.
12. Shedd, *Homiletics*, 187.
13. Chapell, *Christ-centered*, 138.
14. Ibid., 138.
15. Wiersbe, *Dynamics*, 61–62.
16. Larsen, *Anatomy*, 77.
17. Skinner, *Teaching Ministry*, 171.
18. Wood, *Workshop*, 22.
19. Larsen, *Telling*, 102.
20. Ibid., 97.
21. Olford and Olford, *Anointed*, 209.
22. Buttrick, *Moves*, 71.

Words to Live and Preach By

Trusting in a Trustworthy God

*Trust in the Lord with all your heart, and do not lean on
your own understanding. In all your ways acknowledge Him,
and He will make your paths straight. Do not be wise in your own eyes;
fear the Lord and turn away from evil. It will be healing to your body,
and refreshment to your bones.*
PROVERBS 3:5–8

*Do not be afraid of sudden fear, nor of the onslaught of the wicked
when it comes; for the Lord will be your confidence,
and will keep your foot from being caught.*
PROVERBS 3:25–26

*I have directed you in the way of wisdom; I have led you
in upright paths. When you walk, your steps will not be impeded;
and if you run, you will not stumble.*
PROVERBS 4:11–12

*The way of the Lord is a stronghold to the upright, but ruin
to the workers of iniquity. The righteous will never be shaken,
but the wicked will not dwell in the land.*
PROVERBS 10:29–30

*In the fear of the Lord there is strong confidence, and his children
will have a refuge. The fear of the Lord is a fountain of life,
that one may avoid the snares of death.*
PROVERBS 14:26–27

Better is a little with the fear of the Lord,
than great treasure and turmoil with it.
PROVERBS 15:16

Commit your works to the Lord, and your plans will be established.
The Lord has made everything for its own purpose,
even the wicked for the day of destruction.
PROVERBS 16:3–4

The mind of man plans his way, but the Lord directs his steps.
PROVERBS 16:9

He who gives attention to the word shall find good,
and blessed is he who trusts in the Lord.
PROVERBS 16:20

The name of the Lord is a strong tower;
the righteous runs into it and is safe.
PROVERBS 18:10

The fear of the Lord leads to life,
so that one may sleep satisfied, untouched by evil.
PROVERBS 19:23

The fear of man brings a snare,
but he who trusts in the Lord will be exalted.
PROVERBS 29:25

9

Sermon Structure's Functional Means

SUBSTRUCTURE

Substructure as the Ties to the Biblical Text

MORE OFTEN THAN NOT, it is through the means of substructure that the expositor is allowed to be in the text, get with the text, and stay with the text while at the same time to preach a clear, unified sermon with insightful diversity. Expository preaching provides substantial advancement of thought by preaching the text, not preaching about the text, nor preaching from the text, but preaching the text which entails a thorough examination of the passage. Such thorough examination necessitates substructure to clarify and organize the insights brought out in the exposition of the passage. The issue at hand for the expository preacher is simply this—he must open up the Word of God and explain it! Expository preaching is all about God's Word, not therapeutic talk, political palaver, and moralistic drivel, all of which are but "sawdust for the soul!" An accurate, understanding of the biblical text is what the expositor is all about! Therefore, substructure is crucial.

It is at the point of textual engagement, where the details of the biblical text are examined, that the goals of preaching—to inform; to interest; and to persuade—begin to be accomplished in a decisive way. Augustine wrote that the interpreter and teacher of the Scriptures, the defender of the true faith and the vanquisher of error, must win over the antagonistic, rouse the apathetic, and make clear to those who are not conversant with the matter under discussion what they should expect. As listeners need information, there must be a presentation of the facts to make the matter under discussion more familiar. To clarify disputed issues there must be rational argument and deployment of evidence.[1]

The clarifying argumentation of evidence cannot take place without engaging the text and staying in the text in order to process the passage thoroughly. Yet the thorough examination of the text and the insight drawn out from the details of the passage must be managed in a way that is conducive to true understanding. As Augustine wisely inquired, "Who does not realize that a person who is not understood cannot be listened to either with pleasure or with obedience?"[2] When the sermon is the exposition of the substance of a biblical text, the sermon will quite naturally take on the form or the structure of the biblical text.[3] In other words, "The sap of the text should reach the farthest twig of the sermon."[4] The structure, specifically the substructure, reflecting the substance of the details of the passage help to provide the clarity needed to allow interest and persuasion to become realities.

John Wood is correct as he supports the need to have well-ordered structure in our preaching. There will always be people who appreciate the clarity of orderly thought demonstrated by main assertions and minor modification to the main assertions being presented. Vague, meandering thought has little to commend it. Wood states,

> We have a duty to our calling to uphold certain tried and tested standards in the pulpit. And we should recognize the fact that not *all* those who listen to us have succumbed to the thoughtless irrationalism of our disjointed age. The truth of God is meant to be clear and arresting.[5]

The substructure not only allows the expositor to stay in the text but it allows him to preach well. One must certainly lament a preacher who, as "an old man listening to a thirty-year-old tape of his younger self and agonizing over the discovery that then and now he has 'nothing to say.' This is the solemn possibility that should drive every preacher back to the Word of God."[6] It is the preaching of the Bible that is essential for true effectiveness in preaching.

Effective preaching, preaching which gets its substance and structure from the text, gets its unction from above since unction implies a vital insight into the truth.[7] The preacher's substructure is the conduit through which the preacher can channel the vital insights he has discovered in the biblical passage to those who hear him preach.

Just as a sermon proposition is understood fully through the means of the main structure of the sermon, so a main point is understood through the means of the substructure. The substructure establishes the meaning of the preacher's main structure, and more importantly, the meaning of the biblical text the preacher is expounding. I believe it is not possible to exaggerate the need that exists for thorough, effective exposition of the Bible. David L. Larsen is absolutely right in his assertion that,

> Harry Emerson Fosdick tragically led a previous generation away from biblical content. The "life-situation" preachers (such as Charles F. Kemp) followed and left millions starving spiritually. Now voices calling many to a similar crusade for "reaching people" in our time expose us to grave new danger.[8]

The needed response is not simply a changed focus upon the Bible as the center of attention. The renewed focus upon the Bible must result in the exposition of its contents—exposition that the hearers can track with and understand while a text is being micromanaged through the most careful scrutiny of the smallest details of the passage.

The statements of a sermon's main structure must be general in nature. The need for the statements of the main structure is to summarize the full meaning of details of a verse or several verses of Scripture. Through the means of the substructure of the sermon, the sermon moves from the more generalized thought of the main structure to the more detailed and specific thought which makes a tighter logical connection with specific areas of the preaching text.

> Summed up in a single word, the function of generals is to convey understanding. We may say that in a sermon the purpose of a generalization is to cause our hearer to understand some phase of reality. On the other hand, the function of particulars is to present concrete details of the phase of reality... Generalization interprets reality, comprehends it in large masses, while particularity evokes reality by means of concrete details.[9]

This movement of thought from the general to the more specific is an essential matter for preaching, especially expository preaching. Grady Davis wrote,

> Poor preaching may fall into either of two opposite faults. It may move too exclusively among particulars and never tie the particulars together into adequate generalizations. Conversely, it may consist too exclusively of generalities, not glittering generalities, just vague, fuzzy generalities—one general assertion after another, from which nothing stands out as more important than the rest.

> Good thinking moves in both directions. It usually begins with particulars and goes to generals, the process of induction. But good thought, especially when being communicated, never remains general for long. After it has generalized, it moves back again to particulars.[10]

Likewise, Haddon Robinson says, "Many sermons are like a bag of confetti broadcast over a congregation. They are a group of tidbits. They are not held together by any overriding generalizations. But more often, we have generalizations that are not tied down to life. *Good sermons go from that which is abstract to that which is concrete, from generalities to that which is specific.*" (Italics added)[11]

The substructure helps the preacher move from the more generally stated truth of the main point, to the more specific, varied detailed matters of the biblical text. Olford is correct as he writes, "A clear identifiable sense of movement can aid greatly in providing clarity. The more complex a message, generally speaking, the greater the need for clear movements to guide the listener through an expository sermon."[12]

It is the substructure of an outline where the detailed content of a text can be organized to provide progression of the sermon that allows for advancement of thought. "You can't say everything at the same time! There has to be a sequence, and the guiding principle for the sequence and movement of a message should be the truth-movement of the text."[13]

The Need for Stringent Textual Connection

Preaching for many years now has become an endeavor that is so disconnected to the Bible, or marginally connected to the Bible, that the most often quoted and revered definition of preaching is that spoken by Phillips Brooks in his 1877 Yale Lectures on preaching and subsequently recorded in his book entitled *On Preaching*. Brooks said preaching was "truth through personality." Actually the widest consideration of what Brooks spoke will not extricate him from a gross over-simplification of preaching.

> What, then, is preaching, of which we are to speak? It is not hard to find a definition. Preaching is the communication of truth by man to men. It has in it two essential elements, truth and personality. Neither of those can it spare and still be preaching ... And

preaching is the bringing of truth through personality. It must have both elements.[14]

I certainly can appreciate Brooks's two elements in preaching—truth and personality—and would not dispute the crucial nature that both have in preaching. But isn't preaching, at least expository preaching, quite a bit more than truth through personality? I believe it is and it must be! Peter Adam wrote concerning Brooks's definition of preaching, "But this is general enough to include the stand-up comic or a good actor!"[15] Personality through comedy or drama is not preaching. What then is required so that the combination of truth and personality will equate preaching in its fullest sense? Is it not personality and truth that is examined thoroughly, explained carefully, and understood clearly in its textual context and applied in its contemporary context that equates expository preaching, preaching in its fullest sense?

All preaching, which includes expository preaching, will include the personality of the preacher. However, expository preaching is preaching that explains a passage, not just the main truths found in a passage. Explaining a passage requires dealing with the totality of the text. This means then, that the substance of the text, though related to the main points derived from the text, will relate more directly to the more specific headings found under the main points. The main points provide general statements of theological principle. Understanding of a passage must begin with these foundational assertions. Substructure, because of the specific modifications they make to the main points, allows the main points, and therefore the passage, to be understood with greater clarity.

Substructure as the Predominant Preaching Points

It is through the means of the substructure that the preacher actually preaches expositionally, which is preaching with a high degree of textual scrutiny. It is through the means of the substructure that the text is actually dismantled for a thorough examination of its contents. Therefore, the "preaching points" are typically the points of the substructure rather than main structure. In expository preaching, each sub point is a biblical feature that supports a precise aspect of the main point. This means that sub points, which typically are the preaching points, are the crucial thought pegs that take the preacher and the hearers to the portion of the biblical text that supports the main point in a very specific way. "Sub points point to an aspect of the text that will substantiate or develop the premise behind the main point."[16] This requires the preacher to cite the precise portion of the text where the content of the passage can be discovered that supports the sub point, and thereby, developing an understanding of the sermonic main point as well as understanding the passage of Scripture being expounded. The exposition of a passage, most commonly, is unfolded sequentially in a point by point manner, both at the level of main structure and substructure.

A point of main structure certainly can be a preaching point if there are no sub points attending the main point. This does happen occasionally. However, it is usually the case that a main point, or a statement of theological principle, can be understood and validated only as the many small details of a text are treated. A preaching point is the point of textual engagement. Therefore, a preaching point, whether a point of main structure or substructure, must always be accompanied by a verse citation, or a verse-portion citation, that makes it clear to the hearers where the preaching point was derived from the text being expounded.

The Nature and Implementation of Sub points

One can preach in an expository fashion only as the text is being processed thoroughly. Therefore, a true expositor will be preaching most often by the tremendously significant means of substructure. Bryan Chapell provides some helpful clarifying statements regarding the nature and implementation of substructure in expository preaching. He suggests: sub points organize and develop the thought of the main point; not all points need sub points; there is no standard number of sub points which a point should have; the number of sub points does not have to be the same for each point; when sub points are used there should be more than one.[17]

Examples and Assessment of Substructure

A few examples of substructure might be helpful at this point. For the sake of continuity, let's look at the substructure of two outlines referred to above.

To Live As A Child of God You Must . . .

I. Pray Persistently for the Unique Necessities of Your Life

    A. The Limited Participants of Prayer (7–8)

    B. The True Character of Prayer

        1. It is persistent (7–8)

        2. It is intense (7–8)

    C. The Diversified Scope of Prayer

        1. Its unrestricted scope (7–8)

        2. Its implied scope (9–10)

    D. The Promised Effectiveness of Prayer (7–8)

II. Trust Unquestionably in the Perfect Faithfulness of Your God

    A. God's Faithfulness Demanded by His Character (9–11b)

    B. God's Faithfulness Demonstrated by His Gifts (11c)

III. Strive Exclusively for the Equitable Treatment of Your Neighbor

    A. Common Humanity Compels Equitable Treatment (12b, c)

    B. Basic Obedience to God's Word Requires Equitable Treatment (12d)

    C. God's Example Inspires Equitable Treatment (12a)

Several observations should be apparent regarding the substructure of this outline. First of all, the first main point has four sub points; the second main point has two sub points; and the third main point has three sub points. In regards to the actual preaching points of the outline, the first main point has six; the second main point has two; and the third has three. In the first main point, the second and third sub points are subdivided, yielding two preaching points for each of these points of substructure.

The first main point—To live as a child of God you must pray persistently for the unique necessities of your life—can be understood and validated only as verses 7–10 are explained, which addresses the participants of prayer, the character of prayer, the scope of prayer, and the effectiveness of prayer. Likewise, the second and third main points are understood through the more specific assertions reflected in the substructure, which require examination of specific portions of the text under scrutiny.

The second main point—To live as a child of God you must trust unquestionably in the perfect faithfulness of your God—can be understood and validated only as verses 9-11 are explained, which addresses the fact that God's faithfulness is demanded by his character and demonstrated by his gifts.

The third main point—To live as a child of God you must strive exclusively for the equitable treatment of your neighbor—can be understood and validated only as verse 12 is explained, which addresses the fact that equitable treatment of your neighbor is compelled by common humanity, required by the Word of God, and inspired by God's example. Though it is the main structure that must be understood and remembered, as the sermon is being preached and after the sermon has been preached, it is the substructure that allows these statements of theological principle to be comprehended fully and corroborated textually.

Substructure is especially helpful when the main structure has been highly generalized in order to establish the unity within a text of significant diversity. Notice how the substructure, which deals with specific concepts not even mentioned in the main structure, help to make sense of the main structure that is necessarily general in order to establish instruction regarding the broad concept of sin. Recall that the plural noun proposition of this sermon is: In this passage Jesus gives 3 correctives for common misperceptions regarding sin.

I. You Must Identify Sin as an Internal Disposition
　A. The Basic Understanding of the Law Regarding Murder (21)
　B. The General Ignorance of the Law Regarding Murder
　　1. Every act of sin has an attitudinal predecessor (22a)
　　2. Every act of sin has various manifestations
　　　a. apparent disregard (22b)
　　　b. obvious hostility (22c)

II. You Must Equate Sin against Man as Sin against God
　A. The Corruption of True Worship
　　1. Sin which I can consciously identify (23a)
　　2. Sin which has affected others (23b)
　B. The Correction for True Worship
　　1. Understanding that true worship is conditional (24a)
　　2. Understanding that true worship requires a sequence (24b)

III. You Must Act to Minimize the Consequences of Your Sin
   A. The Time for Taking Action (25a)
   B. The Purpose for Taking Action (25b)
   C. The Incentive for Taking Action (26)

In the first point, the internal disposition of sin is the broad concept that is to be understood. But the substructure, as well as the text, deals with sin much more specifically. Murder and anger are addressed. But when the far more specific treatment of physical murder and attitudinal murder—anger—are expounded, it is important to understand and relate these specific sins to the issue at hand, which is—sin must be identified as an internal disposition, not just an outward expression of wrongdoing.

It is through the use of substructure that the general nature of the statement of theological principle and the specific issues of the biblical text can receive a mutually beneficial treatment. The text of verse twenty-one deals with an Old Testament citation with which all were familiar, as well as, the understood consequences to be received for violating this portion of Old Testament Law. The exposition of this verse of the preaching passage is dealt with under the statement of substructure—the basic understanding of The Law regarding murder.

Verse twenty-two deals with the strong assertion of the Lord that anger is in fact a violation of the law pertaining to murder but they never understood neither the culpability of anger nor the consequences of anger. The second sub point—the general ignorance of the law regarding murder—is a crucial statement in order to understand what the Lord is pointing out in his instruction. To help clarify the assertion of this sub point, as well as, expound this verse, two points of sub substructure are used—"Every act of sin has an attitudinal predecessor" and "Every act of sin has various manifestations." The second sub sub point, dealing with various manifestations of sin, received further clarification and textual treatment through two points of smaller substructure—"apparent disregard" and "obvious hostility." The apparent disregard is borne out by a situation where one would address another by the term "Raca." The obvious hostility is reflected by one's addressing another by the term "You fool."

The correction Jesus provides for the common misperception regarding sin, in this instance the sin of murder, is that murder entails more than the taking of one's life physically but also entails murdering or assassinating one's character through disregard or hostility. The internal disposition of sin, anger, is the driving force behind murder—whether it is an attack on one's physical life or one's character. The main thrust of Christ's instruction, the corrective component for a common misperception regarding sin, is that sin must be identified as an internal disposition. And so it goes for the remaining points of this sermon and other sermons.

Substructure and Sermon Structure Quality

The main structure can be understood and validated, as well as the text examined and explained, most profitably through the use of substructure. Qualitative sermon structure will possess main structure and substructure. Expressing this in the terms of general versus specific components of thought, Grady Davis wrote:

> But if it is true that no good sermon can exist without adequate generalizations, it is equally true that no sermon can be good without particulars. Generals and particulars do not have the same function in communication. Each has its own separate function, and each is important. We cannot say that one is more important than the other. Each is indispensable in its place.[18]

The broader generalizations of the main structure develop the unity and progression of the sermon while the narrower specifications of the substructure develop the understanding of the points of main structure and the understanding of the text from which they were drawn.

Cautions Regarding Substructure

EXCESSIVE DIVISION

Typically, it is through substructure that there can be enough biblical insight perceived so as to make specific and meaningful application of the truth to the lives of the hearers. Most commonly, substructure is the place where preaching actually happens. However, as with anything, if it is carried too far it will no longer be of any service or value. If substructure is excessively developed then preaching will be scuttled and confusion will take over. Expository preaching and textual understanding cannot thrive when there is a sermon structure that is divided too finely. As one man appropriately remarked,

> Some ministers "do with their texts, as the Levite with his concubine–cut, and carve it into so many several pieces." Some sermons exhibit a body, owing to the multitude of divisions and sub-divisions, is wholly unsuited to the purposes of persuasive discourse. They are good illustrations of the infinite divisibility of matter, but produce no conviction in the popular mind. This fault will be avoided, if the sermonizer asks, in respect to each and every head or division: "Does this proposed head really tend to prove the proposition, and does it afford a positively new item of proof, that is not contained in any other head?"[19]

The same author wisely commented upon the amount of divisions and subdivisions a sermon should have. Though he suggested that, "no stiff rule can be laid down" in reference to number, the maxim is, "Amplify, rather than multiply." By this he meant,

> The preacher should not leave a point until he has made the common mind feel the whole sum of its force. The instant he has done this, he should drop it. It is not enough to barely state a point. It should be fully unfolded. It should revolve in the preacher's mind, and in the hearer's mind, until all that is latent in it has been elicited.[20]

An additional, yet similar, caution was sounded,

> It is best to limit the number of subdivisions lest the outline tend to make the text seem more complex than it really is. The object ought to be to simplify the structure so as to provide to every listener an insight into the skeleton and linking sinews of the text.[21]

Qualitative sermon structure is achieved through the means of substructure that is wisely limited by the preacher. It is at the level of substructure that a preacher can get too detailed, in the notes he takes with him to the pulpit (or in his memory), and in the pulpit where he seeks to communicate a structure that it too complicated. In the preparation of an outline it is well for each man to prepare only as much as he can really command and use, without too much reference to it while he is in the act of speaking. The preacher, who prepares a very elaborate outline, is handicapped from the start.[22]

An elaborate outline, with finely divided and highly-refined sub points, can become the preacher's pride parade as he seeks to showcase and draw attention to his well-synthesized outline instead of using the outline as a means to bring light to God's Word. The man who has the unique ability to synthesize the details of a text into an outline of sophisticated main and substructure, especially, runs a very real risk of crafting a guide to the text that will hoard attention to itself to the extent that it obfuscates rather than clarifies the text. Warren Wiersbe's counsel and comments regarding sermon outlines are worthy of consideration and personal application.

> By all means organize the message so you know where you're going and how to get there. But don't preach the outline. Use it as a means of conveying God's truth to the minds and hearts of the listeners. The "points" of an outline should be like "pegs" on which people can hang God's truth, or, to change the analogy, like "picture frames" into which they can put the images that reveal God's truth. An outline lets us maintain order, progress, and purpose in the message; but an outline isn't a message.
>
> I get the impression from hearing some preachers that they want me to notice the outline rather than the message, the "package" rather than the contents of the package. They're proud of the outline and keep referring to it. "Look at my great outline! Notice especially my clever alliteration!" But this only distracts from the message itself. Preaching isn't reading a road map; it's taking people on a journey.[23]

Through the use of extensive substructure the sermon outline can become the outstanding accomplishment of the preacher, so that it may be sadly but truthfully said—he created an incredible outline, but his exposition of the text was not nearly so incredible because the outline got in the way of the text to the point that the text had to remain in the shadow of the outline. This must not happen.

When the substructure begins to dominate the sermon the substructure is overemphasized. A biblical text that is understood well will be divided into substructure which consists of supporting details which relate to and develop the large assertions of a passage. But just because sub points can be discovered and organized does not mean they have the right to be used in an adverse way in a message. Substructure will never be used in an inappropriate manner if the following "eight musts of substructure" are honored. Sub points must develop, not dominate thought.

Sub points must support, not supplant the main assertions. Sub points must drive the hearers back to the text, not draw attention to themselves. Sub points must be used to explain the passage, not to exalt the preacher. Sub points must clarify the message, not cloud or confuse the message. Sub points must empower, not enfeeble a sermon. Sub points must be admired for their profitability in a sermon, not for their presence in a sermon. Sub points must be valued for the insight they instill, not for the attention they attract. If the sub points do not enhance the exposition of the text, then the sub points must be eliminated from the expository sermon outline.

Insufficient Division

Without sufficient main structure and substructure, in particular, the insights divulged in expository preaching can become a rather amorphous and copious amount of data. The insights cannot be affixed to any sufficiently specific point being made about the text. The preacher seems to be lost in a protracted discussion of something the hearers cannot pinpoint precisely. His discussion will become needlessly belabored in the mind of the hearers since they cannot comprehend how the information being discussed advances the thought and provides progression for the sermon. "Information, unless it is under the regulation and guidance of a strongly methodizing ability, and true rhetorical talent, leads to prolixity as inevitably as sheer ignorance."[24]

The substructure, because it deals with the details and specifics of a biblical text, has a unique potential to bring about the best treatment of the subject-matter of the passage. Again, Grady Davis is insightful as he writes:

> If the subject is central to the text, it will illuminate the details of the passage and will in turn be illuminated by them, resulting in a true exposition of the text.
>
> Often the beginner, by main force and diligent labor, blows up his idea into an artificial shape, when all the time the lines of its natural expansion lie there unnoticed in the text. This is misdirected effort, zeal not according to knowledge.[25]

Undoubtedly this would be a common trait of one's preaching in the early years but it is also true of men who have preached for decades but are not expositors of the Bible. Their consistent practice is not that of thoroughly processing a text but rather the practice of garnering a few ideas from the text to say many things that have little or nothing to do with the passage which they so casually and carelessly treat. The text with all of its unlocked potential, and the substructure which would have served as an insightful guide to unleash the specific and fitting treatment the subject had a right to receive, is ignored. The congregation then must be edified regarding the subject-matter of the text, not according to the God-given instruction of the textual data but according to that which the preacher decided to offer them in lieu of the text.

Appropriate Division of Substructure

C. J. Ellicott says it is impossible to lay too much stress on the orderly organization of a sermon. He suggests that sermons might be put into two distinct classes—"vertebrate and molluscous." About these two types of sermons he writes:

> Sermons of the molluscous kind produce little impression on a congregation; for this simple reason that it is impossible to attend to them. For purposes of real instruction, sermons must be vertebrate. When you see and admire a horse moving vigorously and easily along the road, you do not see his bones and muscles; but you know that if the bones and muscles were not there and fitted in a very orderly manner, there would be nothing to admire. So in a good sermon there must be a skeleton, though the skeleton need not be seen. By all means make use even of abundant drapery, if you please; but be sure that there is a true skeleton underneath. The richest drapery placed upon a mere stick is only a scarecrow.[26]

The use of substructure to provide clear understanding to the textual scrutiny afforded by true expository preaching is important for the biblical expositor. Most importantly the substructure will be the means to help hearers to grasp the meaning of the passage being expounded.

Bible expositor G. Campbell Morgan affirmed the role of the sermon outline to provide the hearers, even hearers who are already well-versed and knowledgeable of Scripture, with definitive insight regarding a text being expounded. It was the view of Morgan that,

> Large numbers of persons who have been accustomed to read the Bible, and to listen to preaching all their lives, have the loosest possible acquaintance with the details of Biblical history, and their concepts of doctrinal truth are extremely vague. They are grateful to any man who will make their knowledge of the exter-

nal facts of Holy Scripture definite, and who will give sharpness and form to the outlines of their conceptions of truth.²⁷

The substructure is necessary to provide the only development that should be forthcoming in an expository sermon, that which is required by the passage being expounded by virtue of the details contained in the text.

Only the expository preacher can provide the necessary development and expansion of a biblical text through the use of substructure that brings clarity to the various components of a passage. Donald Miller advocates that sermon should embody the truest and most basic conception of "development" as defined by Webster's New International Dictionary—"An expansion by means of which all the elements contained in a given concept are made explicit."²⁸ In applying this definition to preaching Miller writes:

> In the case of a sermon, the "given concept" should be the theme of the portion of Scripture on which it is based. To develop this concept is to take the various elements of which it is composed, arrange them clearly and simply, and set them forth in such a way that the hearer has a grasp of this particular emphasis of scripture, and no other. The theme of the sermon should be the theme of the scripture on which it is based. This theme should be developed in harmony, either directly or indirectly, with the development of the passage in the biblical record. This would not seem to be asking too much from men whose task it is to be expositors of the Bible.²⁹

Insisting that the structure of an expository sermon will of necessity convey the development of the passage from which it is drawn, if the sermon is truly expository, Miller contends that,

> The development of thought in a biblical passage is one of the most effective safeguards against the excesses of allowing the preacher's imagination free play. It does not stifle imagination, but bridles it so that its course is directed on the Bible's highway of thought rather than on the byways of the preacher's cleverness.³⁰

Appropriate division of a sermon, evidenced through main and substructure, is helpful to distill the major assertions of the passage from the supporting material of the passage which serve to validate the major assertions as the main thrusts of the passage. The structure helps those who hear the sermon keep track of the development of the passage the expositor desires to bring out in the process of biblical exposition. Good sermon structure is indeed an ally to the expositor and a friend to the hearers of expository sermons.

The following sermon[31] from James 1:5 by the Puritan preacher, Thomas Manton, demonstrates common traits of Puritan preaching—many points from a brief verse of Scripture resulting in thorough scrutiny of the text, and a propensity for meticulous division of thought demonstrated by substructure. Fortunately, in this instance, the sermon consisting of twelve main points only had substructure in three of the main points. And of the three points containing substructure, only one had substructure that was divided extensively.

I. All Men Are Concluded under the Estate of Lacking.

II. Want and Indigence Put Us upon Prayer, and Our Address to Heaven Begin at the Sense of Our Own Needs.

III. There Is Need of Great Wisdom for the Right Managing of Afflictions.

    A. To discern of God's end in it, to pick out the language and meaning of the dispensation.

    B. To know the nature of the affliction, whether it be to fan or to destroy; how it is intended for our good; and what uses and benefits we may make of it.

    C. To find out your own duty; to know the things of obedience in the day of them.

    D. To moderate the violences of our own passions.

        1. Get wisdom if you would get patience.

        2. To confute the world's censure.

        3. Would ye be accounted wise? Show it by the patience and calmness of your spirits.

IV. In All Our Wants We Must Immediately Repair to God.

V. More Particularly Observe, Wisdom Must Be Sought from God.

VI. God Will Have Everything Fetched Out by Prayer.

VII. Asking Yieldeth A Remedy for the Greatest Wants.

VIII. God's Dispensations to the Creatures Are Carried in the Way of a Gift.

IX. The Proposals of God's Grace Are Very General and Universal.

X. God's Gifts Are Free and Liberal.

   A. Do not straiten God in your thoughts.

   B. Let us imitate our Heavenly Father, and give liberally—with a free and native bounty; give simply, not with a double mind.

XI. Men Are Apt to Upbraid but not God.

   A. God gives in quite another manner than man doth.

   B. God does not reproach his people with the frequency of their addresses to him for mercy, and is never weary doing them good.

XII. One Asking Will Prevail with God.

Nineteen preaching points were advanced in this sermon from one single verse of Scripture. The question is this—did all of these preaching points come from this one verse? If so, it would be helpful to see from where, in the verse, they were drawn. If they were all drawn from the text then appropriate division might stand a chance of being a reality. If, however, the preaching points cannot be tied to the text then excessive and inappropriate division would be the inescapable reality.

THE LAWS OF SERMON STRUCTURE

To summarize our discussion of sermon structure let's consider some laws of putting an outline together. These laws represent a quick checklist of criteria designed to incorporate a quality control devise for arranging and delivering sermon structure. Though the purpose of this book is not directed toward the delivery of the sermon, a few of the laws of sermon structure do not relate to the formulation of the sermon structure but rather the presentation of the structure in the delivery of the sermon. The laws which are related to delivery rather than arrangement will be indicated by an asterisk.

   1. There must be three components of a sermon proposition: a subject; a complement; and a number. There may be four components of a sermon proposition if the plural noun is

only a part of the complement rather than the essence of the complement.
2. There must be equivalence between the sermon proposition and the main structure of the sermon outline.
3. There must be a tight, logical connection between the proposition and the main structure of the sermon outline.
4. The main structure of the sermon outline must synthesize the sermon in construction and delivery.
5. There must be two or more points in the main structure of the sermon outline.
6. The main structure of the sermon must be in full sentence form: either interrogative or declarative statements.
7. The main structure must be cast in the present tense, or occasionally the future tense.
8. The main structure must consist of statements of theological principle.
9. There must be a "peak" in each point of the sermon outline.*
10. The points of main structure must provide distinction in their unity.
11. There must be no manipulation of the main structure to provide balance of time between the points of the sermon.*
12. The sequence of the main structure is determined by the purpose for, or the progression of, the sermon.
13. There must be no loss of meaning or accuracy in wording the main structure or substructure by attempting to secure symmetry or alliteration.
14. The preaching points, whether main structure or substructure, must be documented by verse, or verse portion, citation.
15. The substructure of the sermon outline must provide analysis of the points of the main structure.
16. There must be a plurality in order to form an identifiable level of substructure. In other words: for every "A" there must be a "B"; for every "1" there must be a "2"; for every "a" there must

be a "b"; for every "1)" there must be a "2)"; for every "a)" there must be a "b)"; for every "(1)" there must be a "(2)"; for every "(a)" there must be a "(b)".

17. There must be a greater indention for each successive level of substructure.

I.
   A.
      1.
      2.
         a.
         b.
            1)
            2)
               a)
               b)
                  (1)
                  (2)
                  (3)
                  (4)
   B.
      1.
      2.
II.
   A.
   B.

18. The predominant transition to a subsequent point of main structure is the repetition of the preceding points of the main structure.*

19. The transitional statement to a subsequent point of main structure must contain the complement of the sermon proposition.*

Good organization, which is the result of careful preparation and based upon clear thinking, is invaluable for preaching. Warren Wiersbe recounts:

> One of the greatest encouragements I ever received in my years of preaching came from a lad about ten years old who approached

me after a worship service, looked up at me, and said, "I understood every word you said." It was like getting the Pulitzer prize. We preach to be understood, and that involves clear thinking, careful preparation, and organization—and the kind of delivery that makes people want to listen.[32]

Good sermon structure is obtainable but it is not obtained easily. Hard work and clear thinking are necessary in order to produce sermon outlines that will be serviceable to those who hear sermons and to those who preach them.

In the effort to provide concrete understanding of the kind of sermon structure which has been advocated in this book, notice how Bible expositor Dr. David Jeremiah, Pastor of the Shadow Mountain Community Church in El Cajon, California exemplifies so well the instruction provided in the previous chapters. Five sermon outlines used by Dr. Jeremiah are provided below. These sermons were aired on Dr. Jeremiah's radio ministry "Turning Point." Dr. Jeremiah is an excellent expository preacher and is consistently outstanding in the sermon structure he uses in his preaching. Two of the sermon outlines below are from sermons in which a biblical topic was being expounded. Therefore, selected verses were used as the basis for the preaching points and these selected verses were not included below. Verse citation is provided for the preaching points in the examples below when the sermon was an exposition of a biblical text.

Before It's Too Late, Ecclesiastes 11–12

I.   Life Is Uncertain, Embrace It! (11:1-6)

   A.   Diversify your investments (11:1-2)

   B.   Be diligent in your involvement (11:3-6)

II. Life Is Short, Enjoy It! (11:7—12:7)

   A.   Experience each day totally (11:7-8)

   B.   Enjoy your youth thoroughly (11:9-10)

   C.   Express your faith thoughtfully (12:1-2)

   D.   Embrace your aging thankfully (12:3-7)

III. Life Is Mysterious, Examine It! (12:9-12)

   A.   Wisdom comes through instruction (12:9)

    B. Wisdom comes through insight (12:10)

    C. Wisdom comes through inspiration (12:11-12)

IV. Life Is Obedience, Express It! (12:13-14)

Love's Power over Envy, Selected Passages

I. Jealousy and Envy Travel in Possession Circles

II. Jealousy and Envy Travel in Power Circles

III. Jealousy and Envy Travel in Performing Circles

IV. Jealousy and Envy Travel in Professional Circles

V. Jealousy and Envy Travel in Paternal Circles

A Door of Hope, Psalms 42-43

I. Hope Is Most Alive When Everything Seems Hopeless (42:3-7, 9-11, 43:4, 6)

II. Hope for the Future Is Built on the Past (42:4, 6)

III. Hope Sings When It Feels Like Crying (42:4, 5, 8, 11, 43:5)

When Strings Turn to Wings, Selected Passages

I. Perspective Is Everything

II. Postponed Response Brings Parental Regrets

III. Pain Is a Part of the Family Process

IV. Prayer Is the Greatest Thing You Can Do

V. Parents Need to Take the Initiative in Staying Close

VI. Plan for Your Children to Return

VII. Prioritize Your Own Lives Again

VIII. Parenting Really Is Forever

What the Bible Teaches about Prayer, Matthew 6:9-14

I. Praise God First in Your Praying (6:9)

II. Then Bring Your Priorities before Him (6:10)

III. Then Ask God for Your Provisions (6:11)

IV. Then Deal with Your Personal Relationship Challenges (6:12, 14)

V. Then Ask God for Protection (6:13)

A preacher's understanding of the content of a sermon will affect his disposition toward the content of that sermon. His disposition toward the content of his sermon will impact his expression of that content which will affect the reception of that content by his hearers. With so much at stake, it may truly be a preacher's most valuable sacrifice to produce outlines that help hearers understand God's Word through the preaching of his sermons. If one can do this, not occasionally, but consistently throughout the years of one's preaching then the toil and diligence of one's efforts will not be in vain. How blessed is the man who personally experiences that which is available for all who seek to minister to others through the spoken word, just as the Scripture itself affirms—"The heart of the wise teaches his mouth, and adds persuasiveness to his lips" and "A man will be satisfied with good by the fruit of his words, and the deeds of a man's hands will return to him."

To see how all of the elements of sermon structure are evaluated in a sermon, refer to the sermon evaluation sheet at the end of this chapter.

CONSIDER THE FOLLOWING QUESTIONS

1. What is it that substructure, as a means, allows for an expository preacher and what is it that expository preaching provides through substructure?

2. What are the goals of preaching and how are they begun to be accomplished in a decisive way?

3. Augustine's conviction that "a person who is not understood cannot be listened to with pleasure or with obedience" prioritizes what two requirements needed to produce "the clarifying argument of evidence"?

4. What quotation clarifies the sought after reality that when the sermon is the exposition of the substance of a biblical text, the sermon will quite naturally take on the form or the structure of the biblical text?

5. How is the substructure's function in relation to the main structure similar to the main structure's function in relation to the sermon proposition?

6. What does the much needed renewed focus on the Bible require and how is this facilitated by the means of substructure?

7. How does Grady Davis depict poor preaching and what is the corrective measure he suggests?
8. What is accomplished by means of a sermon's substructure and how does this relate to Haddon Robinson's assessment of what constitutes "good sermons"?
9. What needs to be added to Phillips Brooks's definition of preaching in order to equate expository preaching, preaching in its fullest sense?
10. How is a preaching point defined and what level of sermon structure typically constitutes a preaching point and why is this so?
11. What must a preacher make sure accompanies each preaching point, whether a point of main structure or substructure, and why is this so?
12. Beyond the function to "organize and develop the thought of the main point," what four clarifications does Bryan Chapell provide for substructure?
13. What is it that qualitative sermon structure possesses and why is this so?
14. What do the main structure's broader generalizations develop as contrasted to the development of the substructure's narrower specifications?
15. What two cautions must be honored when incorporating substructure?
16. What condition prevents expository preaching and textual understanding from thriving?
17. What maxim provides wise counsel in reference to the number and treatment of main structure and substructure?
18. What may cause a preacher to produce an elaborate outline containing finely divided substructure?
19. What is the content of Warren Wiersbe's worthy counsel regarding sermon outlines?
20. What are the "eight musts of substructure" that, if honored, will prevent sub points from being used in an inappropriate manner?

21. What are the unproductive results for the hearer of a sermon without sufficient structure, especially substructure?

22. What is the common trait and consistent practice of preachers in their early years of preaching as well as preachers who have preached for many years but are not Bible expositors?

23. What is the basis of Donald Miller's contention that developing the thoughts of the text are effective "safeguards" and "bridles" for a preacher?

24. How is good sermon structure, evidenced by appropriate division of main and substructure, "an ally to the expositor and a friend to the hearers of expository sermons"?

I. INVENTION, ARRANGEMENT
A. Introduction .... Grade: _____/15
    Gets Attention .... _____/1
    Secures Interest .... _____/4
    Indicates Purpose of the sermon .... _____/2
    Orientation to subject .... _____/1
    Summarization of Biblical context .... _____/2
    Connection to previous message .... _____/1
    Proposition stated clearly .... _____/1
    Proposition synthesized fully .... _____/1
    Proposition repeated .... _____/1
    Transition from proposition to first point .... _____/1
    Length appropriate, necessary .... _____/0

B. Body
    Skeleton .... Grade: _____/15
        Main points principlized fully, clearly .... _____/2
        Main points stated clearly .... _____/2
        Main points incorporating the proposition .... _____/2
        Main points expressed in complete sentences .... _____/2
        Subordinate structure related to preaching text .... _____/2
        Supporting material related to main/sub points .... _____/1
        Transitions between points clear .... _____/1
        Structure repeated effectively .... _____/3
    Flesh and Muscles .... Grade: _____/18
        Lexical Description effective .... _____/3
        Grammatical description effective .... _____/3
        Syntactical description supportive .... _____/3
        Theological description effective .... _____/3
        Theological corroboration persuasive .... _____/3
        Attention directed to words of passage/cr. refs .... _____/3
    Vital Organs .... Grade: _____/20
        Illustrations appropriate, effective .... _____/8
        Application pointed, forceful .... _____/8
        Dialogue/Argumentation clear, cogent .... _____/4

C. Conclusion .... Grade: _____/15
    Transition to conclusion clear .... _____/1
    Synopsis of the structure of the sermon .... _____/2
    Closing appeals clear, forceful .... _____/5
        (Obedience encouraged, disobedience rebuked)
    Clenching element of persuasion .... _____/3
    Purpose of the sermon fulfilled .... _____/1
    Appeal to unbelievers incorporated .... _____/3
    Length appropriate, necessary .... _____/0

D. Sermon Emphasis (Intro, Illust, Appl, Concl) .... Grade: _____/4

II. DELIVERY, STYLE, MEMORY
A. Oral Presentation .... Grade: _____/2
    Varied intensity .... _____/1
    Varied projection .... _____/1
    Natural, conversational voice quality .... _____/0
    Varied pitch .... _____/0
    Varied rate .... _____/0
    Appropriate, meaningful pauses .... _____/0

B. Physical Presentation .... Grade: _____/2
    Gestures appropriate, natural .... _____/0
    Eye contact varied, purposeful .... _____/2
    Mannerisms non-distracting .... _____/0
    Bodily animation natural, energetic .... _____/0
    Facial expressions engaging .... _____/0

C. Rational Presentation .... Grade: _____/3
    Progression of message adequate .... _____/1
    Advancement of message adequate .... _____/1
    Familiarity with content of message obvious .... _____/1
    Notes referred to briefly .... _____/0
    Notes handled inconspicuously .... _____/0

D. Pathos .... Grade: _____/3
    Passion (message processed through heart) .... _____/3
    Enthusiasm concerning the message .... _____/0
    Tone of the message corresponding to content .... _____/0
    Life, vitality .... _____/0

E. Language .... Grade: _____/3
    Concrete, specific language .... _____/0
    Interesting expression, sense appeal .... _____/2
    Direct address .... _____/1
    Correct vocabulary .... _____/0
    Correct grammar .... _____/0
    Correct pronunciation .... _____/0

Grade Total _____

Estimated Error Due To Grader Subjectivity (-3, -2, -1, 0, 1, 2, 3)
Final Grade _____

ENDNOTES

1. Augustine, *On Christian Teaching*, 103–4.
2. Ibid., 141.
3. Pierson, *Divine Art*, 108.
4. Massey, *Designing*, 32.
5. Wood, *Workshop*, 13.
6. Larsen, *Telling*, 110.
7. Pierson, *Divine Art*, 108.
8. Larsen, *Telling*, 111.
9. Davis, *Design*, 246.
10. Ibid., 247.
11. This quotation was taken from a series of lectures given by Haddon Robinson at Conservative Baptist Theological Seminary. Unfortunately, I failed to record in my notes such pertinent particulars as the date and title of the lecture.
12. Olford and Olford, *Anointed*, 142.
13. Ibid., 142.
14. Brooks, *On Preaching*, 5.
15. Adam, *Speaking*, 59.
16. Chapell, *Christ-centered*, 151.
17. Ibid., 152.
18. Davis, *Design*, 246.
19. Shedd, *Homiletics*, 188–89.
20. Ibid., 189–90.
21. Kaiser Jr., *Exegetical*, 159.
22. Brown, *Art*, 89.
23. Wiersbe, *Imagination*, 315.
24. Shedd, 141.
25. Davis, *Design*, 80–81.
26. Ellicott, *Homiletical*, 61.
27. Morgan, *Preaching*, 83–84.
28. Miller, *Way*, 110.
29. Ibid., 110–11.
30. Ibid., 103.
31. Manton, "Discipline," 44–45.
32. Wiersbe, *Dynamics*, 68.

Bibliography

Abbott, Lyman. *The Christian Ministry*. Boston: Houghton, Mifflin, 1905.
Adam, Peter. *Speaking God's Word*. Downer's Grove, Illinois: InterVarsity, 1996.
Alexander, J. W. *Thoughts on Preaching*. Carlisle, Pennsylvania: Banner of Truth, reprint, 1988.
Allen, Ronald J. and Bartholomew, Gilbert L. *Preaching Verse by Verse*. Louisville, Kentucky: Westminster John Knox, 2000.
Awbrey, Ben. *How Effective Sermons Begin*. Ross-shire, Scotland, UK: Christian Focus, 2008.
Baxter, Richard. *The Reformed Pastor*. Carlisle, Pennsylvania: Banner of Truth, reprint, 1979.
Beecher, Henry Ward. *Yale Lectures on Preaching: Three Volumes in One*. Boston: Pilgrim Press, n.d.
Behrends, A. J. F. *The Philosophy of Preaching*. New York: Charles Scribner's Sons, 1890.
Bickel, R. Bruce. *Light and Heat: The Puritan View of the Pulpit*. Morgan, PA: Soli Deo Gloria, 1999.
Blackwood, Andrew W. *Expository Preaching for Today*. Grand Rapids: Baker, 1980.
———. *The Fine Art of Preaching*. Grand Rapids: Baker, 1976.
———. *The Preparation of Sermons*. New York: Abingdon, 1948.
Borgman, Brian. *My Heart for Thy Cause*. Ross-shire, Great Britian: Christian Focus, 2002.
Brastow, Lewis O. *The Modern Pulpit: A Study of Homiletic Sources and Characteristics*. New York: Hodder & Stoughton, 1906.
Bridges, Charles. *The Christian Ministry*. Carlisle, Pennsylvania: Banner of Truth, reprint, 1991.
Broadus, John A. *A Treatise on the Preparation and Delivery of Sermons*. New York: A. C. Armstrong and Son, twentieth ed., 1893.
Brooks, Phillips. *On Preaching*. New York: Seabury Press, reprint, 1964.
Brown, Charles Reynolds. *The Art of Preaching*. New York: Macmillan, 1932.
Bryson, Harold T., and Taylor, James C. *Building Sermons to Meet People's Needs*. Nashville: Broadman, 1980.
Burrell, David James, *The Sermon: Its Construction and Delivery*. New York: Revell, 1913.
Buttrick, David. *Homiletic Moves and Structures*. Philadelphia: Fortress, paperback edition—second printing, 1988.
Carrick, John. *The Imperative of Preaching*. Carlisle, Pennsylvania: Banner of Truth, 2002.
Chapell, Bryan. *Christ-centered Preaching*. Grand Rapids: Baker, 1994.
Clowney, Edmund P. *Preaching and Biblical Theology*. Phillipsburg, New Jersey: Presbyterian and Reformed, 1979.
Cox, James W., editor, and Cox, Kenneth M., associate editor. *Best Sermons 1*. San Francisco: Harper & Row, 1988.

Cox, James W. *Preaching*. San Francisco: Harper, 1985.
Craddock, Fred B. *Overhearing the Gospel*. Nashville: Abingdon, 1978.
Daane, James. *Preaching With Confidence*. Grand Rapids: Eerdmans, 1980.
Dabney, Robert L. *Sacred Rhetoric*. Chatham, Great Britain: W & J Mackay, 1870. Reprint edition, Carlisle, Pennsylvania: Banner of Truth, 1979.
Dargan, Edwin Charles. *The Art of Preaching in the Light of Its History*. Nashville: The Sunday School Board of the Southern Baptist Convention, 1922.
Davies, George Jennings. *Papers on Preaching*. London: George Bell and Sons, third edition, 1883.
Davis, Henry Grady. *Design for Preaching*. Philadelphia: Fortress, 1958.
Demaray, Donald E. *Proclaiming the Truth*. Grand Rapids: Baker, 1979.
Elliott, Mark Barger. *Creative Styles of Preaching*. Louisville, Kentucky: Westminster John Knox, 2000.
Ellicott, C. J. *Homiletical and Pastoral Lectures*. New York: A. C. Armstrong & Son, 1880.
Emery, Donald W. *Sentence Analysis*. Chicago: Holt, Rinehart and Winston, 1961.
Etter, John W. *The Preacher and His Sermon: a Treatise on Homiletics*. Dayton, Ohio: United Brethren Publishing House, 1885.
Evans, William. *How to Prepare Sermons and Gospel Addresses*. Chicago: Moody, 1913.
Exell, Joseph S., editor. *The Biblical Illustrator*, Vol. 22. Grand Rapids: Baker, third printing, 1977.
Fant, Jr., Clyde E., and Pinson, Jr., William M. *20 Centuries of Great Preaching*, Volume Two. Waco: Word, 1971.
Fenelon, Francois. *Dialogues on Eloquence*. Translated by Wilbur Samuel Howell. Princeton, New Jersey: Princeton University Press, 1951.
Genung, John F. *Outlines of Rhetoric*. Boston: Ginn & Company, 1903.
Gibbs, Alfred P. *The Preacher and His Preaching*. Kansas City, Kansas: Walterick, 1939.
Greidanus, Sidney. *The Modern Preacher and the Ancient Text*. Grand Rapids: Eerdmans, 1988.
Hall, E. Eugene and Heflin, James L. *Proclaim the Word*. Nashville: Broadman, 1985.
Halvorson, Arndt L. *Authentic Preaching*. Minneapolis: Augsburg, 1982.
Hamilton, Donald L. *Homiletical Handbook*. Nashville: Broadman, 1992.
Hendricks, Howard G. *Say it with Love*. Wheaton, IL: Victor, 1973.
———. *Teaching to Change Lives*. Portland, OR: Multnomah, 1987.
Holland, Withrow T. *The Structure of Sermons*. Orlando, Florida: LeRoi, 1974.
Hoppin, James M. *Homiletics*. New York: Funk & Wagnalls, 1883.
Jones, Owen. *Some of the Great Preachers of Whales*. London: Tentmaker, third printing, 1997.
Jowett, J. H. *The Preacher: His Life and Work*. New York and London: Harper & Brothers, 1912.
Kantenwein, Lee L. *Diagrammatical Analysis*. Winona Lake, IN: BMH Books, 1979.
Kaiser, Walter C., Jr. *Toward an Exegetical Theology: Biblical Exegesis for Preaching and Teaching*. Grand Rapids: Baker, 1981.
Kerr, Hugh Thomson. *Preaching in the Early Church*. New York: Revell, 1942.
Kidder, Daniel P. *A Treatise on Homiletics, Designed to Illustrate the True Theory and Practice of Preaching the Gospel*. London: Dickinson & Higham, 1873.
Killinger, John. *Fundamentals of Preaching*. Minneapolis: Fortress, second ed., 1996.
Kistler, Don, General Editor. *Feed My Sheep*. Morgan, Pennsylvania: Soli Deo Gloria, 2002.

Bibliography

Koller, Charles W. *Expository Preaching without Notes*. Grand Rapids: Baker, 1962.
Kroll, Woodrow. *Prescription for Preaching*. Grand Rapids: Baker, 1980.
Larsen, David L. *The Anatomy of Preaching*. Grand Rapids: Baker, 1989.
———. *Telling The Old Old Story*. Wheaton, Illinois: Crossway, 1995.
Lenski, R. C. H. *The Sermon: Its Homiletical Construction*. Grand Rapids: Baker, reprint, 1968.
Lewis, Ralph L. and Lewis, Gregg. *Inductive Preaching*. Westchester, IL: Crossway, 1983.
Lloyd-Jones, D. Martyn. *Preaching and Preachers*. Grand Rapids: Zondervan, 1972.
Logan, Jr., Samuel T., editor. *The Preacher and Preaching*. Phillipsburg, New Jersey: Presbyterian and Reformed, 1986.
Luccock, Halford E. *In the Minister's Workshop*. New York: Abingdon-Cokesbury, 1944.
MacArthur, John, Jr. *Rediscovering Expository Preaching*. Dallas: Word, 1992.
Massey, James Earl. *Designing the Sermon: Order and Movement in Preaching*, edited by William D. Thompson. Nashville: Abingdon, 1980.
McComb, Samuel. *Preaching in Theory and Practice*. New York: Oxford University Press, 1926.
McDill, Wayne. *The 12 Essential Skills for Great Preaching*. Nashville: Broadman & Holman, 1994.
Miller, Calvin. *Marketplace Preaching*. Grand Rapids: Baker, 1995.
———. *Spirit, Word, and Story*. Grand Rapids: Baker, 1996.
Miller, Donald G. *The Way to Biblical Preaching*. New York: Abingdon, 1957.
Morgan, G. Campbell. *Preaching*. Grand Rapids: Baker, 1974.
———. *The Westminster Pulpit, Volume VII*. Grand Rapids: Baker, reprint, n.d.
Niles, D. T. *The Preacher's Task and the Stone of Stumbling*. New York: Harper & Brothers, 1958.
Olford, Stephen F., and Olford, David L. *Anointed Expository Preaching*. Nashville: Broadman & Holman, 1998.
Oxnam, Bromley. *Effective Preaching*. New York: Abingdon, 1929.
Pattison, T. Harwood. *The Making of the Sermon*. Valley Forge: Judson, 1941.
Phelps, Austin. *The Theory of Preaching: Lectures on Homiletics*. New York: Charles Scribner's Sons, 1882.
Pierson, Arthur T. *The Divine Art of Preaching*. London: Passmore And Alabaster, 1892.
Rummage, Stephen Nelson. *Planning Your Preaching*. Grand Rapids: Kregel, 2002.
Saint Augustine. *On Christian Teaching*. Translated by R. P. H. Green. New York: Oxford University Press, 1997.
Scherer, Paul E. *For We Have This Treasure*. Grand Rapids: Baker; paperback edition, 1976.
Shedd, William G. T. *Homiletics and Pastoral Theology*. New York: Scribner, Armstrong & Co., eighth ed., 1876.
Skinner, Craig. *The Teaching Ministry of the Pulpit*. Grand Rapids: Baker, second printing, 1981.
Sleeth, Ronald E. *Persuasive Preaching*. New York: Harper & Row, 1956.
Smyth, J. Paterson. *The Preacher and His Sermon*. New York: Doran, 1922.
Spence, H. D. M. and Exell, Joseph S., editors. *The Pulpit Commentary*, Vol. 21. Grand Rapids: Eerdmans, 1950.
Spurgeon, C. H. *Lectures to My Students*. Grand Rapids: Zondervan, new edition, 1954.
Stott, John R. W. *Between Two Worlds*. Grand Rapids: Eerdmans, 1982.
———. *The Preacher's Portrait*. Grand Rapids: Eerdmans, 1961.

Thompson, James W. *Preaching Like Paul*. Louisville, Kentucky: Westminster John Knox, 2001.
Van Cleave, Nathaniel M. *Handbook of Preaching*. San Dimas, CA: L.I.F.E. Bible College, 1983.
Vines, Jerry and Shaddix, Jim. *Power in the Pulpit*. Chicago: Moody, 1999.
Vinet, Alexander. *Homiletics; or the Theory of Preaching*. Translated and edited by Thomas H. Skinner. New York: Ivison, Blakeman, Taylor & Co., 1880.
Vos, Howard F. *Effective Bible Study: a guide to sixteen methods*. Grand Rapids: Zondervan, twentieth edition,1980.
Wardlaw, Don M., editor. *Preaching Biblically*. Philadelphia: Westminster, 1983.
White, R. E. O. *A Guide to Preaching*. Grand Rapids: Eerdmans, 1973.
Whitesell, Faris D. *Power in Expository Preaching*. n.p.: Revell, 1963.
Wiersbe, Warren W. *The Dynamics of Preaching*. Grand Rapids: Baker, 1999.
———. *Preaching and Teaching with Imagination*. Wheaton, Illinois: Victor, 1994.
———. *Treasury of the World's Great Sermons*. Grand Rapids: Kregel, reprinted, 1982.
Wiersbe, Warren W. and Perry, Lloyd M. *The Wycliffe Handbook of Preaching and Preachers*. Chicago: Moody, 1984.
Willingham, Ronald L. *How to Speak so People Will Listen*. Waco, TX: Word, 1968.
Wilson, Gordon. *Set for the Defense*. n.p.: Western Bible & Book Exchange, 1968.
Wood, John. *The Preacher's Workshop*. London: Tyndale, 1965.

www.ingramcontent.com/pod-product-compliance
Lightning Source LLC
Chambersburg PA
CBHW071232230426
43668CB00011B/1400